Grades K-6

SPECTACULAR Guidance Activities for kids

By Diane Senn, Ed.S.

youthlight inc.

Chapin, SC 29036

Design and Layout by Amy Rule
Project Editing by Susan Bowman and Brian C. L

ISBN: 978-1-59850-083-7

Library of Congress Number
2010920669

10 9 8 7 6 5 4 3
Printed in the United States

Acknowledgement

A SINCERE THANK YOU TO THE FOLLOWING...

To Amy Rule, the graphic artist, who graciously and willingly worked with me to create the BULLY FREE ISLAND and the PROBLEM SOLVING POND posters to use in my own school program. And later as the book was developed, added these posters and created the CAREER VILLAGE poster. I appreciate Amy's talent, her creativity, and her ability to bring "life" to the pages of the book. Thank you.

To the students and faculty of Crowders Creek Elementary who continue to support, encourage, respond to, assist with, and appreciate the activities and programs. Thank you.

To Betts Gatewood and Kathy McElvenny who gave of their time and effort to read, give feedback, and edit the work. Thank you for listening and reviewing activities, and for your willingness and support you have given.

To Bob and Susan Bowman, presidents of YoughLight, Inc., for their support, encouragement, and belief in this project.

To my husband Stan, for his unconditional love, support, and his faith in me that I could accomplish this task. Thank you for listening, providing feedback, and giving encouragement when needed.

And most importantly we give honor and thanks to God, our guiding light.

Table of Contents

INTRODUCTION

This book provides activities that can be used as part of a school counseling program, can be used by other school personnel or by any helping professional with the intent to help our children maximize their potential in the areas of living (personal/social development), learning (academic development), and working (career development). **The activities are divided into the three domains of our ASCA (American School Counselor Association) National Standards for Students.** It is our standards that guide school counseling programs to implement strategies and activities for personal and social growth, to provide support and maximize each student's ability to learn, and to provide the foundation for gaining skills, attitudes and knowledge that enable students to make a successful transition from school to the world of work.

My intent with the **activities** is to provide a brief (15-20 minutes), easy to use, creative activity that can be expanded upon, streamlined or combined with other activities to fit your need. **The activities can be utilized in class lessons, with individuals, in small group counseling, and in some cases can be shared through school-wide programs.** It is up to you as to which age students and in what setting the activity would work best for your program. I don't want our thinking to limit a particular activity for a particular grade or for a particular delivery system. I have found through the years that what I have used in a classroom lesson, I also find successful in small group and with individuals and at times the same activity, with some modifications, can be shared at assembly programs or morning announcements.

I hope you will enjoy the activities provided and that the activities will help you connect with our children assisting in their personal, social, academic, and career growth.

Activities for LIVING

Personal and Social Development

We can make a difference in the lives of children!

FEELINGS

Feelings are a part of who we are, our everyday living, and problems that arise. Being able to target our feelings is the building block necessary for learning how to manage the feeling. This section provides activities for feeling exploration as well as guiding toward healthy and appropriate ways to manage our feelings.

Activity 1 | Activity for LIVING | Feelings

A Rainbow of Feelings

Overview: To provide an awareness and appreciation of our feelings.

Materials

- ✓ Glass prism
- ✓ Flashlight
- ✓ Copy of the *A Rainbow of Feelings* worksheet

Procedures

1. Ask: **Have you ever seen a rainbow in the sky? What do you know about rainbows?** You may choose to include in your discussion the following depending on the age of the student:
   - ✯ The science of the rainbow is "refraction" which is the bending and reflecting of the sunlight as it passes through water droplets producing the various colors.
   - ✯ The seven colors (spectrum) of the rainbow are: red, orange, yellow, green, blue, indigo, and violet.
   - ✯ Rainbows have no end because they are circles. You can see the complete circle of a rainbow from an airplane but not from the ground.

2. Demonstrate the spectrum of colors by using a prism and the sunlight or a flashlight. (Explain that the prism is a substitute for the raindrops). Move the prism to catch the light to display the spectrum of colors on the wall or ceiling. Have the students discuss or draw and color what they see.

3. Share: **We can think of ourselves as being like a prism or a raindrop and as we go through life with the light shining we show our different feelings or colors of our rainbow.** Relate the different colors to various feelings such as: red – mad; orange - frustrated; yellow – happy; green – scared; blue – sad; indigo – proud; violet – shy. You or the student may choose different feelings for different colors, the point is that we are made up of all kinds of feelings both pleasant and unpleasant.

4. The feeling words related to the colors of the rainbow provide a beginning feelings vocabulary. Further this discussion by asking the student(s) to give feeling situation examples, by role playing, and discussing and modeling body language associated with the different feelings. For older students, they may brainstorm additional feeling vocabulary

words associated with the main word. It is important for children to build an extensive feelings vocabulary. Accurately identifying often complex feelings is the key to successfully managing the feeling.

5. Complete *A Rainbow of Feelings* worksheet.

Additional Ideas

Convey the point that just as you can't take a color out of the rainbow – you can't get rid of a feeling you may be having, instead you learn to manage the feeling.

A student may choose to color their world to express their feelings by drawing a picture and using color to symbolize their feelings, or draw their body outline and then add different colors to communicate how they may be feeling.

For an added reminder or visual for students of our 'rainbow of feelings inside of us', you may purchase a rainbow mouth coil (typically sold by magic trick suppliers) and demonstrate. I typically have the mouth coil in my hand, put my hand with the coil up to a student's ear, and then pull the rainbow coil out from my hand giving the visual of the rainbow of feelings inside of the person.

You may vary the activity by creating an additional analogy of 'the beauty of the rainbow after the storm' related to 'finding the good (beauty) in a difficult event (storm) in our life'.

OR the thought that 'Rain is a part of Rainbow'.

HAVE FUN BUILDING ON THE RAINBOW CONCEPT!

A Rainbow of Feelings

WORK SHEET

Directions: *Add color to the rainbow below. Then, label each color with a feeling and add a feeling face. Next, think of a situation and how you felt or are feeling. Color the body outline with the feeling color and complete the sentence in the clouds.*

ALL OF MY FEELINGS MAKE UP THE BEAUTY OF WHO I AM!

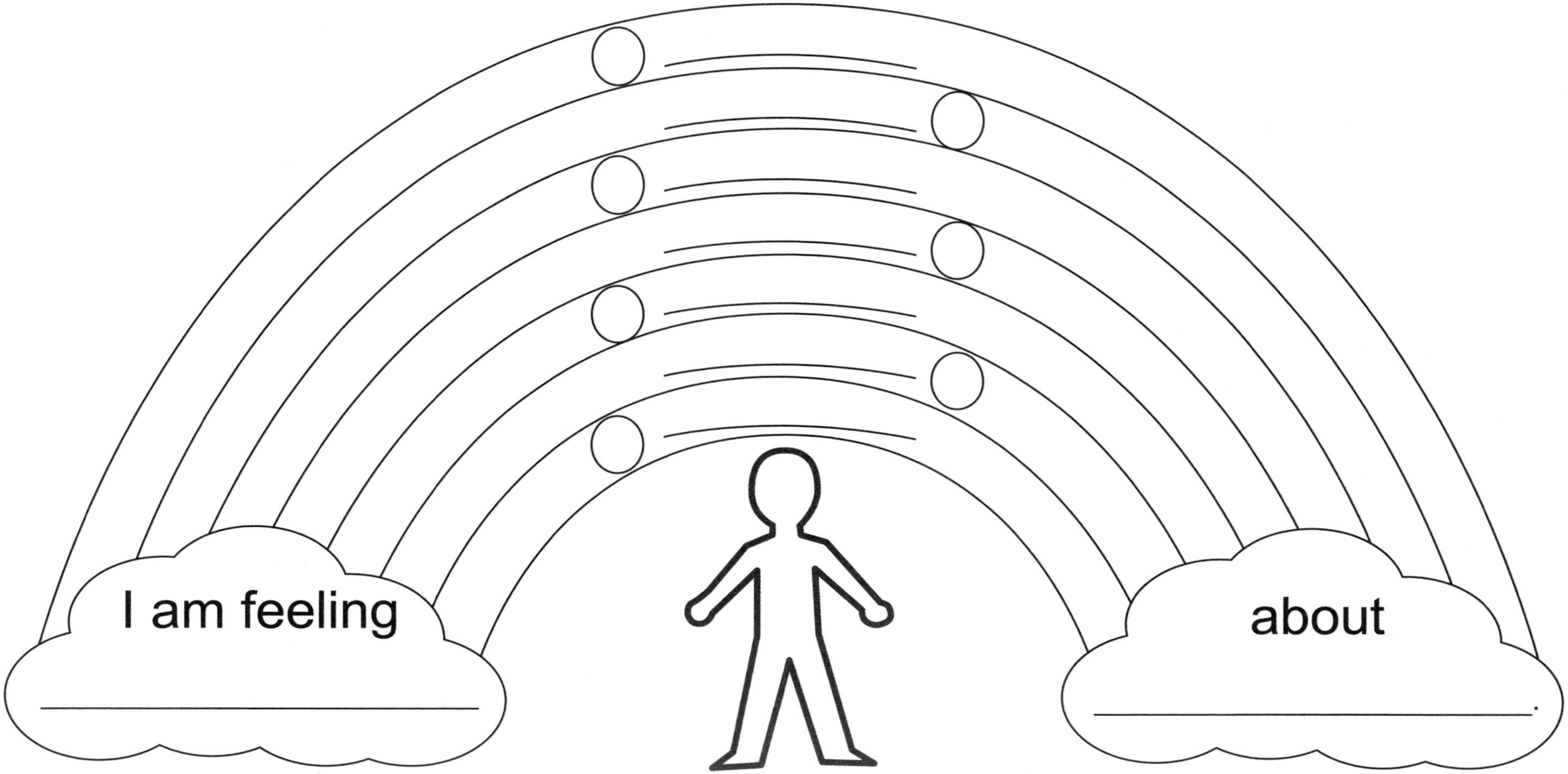

Activity 2

Activity for LIVING

Feelings

Crayon Magic*

Overview: This activity encourages the acknowledgement of all feelings and explores healthy ways to manage our unpleasant feelings.

Materials

- ✓ Box of 8 count crayons with a window or opening on the front of the box
- ✓ Scissors
- ✓ Clear tape
- ✓ Copy of the *Crayon Magic* worksheet

Preparation**

Remove the crayons from the box and cut them in half (measure the cut so that when the crayons are placed back in the box they fall below the opening). Tape the bottom of the crayons together with clear tape and place back in the box.

Procedures

1. Turn the box upside down, then pinch or hold tight with your fingers and thumb the bottom half of the box as you turn the box upright. The crayons showing through the window give the appearance of a box of full crayons. Display, what appears to be a full box of crayons, for the students to see as you relate the multi-colored box of crayons to our many feelings, both pleasant and unpleasant. Have the students share their thoughts about the different feelings and connect a color to a feeling. For example: 'yellow' may stand for 'happy'; 'blue' for 'sad'; 'red' for 'mad'; 'orange' for 'excited'; 'green' for 'jealous', 'purple' for 'afraid', etc. There is no set color for a feeling so whatever relationship you choose is fine. (If needed, you may go into more detail about feelings by asking for examples of the feelings, role-playing, and sharing the body language of that feeling.)

2. Ask: **Have you ever been so sad and are tired of feeling a certain way that you wish for all of your feelings to go away?** As you say this, turn the front (window) of the box to the back away from your audience and release the tightness of your hold on the box so that the half crayons drop to the bottom below the window. Turn the box back to the audience and it appears that the crayons have disappeared.

* adapted from R. Bowman, 2004, *The Magic Counselor*, Chapin, SC: YouthLight, Inc.
** Disappearing Crayons can be purchased through YouthLight, Inc. 1-800-209-9774

3. Say: **Not only did our blue crayon, our 'sad' feeling, go away but all of our other feelings did also. I don't think we want all of our feelings to go away… I want to enjoy feeling happy and excited. So it looks like we need to get all of our feelings back and instead learn how to manage our unpleasant feelings. I need your help. On the count of 3 say, "Feelings, feelings, come back all."** As the students are calling for the feelings to return, turn the box window away from the audience and upside down. Then pinch or hold tight with fingers and thumb the bottom half of the box as you turn the box upright, with the window facing the audience to show that the crayons have reappeared.

4. Say: **Now that we have our feelings back we need to learn how to manage our unpleasant feelings. What are some healthy ways that we can manage our sad feelings?** Brainstorm different ways. (You may choose to focus on other feelings with the crayon trick such as mad, afraid, or worried).

5. Complete the *Crayon Magic* worksheet.

Crayon Magic

WORK SHEET

Directions: *Complete the feeling situation box, next label your crayon with a feeling word and add color to your feeling crayon, then complete "Healthy ways to manage my feeling."*

FEELING SITUATION

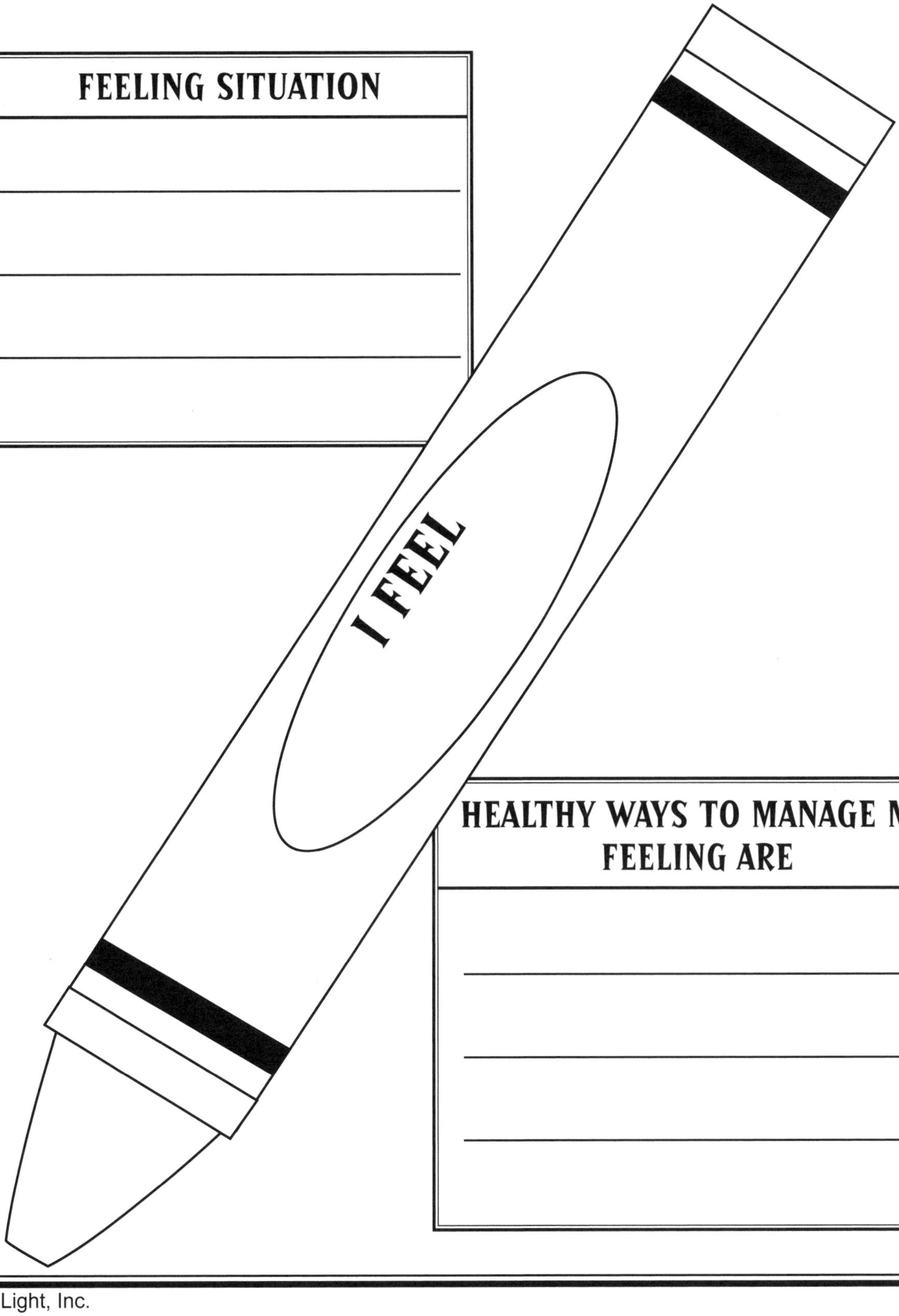

HEALTHY WAYS TO MANAGE MY FEELING ARE

Activity 3 | Activity for LIVING | Feelings

The Printout for Feeling Management

Overview: This activity provides for feeling identification and finding appropriate ways to manage our feelings.

Materials

✓ Copy of *The Printout for Feeling Management* Worksheet

Procedures

1. Brainstorm together a list a feeling words. Expand your discussion by asking students to give examples and show the body language that may accompany each feeling.
2. Say: **I am going to share some examples of ways people may handle their feelings. Give me a 'thumbs up' if it is an okay way to deal with our feelings or a 'thumbs down' if it is not an okay way to manage our feelings.**
   - ☆ When feeling sad, you choose to say mean things to another person trying to make them feel sad too.
   - ☆ When you are angry, you choose to take out your anger on the person by shoving them.
   - ☆ When you are angry, you choose to sit down, take deep breaths and tell yourself to calm down.
   - ☆ When you are feeling sad, you choose to sit in front of the TV all day.
   - ☆ When you are feeling sad, you choose to get busy doing something fun to get your mind off of the sad feeling.
   - ☆ When you are afraid that you will get in trouble about the broken window, you choose to lie about it.
   - ☆ When you are angry that you don't get your way, you choose to pout about it.
   - ☆ When you are sad that you don't get to do something you really wanted to do, you whine about it.
   - ☆ When you are upset, you choose to go to an adult you trust and talk it out.
   - ☆ When you are frustrated that you don't understand your math work, you choose to crumple up the paper and yell, "I quit!".
3. Share: **Let's review *The Printout for Feeling Management* Worksheet for more ideas on 'thumbs up' ways to manage our feelings.** Review the worksheet adding any additional feelings and ways to handle the feelings. Next, allow time for students to complete the printout by adding a feeling situation and a positive outcome.

The Printout for Feeling Management

WORK SHEET

Describe the situation:

____

____

FEELINGS	WAYS TO HANDLE MY FEELINGS
- Sad	- Take a deep breath and count to calm down.
- Mad	- Talk to a friend or adult you trust.
- Happy	- Listen to music or sing to improve your mood.
- Scared	- Do a physical activity like jumping rope or running.
- Worried	- Write or draw a picture about the problem.
- Frustrated	- Be honest and talk with the person in a caring way.
- Overwhelmed	- Read a book or play a game to give your mind a break.
- Annoyed	- _______________________________
- Confused	- _______________________________
- Excited	
- ____________	
- ____________	

Name the feeling:

____

I will handle my feeling by:

____

____

____

You are in charge of what you say and do.

Activity 4

Activity for LIVING

Feelings

Calm the Volcano

Overview: This activity provides an awareness of the damage that our 'out of control anger' can do and reviews the ways to calm our anger.

Materials

- ✓ Picture or video clip of an erupting volcano
- ✓ Board or chart paper/markers
- ✓ Copy of *Calm the Volcano* and *Calm the Volcano – Calm the Body* worksheets

Procedures

1. Ask: **Have you ever seen a picture of a volcano?** Prompt a discussion of volcanoes with pictures or video clips. Explain that inactive volcanoes do no damage to people and property but that erupting volcanoes with flowing hot lava, fire, and ash can hurt people and property in the area.

2. Share: **In a way, we can think of ourselves like a volcano. We may get hot or angry inside. It's normal to feel angry at times but as long as we manage our anger we can be like the inactive volcano handling the steam and pressure. However, if we choose not to handle our angry feelings we explode like an erupting volcano and our 'out of control anger' can hurt people and property.**

3. Ask: **What kind of damage can our 'out of control anger' do?**

4. Establish the following 3 guidelines in managing our anger well.

> ***When I am angry:***
> 1. ***I may NOT hurt MYSELF.***
> 2. ***I may NOT hurt PROPERTY.***
> 3. ***I may NOT hurt OTHERS.***

5. Discuss and make a list of appropriate ways to help calm down our anger – to let off the steam. Review each suggestion on your list and make sure the suggestion meets the three guidelines about anger.

6. Complete the *Calm the Volcano* worksheet.

Calm the Volcano

WORK SHEET

Directions: *Circle the suggestions that would help calm down our angry volcano or let off steam – remember, it needs to meet the 3 guidelines about anger. Strike through the ways that would make our anger worse.*

"That's not fair!"
I can walk away.
I can sit down and take some deep breaths.
"I can handle this!"
"I never get to do anything."
I'll just turn around and walk away.
"He did that on purpose, I'll get him back."
I don't like the consequences of my anger out of control.
I can count to 10 and tell myself to calm down.
"Nobody likes me. I'm no good."
I can listen to music and get in a better mood.
Since I didn't win I'll call her a cheater.
I'm so mad, I'll kick the wall.
I'll just break the toy if they won't let me play.
I can talk to an adult or friend I trust.
When I am angry:
1. I may NOT hurt MYSELF.
2. I may NOT hurt PROPERTY.
3. I may NOT hurt OTHERS.

Calm the Body

WORK SHEET

Directions: *Complete the following listing ways to help our body calm down when we are mad.*

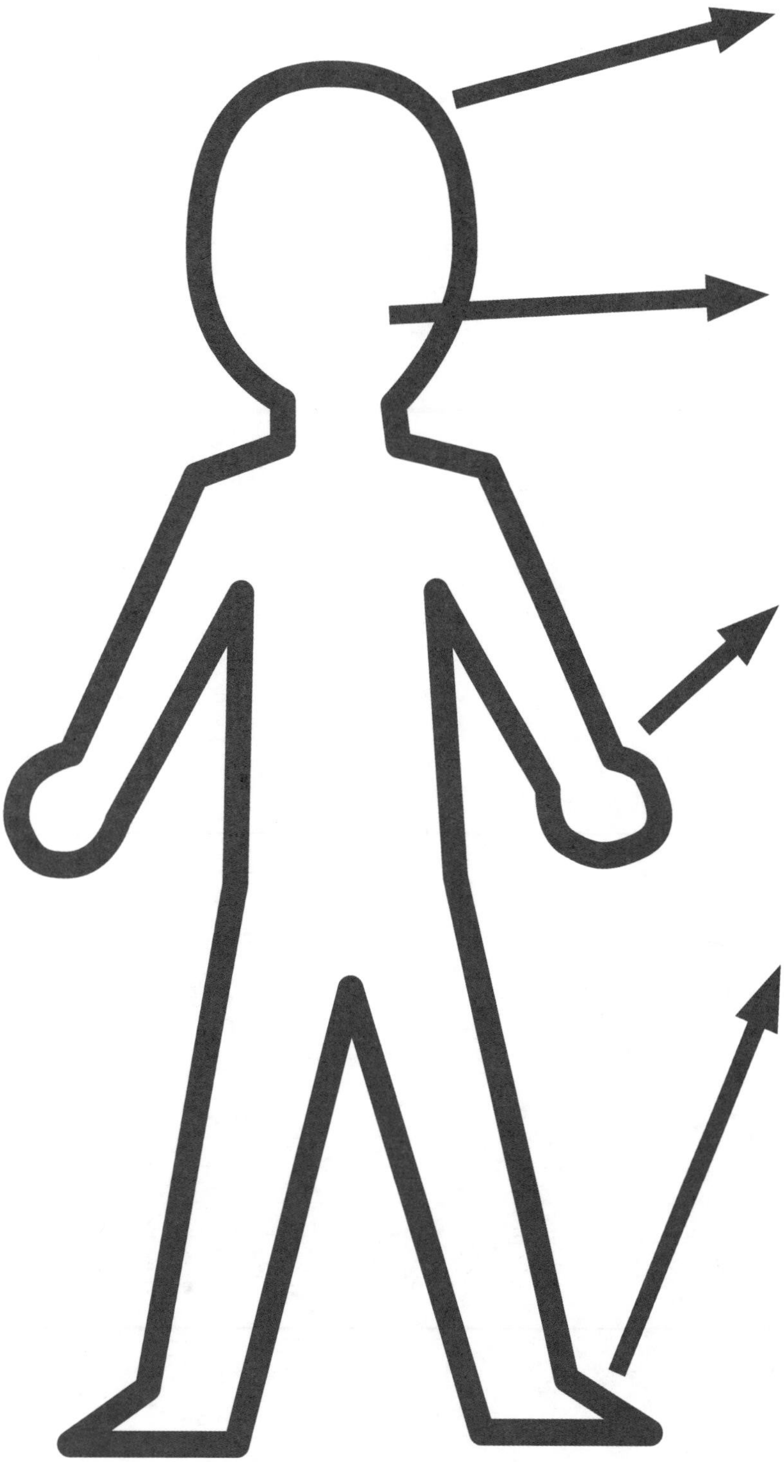

Tell yourself to:

____

____

____

Slow your breathing down by:

____

____

____

Do something okay with your hands like:

____

____

____

Do something active like:

____

____

____

Other things I can do to calm down:

____

____

____

Things Are Looking Up!

Overview: This activity focuses on changing our thoughts and body language to help when we are sad.

Materials

✓ Copy of *Things Are Looking Up!* worksheet for each student and one for demonstration. Follow the directions to cut, assemble, and glue to a popsicle stick.

Procedures

1. Ask the student(s) to complete the following sentence: **Sometimes I'm sad when…** Ask: **What might a person be thinking when he/she is 'sad'? What messages might he/she be saying or thinking in his/her head?**

2. Ask for the student or volunteer to show the body language that might go with feeling sad.

   Include the following:
   - ★ Head down
   - ★ Eyes on the ground
   - ★ Straight or turned down mouth
   - ★ Shoulders slumped

3. Now ask the student to show the body language when the person is no longer sad. Include the following:
   - ★ Head up
   - ★ Eyes forward
   - ★ Pleasant look on face
   - ★ Shoulders up

4. Ask: **What might a person be thinking when he/she is finding a good way to handle their sadness?**

5. To help when we are sad, encourage students to FIRST physically hold their head up, eyes forward, pleasant look on their face, and shoulders up. The physical posture, or looking up, can then trigger the SECOND STEP which is to "rewrite" the message in our head to be more positive and to look on the brighter side.

6. Complete the *Things Are Looking Up!* worksheet.

Things Are Looking Up!

WORK SHEET

Directions: *Complete the sentence on both sheets indicating what each person may be thinking. Cut out all 4 items on these pages (2 people and their hair). Glue the pictures of the 2 people to each side of a popsicle stick with their faces outward. Next tape the hair cutouts to the top of the head so that the hair can be raised to see the messages inside.*

When I am sad,
I keep thinking or
saying to myself that...

When I am sad...

Things Are Looking Up!

WORK SHEET

To help when I am sad...

Activity 6

Activity for LIVING

Feelings

Scary Tales

Overview: This activity identifies and promotes strategies for dealing with imaginary and real fears.

Materials

- ✓ Marker and paper for list making
- ✓ Copy of the *Scary Tales* worksheet
- ✓ Optional: The book, *"How to Get Rid of Bad Dreams"* by Nancy Hazbry and Roy Condy.

Procedures

1. Ask: **Do you know what the word AFRAID means? Show me what your face may look like when you are afraid.**

2. Ask: **What are some other words that mean the same or about the same thing as "afraid"?** (It is important to expand student's feeling vocabulary so they can more accurately assess/describe their feelings in order to effectively manage the feeling).

3. Brainstorm with the student(s) and make a list of things that scare us and things people may be afraid of. Beside each item decide whether it is something REAL or IMAGINED and put an 'R' or 'I' beside each item.

4. Discuss strategies to deal with the IMAGINARY fears. Since they are imaginary and not real discuss how we can use our IMAGINARY POWER to find imaginary, creative, and fun ways to deal with the fear. If you have the book available, read the story, *How to Get Rid of Bad Dreams*. The story gives examples of imaginary, creative and fun ways to deal with imaginary fears. If you are unable to read the book, give them some fun examples such as:

   - ✯ To deal with the fear of a monster under the bed – have your box of shrinking powder on the night stand ready to sprinkle on the monster and shrink him smaller than your pinky.
   - ✯ To deal with the boogie man in the closet – put your favorite music on so he will dance on out of your house. (Finding fun and creative ways helps the student use his/her "power" to conquer the fear.)

5. Next, review those items that are REAL fears. Share with the student(s) that for helping with our REAL fears we need to use our BRAIN POWER. Brainstorm appropriate strategies to deal with or manage the fears listed as real. Keep in mind that real fears may range from afraid about being new or the first day of school to being afraid of natural disasters or dangerous people. Be ready to support and guide. Review safety rules when appropriate. Help the student realize he/she has "brain power" that can be used to help give a sense of control in difficult situations.

6. Complete the *Scary Tales* worksheet

Scary Tales

WORK SHEET

My Scary Tale

IMAGINATION POWER

By: ______________________________

Once upon a time, I woke up in the middle of the night and imagined that under my bed were __________________________. At first I felt ____________________________________ but then I realized I had my IMAGINATION POWER that could help me handle this. So I ____

____. And poof, that took care of my problem. My IMAGINATION POWER saved the day!

In real life one time, I felt scared when ___________________. At first I felt like there was nothing I could do to help with my scary feeling but then I realized I had my BRAIN POWER that I could use to find a good way to handle it. So I _______________________________ _________________________. Thanks to my BRAIN POWER I felt better.

If you have ever felt afraid or scared, here is my advice for you:

____

____

____.

The End

SELF-CONCEPT

Developing and maintaining a positive self-concept is important in being a happy and productive person. So much of our outlook on life is rooted in our own perception of ourselves and our abilities. The activities in this section focus on the development of a healthy self-concept. A strong self-concept will allow us to acknowledge and appreciate our strengths and the things we can do well and develop positive thoughts and skills to deal with life when things do not go *right*.

Activity 7

Activity for LIVING

Self-Concept

I'm Worth a Million Bucks*

Overview: This activity emphasizes the value of each person and focuses on a person's good qualities and strengths.

Materials

- ✓ $20 bill for demonstration purposes
- ✓ Copy of the *I'm Worth A Million Bucks* worksheet

Procedures

1. Display a $20 bill and ask: **Is this $20 bill worth something - is it valuable?** (typically when you first hold up the money you get a reaction.) Next, crumple the bill in your hand, drop it on the floor… and stomp on it. (You typically get a different kind of reaction). Straighten out the bill, display it again, and ask: **Is this $20 bill still worth something – is it still valuable? Did getting crumpled and stepped on take away any of its value?** The answer is "no." The $20 bill is still good – just as valuable.

2. Ask: **Are we important and valuable like $20 or a million bucks? Are there times we may get crumpled? Share some ways we may get crumpled or feel like we have been stepped on?** (Look for examples such as: being teased or picked on, making mistakes, trying to learn something new but failing.)

3. Ask: **Even after we may get crumpled or stepped on, are we still just as important and valuable like that $20 bill or a million bucks?** YES!

4. Complete the *I'm Worth a Million Bucks* worksheet listing the good qualities and strengths. These qualities and strengths are constants that make a person valuable and important and can not be diminished by other's teasing or the mistakes one makes.

REMEMBER, YOU'RE WORTH A MILLION!

* adapted from a concept shared by Lawrence Shapiro

I'm Worth a Million Bucks

WORK SHEET

Directions: *Complete the worksheet adding a picture of yourself, your good qualities, and listing the things you do well.*

Some examples of good qualities are: friendly, respectful, honest, responsible, helpful, caring, cooperative, a positive attitude, etc.

Some examples of things we may do well are: good at math, music, sports, creative writing, drawing, problem solving, peacemaking, organizing, lego building, reading, etc.

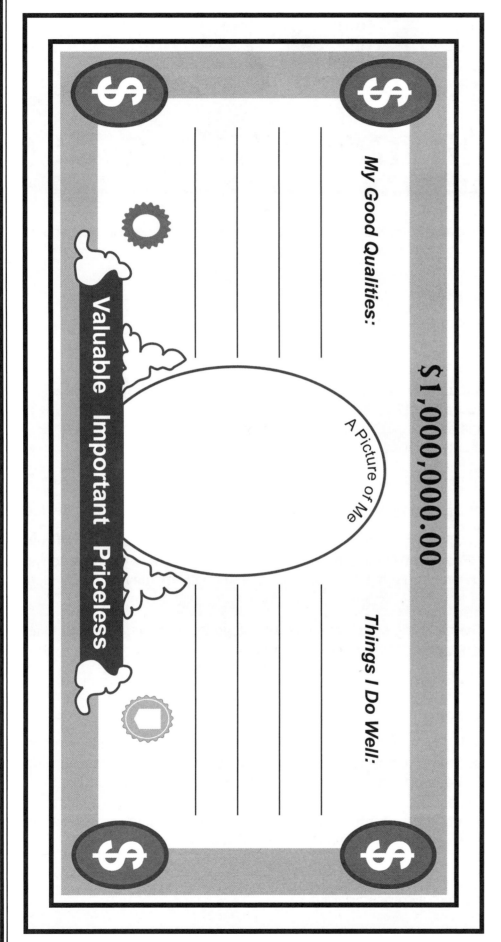

$1,000,000.00

My Good Qualities:

____

____

____

____

A Picture of Me

Things I Do Well:

____

____

____

____

Valuable Important Priceless

Activity 8

Activity for LIVING

Self-Concept

The Treasure Within Us

Overview: This activity promotes the real treasure in life in being the best person we can be.

Materials

✓ Chart paper/board and marker

✓ Copy of *The Treasure Within Us* worksheet

Procedures

1. Ask: **Have you ever read a story or seen a movie about a Treasure Hunt? What all is involved in the Treasure Hunt?** Write the following key items of a treasure hunt on the chart paper/board and ask the students to explain how each item or characteristic is important in a treasure hunt - discuss:

   MAP (Share that a map shows you the path/directions to achieve your goal/treasure.)

   COMPASS (Share that a compass points you in the right direction so you don't get lost.)

   PERSEVERANCE (Define 'perseverance' as "continuing even if something is difficult – refusing to stop". Share that finding the treasure is not always easy, we have to work hard and continue even though it may be difficult, and mistakes may be made along the way.)

   COOPERATION (Share that treasure hunting is usually done with other people, it often takes many to work together to find the treasure.)

   PROBLEM SOLVERS (Share the importance of being good problem solvers in order to handle the problems and obstacles that arise on the treasure hunt.)

2. Ask: **Now that we know the basics of a treasure hunt I want us to relate the treasure and the hunt to the idea that real treasure is not on the outside with jewels and gold but the real treasure in life is on the inside in being the best person we can be. So let's begin the hunt. Review the 5 words on the chart paper/board and now relate them to a different kind of treasure hunt in finding the real treasure in ourselves by being our best.** Include the following information in your discussion:

MAP (Ask how character traits can serve as a guideline or map to follow to be our best. Include the following character traits in the discussion: RESPECTFUL, RESPONSIBLE, HONEST, APPRECIATIVE, CARING, SELF-DISCIPLINED, COURAGEOUS.)

COMPASS (Ask students to share people that they can trust to point them in the right direction. Include parents, teachers, and friends you trust.)

PERSEVERENCE (Discuss mistakes or obstacles that come up in our lives – being teased, difficulty learning something new, family changes, etc. Ask for suggestions of what to do or tell ourselves to overcome the mistakes and obstacles to keep going in the right direction.)

COOPERATION (Share that success is rarely achieved alone, it takes working together with people. Ask when and how cooperation is important – ex. Team sports, classmates, involved bystanders to help each other.)

PROBLEM SOLVERS (Ask what are problems that may come up in life? Ex. Not getting chosen or elected, difficulty learning something new, disagreement with a friend, etc. Discuss ways to be problem solvers in handling the problems.)

3. Complete *The Treasure Within Us* worksheet.

The Treasure Within Us!

WORK SHEET

Directions: *Complete your treasure map by circling the 7 character words hidden on the map and answering the questions on the Compass and in the Key. Remember the treasure is in you!*

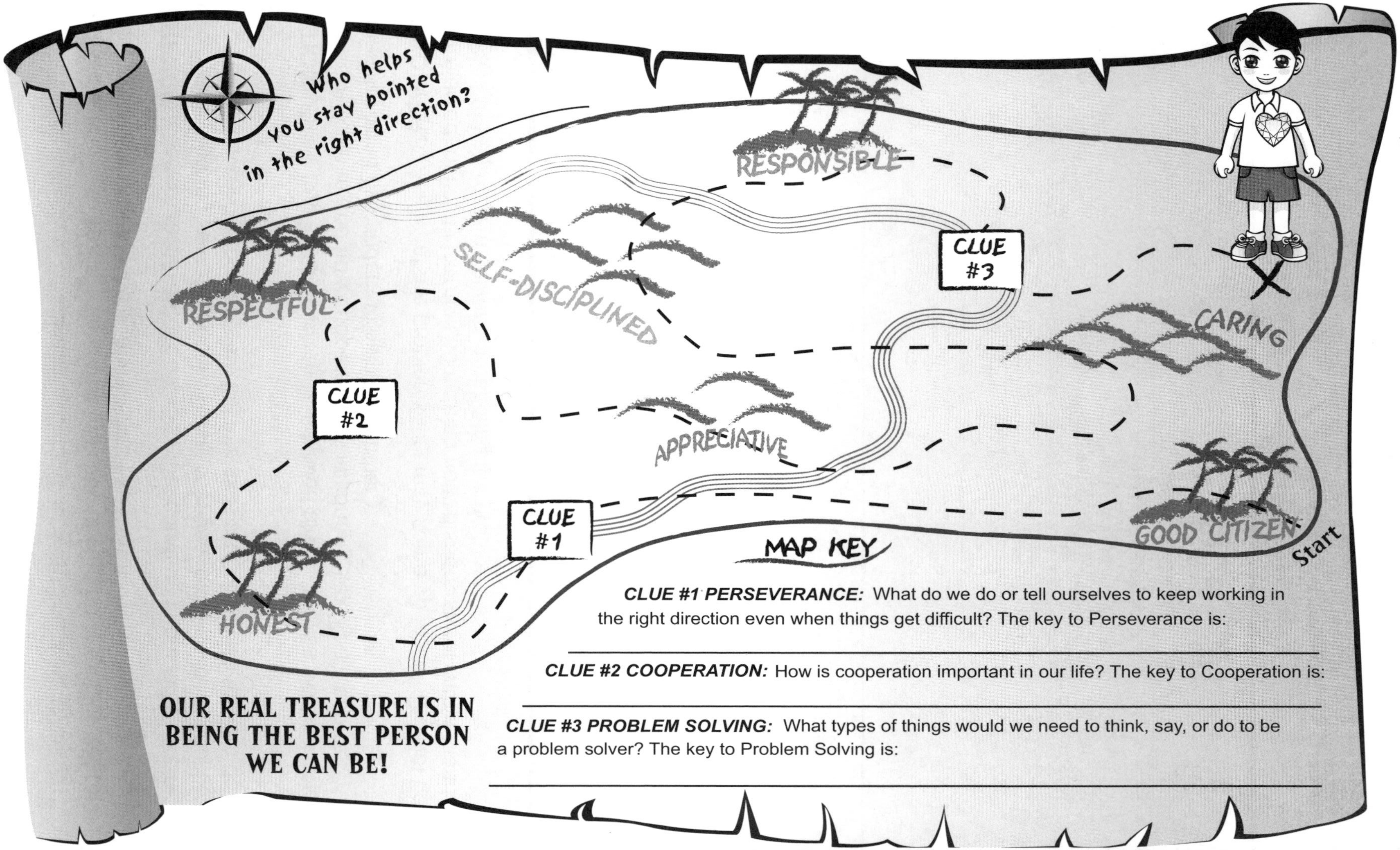

MAP KEY

CLUE #1 PERSEVERANCE: What do we do or tell ourselves to keep working in the right direction even when things get difficult? The key to Perseverance is:

____

CLUE #2 COOPERATION: How is cooperation important in our life? The key to Cooperation is:

____

CLUE #3 PROBLEM SOLVING: What types of things would we need to think, say, or do to be a problem solver? The key to Problem Solving is:

____

OUR REAL TREASURE IS IN BEING THE BEST PERSON WE CAN BE!

Activity 9

Activity for LIVING

Self-Concept

Managing Mistakes

Overview: This activity reviews the importance of learning from our mistakes and trying again.

Materials

- ✓ Eraser for demonstration
- ✓ Copy of *Managing Mistakes* worksheet

Procedures

1. Hold up the eraser and ask: **What is the purpose of an eraser?** Summarize that an eraser is used to correct our work when we make a mistake. Ask: **What are some mistakes you may have made in the past with your work?**

2. Ask: **We've talked about mistakes that we make with our written work but are there other kinds of mistakes we may make? Give examples.** (Examples may include - mistakes with our friends in saying or doing something that isn't nice, forgetting to do a chore at home, not following a rule correctly when playing a game, or when you're learning something new and having difficulty.

3. Ask: **When we make a mistake should we just give up or should we learn from and correct the mistake? Think about a mistake with our written work – when we make a mistake do we just quit or do we erase the work, and try again? When we erase the work and write again do we write the same wrong answer or do we think and write a different answer?**

4. Give an example of a professional basketball player by saying: **When a professional player shoots and misses the shot - does he quit, get mad, and never try again or does he try again?** The answer is 'he tries again'. Analyze with the students what the player may do as he tries again – perhaps the player thinks about how he may have been off in the shot so he can correct it in the future, or he may choose to practice the shot more in between games. Share that making mistakes and *learning* from them is part of getting better.

5. Complete the *Managing Mistakes* worksheet practicing ways to use our "life's eraser" to learn from our mistakes and try again.

Managing Mistakes

WORK SHEET

Directions: *Complete the "life's erasers" by rewriting the mistakes. Share what you could THINK, SAY, and/or DO to learn from the mistake and try again.*

Mistake: I made an F on my test when I didn't read the directions carefully.

What I can THINK: ______________________________

SAY: ______________________________

DO: ______________________________

To learn from my mistake and try again!

Think about this situation and complete the THINK, SAY, or DO

Mistake: I should not have gotten mad and quit the basketball team.

What I can THINK: ______________________________

SAY: ______________________________

DO: ______________________________

To learn from my mistake and try again!

Think about this situation and complete the THINK, SAY, or DO

Mistake: I was so embarrassed when I forgot my lines in the school play.

What I can THINK: ______________________________

SAY: ______________________________

DO: ______________________________

To learn from my mistake and try again!

Think about this situation and complete the THINK, SAY, or DO

Mistake:

What I can THINK: ______________________________

SAY: ______________________________

DO: ______________________________

To learn from my mistake and try again!

Write your own mistake and complete the THINK, SAY, or DO

Activity 10 · Activity for LIVING · Self-Concept

Perfect Isn't Perfect

Overview: This activity seeks to reduce the pressure of unattainable perfection.

Materials

✓ Copy of the story "*Ish*" by Peter Reynolds

✓ Copy of the *Perfect Isn't Perfect* worksheet

Procedures

1. Ask: **Have you ever started to write something, make something, or draw something but you get caught up in it looking "perfect" and you get frustrated with it? What does "perfect" mean?**
2. Introduce the story by sharing: **In our story today, Ramon loves to draw pictures until one day his older brother, Leon, makes a careless remark about Ramon's drawing and from then on Ramon becomes critical of his drawings and tries to make them perfect. His younger sister, Marisol, comes along and has a whole different way of looking at his pictures – let's read to find out.** Share the story.
3. Discuss the story with the following questions:

   - ✯ **What did Leon say about Ramon's drawing and how did Ramon react to what Leon said?**
   - ✯ **What did Marisol do with Ramon's crumpled pictures?**
   - ✯ **What did Marisol think about Ramon's pictures?**
   - ✯ **When Ramon said that his picture was supposed to be a vase of flowers but it doesn't look like one… Marisol exclaimed, "Well, it looks vase-ISH!" What did she mean by that?**
   - ✯ **How did Ramon begin to feel about his drawings when he looked at his pictures in a whole new "ish" way?**
   - ✯ **What does the following saying mean, "Beauty is in the eye of the beholder."**
   - ✯ **What are some things that we can look at "ishfully"?**

4. Ask: **What lesson can we learn from this story? How can this help us in our own lives?** (Emphasize the lesson that what is beautiful and "right" can change with different people's opinions, therefore it is important to appreciate our own work and be proud. Include the importance to focus on what's *right* about our work and what we do rather than pointing out everything we can find wrong. Explore with the student the importance to set realistic goals when learning something new and allowing ourselves time and practice to gain greater skills.)

5. Complete the *Perfect Isn't Perfect* worksheet as you further discuss.

Perfect Isn't Perfect

WORK SHEET

Directions: *Read the following situations sharing your thoughts and advice on how to help the person.*

I NEED YOUR HELP!

I try hard to write a great creative writing story. I want it to be perfect but I end up staring at the blank paper for hours trying to figure out what to write about. And then when I do start I don't like it so I end up starting over again, and again, and again. What can I do?

Signed,
The Struggling Story

Dear Struggling Story,

____

____

____

____

____

____

I NEED YOUR HELP!

I want to learn how to play the piano but it is so hard. I keep missing notes and it sounds so weird. My classmate from school who lives next door came over one afternoon and she heard me practicing. She laughed and rolled her eyes at me. What can I do?

Signed,
Sour Note

Dear Sour Note,

____

____

____

____

____

____

Activity 11

Activity for LIVING

Self-Concept

Flip to the Bright Side

Overview: This activity uses the flip of a coin to encourage us to look for the positives in a situation.

Materials

- ✓ Copy of the *Flip to the Bright Side* worksheet
- ✓ Penny for demonstration *(optional: a penny for each student as a visual reminder of the lesson)*

Procedures

1. Display the coin and ask: **Have you ever flipped a coin to see who goes first? It's only one coin but it does have 2 sides. What are the 2 sides of a coin?** (heads and tails)

2. Ask: **Have you heard the saying, "There's two sides to every situation"?** Share the following situation as a discussion example:

   You've been asked to memorize and share your poem at next week's assembly program and you are worried about 'messing up' in front of the whole school. Point to the "tail" side of the coin first and ask the student(s) to share a negative way to look at or think about the situation. Then turn the coin over to "heads" and ask them to think of and to share a positive way to look at or think about the situation. Explore how one may feel and what their actions and consequences may be as they view the same situations from different sides of the coin or from different thoughts.

3. Ask students: **Have you heard the saying, "Look on the bright side"? What does is mean?** Point out how "looking on the bright side" usually has a better outcome. Explain that today we are going to flip our coin to heads to use our good brain to look at the bright side of the situations.

4. Complete the *Flip to the Bright Side* worksheet, using your good thinking for a bright idea to handle the difficult situations.

5. You may choose to give each student a coin – penny – as a visual reminder of the lesson to "flip to heads to use our good brain" or "flip to the bright side" for difficult situations.

Flip to the Bright Side

WORK SHEET

Directions: *Read the following. Use your good thinking, to "flip to the bright side" finding a positive way to think about or deal with the situations. Write your answers.*

I can't do this. It's too hard.
HEADS UP FOR A BRIGHTER THOUGHT.

That's not fair. She got to go first.
HEADS UP FOR A BRIGHTER THOUGHT.

I didn't get invited to the party. Nobody likes me.
HEADS UP FOR A BRIGHTER THOUGHT.

This picture I drew is ugly.
HEADS UP FOR A BRIGHTER THOUGHT.

I don't want to do my homework.
HEADS UP FOR A BRIGHTER THOUGHT.

I quit. I'll never learn how to hit a baseball.
HEADS UP FOR A BRIGHTER THOUGHT.

FRIENDSHIP

Friends and the ability to make friends is an important part of a child's development. Children need the acceptance and the support of their peers. Making and keeping friends is not as easy as one might think. First you need to learn how to connect with others and then after the initial contact more complex social skills are required to maintain a friendship. This section explores qualities and characteristics that make a good friend, promotes acceptance in differences of others, provides an awareness of how our body language and attitude impact friendships as well as behaviors that can help or hurt friendships, and reviews how and when to resist peer pressure and say 'no' to a friend.

Activity 12

Activity for LIVING

Friendship

Recipe for Friendship

Overview: This activity identifies desired qualities and characteristics valued in a friend and provides an opportunity for the student to reflect on their own friendship qualities.

Materials

- ✓ Measuring cups and measuring spoons typically needed to follow recipes
- ✓ Copy of a recipe for baking a cake
- ✓ Copy of *Recipe for Friendship* worksheet

Procedures

1. Ask: **Have you ever helped bake a cake? How do you know how to bake the cake?** (include following a recipe) **What ingredients typically go in a cake?** (flour, butter, sugar, etc) **What would happen if I put sand in the cake? Or rocks? Sounds like for the cake to be successful I need to follow the recipe and put the right ingredients in the cake.** Discuss how a recipe shows ingredients and the amount that is needed. Display your measuring cups and spoons and review your copy of a recipe to bake a cake.

2. Say: **When it comes to being a good friend we also need to use the right ingredients. Look at our worksheet *Recipe for Friendship*. Let's review the ingredients and strike through any ingredient that would not be helpful in a friendship.** (Discuss each ingredient, quality or characteristic, explaining why or why it would not be helpful in a friendship.) **Using the ingredients that you said were helpful in a friendship, and using the different measuring cups and measuring spoons, create your own recipe for friendship on the worksheet provided**.

3. Ask the students to review their completed recipe for friendship and compare their own friendship behaviors to that of their recipe. Encourage the students to set a goal to adjust or make any changes in their own style so they can be the best friend possible.

Recipe for Friendship

WORK SHEET

Directions: *Review the possible ingredients (characteristics and qualities) for friendship. Strike through the ingredients that would NOT be helpful in a friendship. Choose from the remaining ingredients that would be helpful to create your own recipe for friendship. Cut out your recipe for friendship and display.*

POSSIBLE INGREDIENTS

In the blank spaces, add three other ingredients that may be helpful in a friendship.

Good listener	Helpful	Responsible
Fun to be around	Honest	Breaks the rules
Trustworthy	Spreads rumors	Respectful
Gossips	Funny	Smart
Polite	Talkative	Bossy
Caring	Cooperative	Good sport
Whines	Teases Others	Calls people names
______________	______________	______________

RECIPE FOR FRIENDSHIP

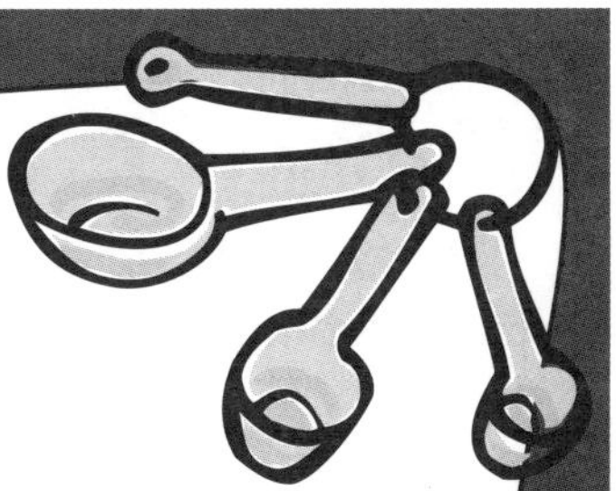

Ingredients: ______________________________

____

____

Directions: ______________________________

____

Review your new recipe for friendship and think about the kind of friend you are to others. Are there any changes you want to work on to be a good friend? If so, what ingredients are you going to add or remove in order for you to be the best friend possible? ______________

____

Activity 13 | Activity for LIVING | Friendship

Runway Model*

Overview: This activity emphasizes the importance of body language in meeting and talking with others.

Materials

✓ Strip of paper for the floor to serve as a 'runway'

✓ Copy of the *Runway Model* worksheet

Procedures

1. Ask: **Have you ever heard that your body talks?** (Explain that it is not the talking with the mouth but talking with the way our body looks. Share that our body can say a lot by the way our face looks and how we move our body.

1. Ask: **Have you been in trouble with mom or dad and your parent doesn't have to say anything but you know, by the way they look, that you have done something wrong?**

2. Demonstrate different feeling messages with your body. Share that when you are connecting with friends and beginning a conversation with someone, you need to have the right *look*.

3. Explain that you need their help pretending to be a runway model. If need be, explain what a runway model does. Place a strip of paper on the floor for the runway. Let the students know that you will whisper to them how they need to look with their face and body when they walk down the runway. Let each person have a turn. Narrate the walk asking questions to the group and discussing how this walk would help or not help to begin a friendly conversation. Begin with the instructions for the **unhelpful body language**, such as:
   - ✭ walk in with head and shoulders down
   - ✭ walk in with eyes not looking at anyone but looking all around the room
   - ✭ walk in a little but turn and look shy
   - ✭ walk (stomp) in with an angry look
   - ✭ walk in pointing and laughing at people

   Next, discuss what would be **helpful body language** such as, good eye contact, head and shoulders up, pleasant look on face, etc. Allow each person to take another turn on the runway but this time they must use the helpful walk. Have the group point out the positives of each person's walk down the runway.

4. Complete the *Runway Model* worksheet for reinforcement.

*adapted from the lesson, "What To Do To Talk With Others" from D. Senn's *Small Group Counseling for Children K-2*, Youthlight 2004.

Runway Model

Directions: *Draw a picture of yourself on the runway showing friendly body language. Then describe helpful body language for connecting with friends by completing the information at the bottom of the page.*

MY FRIENDLY BODY LANGUAGE Includes:

______________________________ ______________________________

______________________________ ______________________________

______________________________ ______________________________

Activity 14

Activity for LIVING

Friendship

What Do I Say?

Overview: This activity helps students develop a repertoire of conversation questions/statements.

Materials

- ✓ Comic strip with the talk bubbles for the characters
- ✓ Copy and cut out for each person the *Talk Bubble* worksheet
- ✓ Copy of the *What Do I Say?* Worksheet

Procedures

1. Display the comic strip, point to a talk bubble, and ask: **Do you know the purpose of a talk bubble on the comic strip?** (Explain that what the character is saying is written inside the bubble.)

2. Hold up a bubble beside your head and explain that when it comes to meeting new people and making friends we need to practice what to say. Write a greeting phrase on your talk bubble and role play for your students how to begin a conversation using your talk bubble phrase.

3. Brainstorm together different questions, phrases, or compliments that can be said when meeting someone and beginning a conversation. You may include such phrases as:

   - ★ Hey, what's up?
   - ★ How are you doing?
   - ★ It's good to see you.
   - ★ Hey, my name's _________, it's nice to meet you.
   - ★ Hi! I like your ________.
   - ★ Do you have any pets?
   - ★ What do you like to do at school?
   - ★ Are you into sports?

4. Distribute a talk bubble to each person. Instruct each student to write a friendly question, phrase, or compliment on their talk bubble that could be used to begin a conversation with another person. Then have the students take turns role playing their conversation starter. Remind students that a pleasant look and sound in the voice while saying the words is also important.

5. Share a copy of the *What Do I Say?* worksheet with each student. Allow time for the students to write a summary or master list of possible statements that can be used to connect with another person.

*adapted from the lesson, "What To Do To Talk With Others" from D. Senn's *Small Group Counseling for Children K-2*, Youthlight 2004.

Talk Bubble

WORK SHEET

What Do I Say?

WORK SHEET

Directions: *In each talk bubble write a friendly question, phrase, or compliment that could be used to begin a conversation with another person.*

Activity 15

Activity for LIVING

Friendship

Beyond the Outside

Overview: This activity uses the special goodfinder glasses to look beyond the outside of a person but instead looks for the good qualities inside the person.

Materials

- ✓ Board or chart paper and markers
- ✓ Pair of oversized glasses often found at dollar stores

Procedures

1. Ask: **Can you tell what kind of a person someone is by looking at them on the outside? Why or why not?** (continue guiding with questions to fully explore that our outside only presents first impressions and does not tell everything about a person).

2. Ask: **What are all the different parts or components that make up who a person is?** Include how a person thinks, their good characteristics and qualities, their behavior in how they choose to treat others, the kinds of things they say to others, etc.)

3. Refer to the board or chart paper and label two columns: SAME and DIFFERENT. Ask students to name ways in which people are the same - things they have in common - and ways in which people are different. Review the list. Point out a main "sameness" is that we all have feelings and emotions. Include in our "differences" that we may look different, talk different, dress different, or think differently. Emphasize the importance of appreciating and respecting each other's differences. Ask: **What is the benefit of people being different?**

4. Display the oversized glasses and explain that these are "special goodfinder glasses" that help us see beyond the outside of a person to who a person really is on the inside in finding the good qualities about a person.

5. Model putting on the glasses, going up to students, and complimenting them on their good qualities. (Ex., "Oh, I see that Samantha is a very caring person who goes out of her way to help others.").

6. Take turns with volunteers putting on the goodfinder glasses and sharing compliments with others – remind them that the compliments need to go beyond what they see on the outside but to who they are on the inside.

7. Ask: **How can this activity help us when hearing about groups of people or when meeting new people?**

Activity 16

Activity for LIVING

Friendship

Roadblocks to Friendship

Overview: This activity reviews the roadblocks or unhelpful responses in friendships and encourages the positive connections.

Materials

✓ Copy of the *Roadblocks to Friendship* worksheet

Procedures

1. Ask: **Are there things we say and do that can hurt or block our friendships with others?** Give examples.

2. **ROLE PLAY:** Ask for volunteers to role play with you. For each situation, set the scene with your volunteer and then you as the adult can demonstrate an unhelpful response from the list below. As you role play an unhelpful response, stop and ask the students to pinpoint and label the unhelpful response. Process with the person you were role playing with how it felt when you were rude or hurtful. Ask students what a more helpful response would have been. Apologize to your volunteer and ask them to replay the situation again with you but this time show you learned from your mistake and instead give a helpful, polite response. As you continue through the role plays with different volunteers – summarize the list of things you have learned - giving the helpful, polite responses.

   Role play situations:

   - ✯ **Pretend we are using the legos together for our project**, then… grab all the legos and pull them to your side. (Replay: Sharing and taking turns fairly)
   - ✯ **Pretend we are talking about what we did over the weekend. Ask your volunteer to go first sharing,** then… interrupt, keep talking and dominate the conversation. (Replay: Good listening)
   - ✯ **Pretend we are on a baseball team together. We are sitting in the dugout waiting to bat**, then…start talking about how great you hit the ball last inning and it was probably better than anyone else could do. (Replay: Complimenting others)
   - ✯ **Pretend we both have just arrived to class that morning. Ask the volunteer to turn to you and say, "Good Morning!"** then… you turn to them with a grumpy look and say, "yea, what's so good about it?" (Replay: Smiles and is pleasant)
   - ✯ **Pretend we are out at recess playing kickball. Ask your volunteer to pretend to kick the ball but miss,** then… say, "what's the matter, even a baby could have kicked that ball." (Replay: Being polite)

Roadblocks to Friendships

WORK SHEET

Directions: *Mark the correct road, following the right path to being a good friend.*

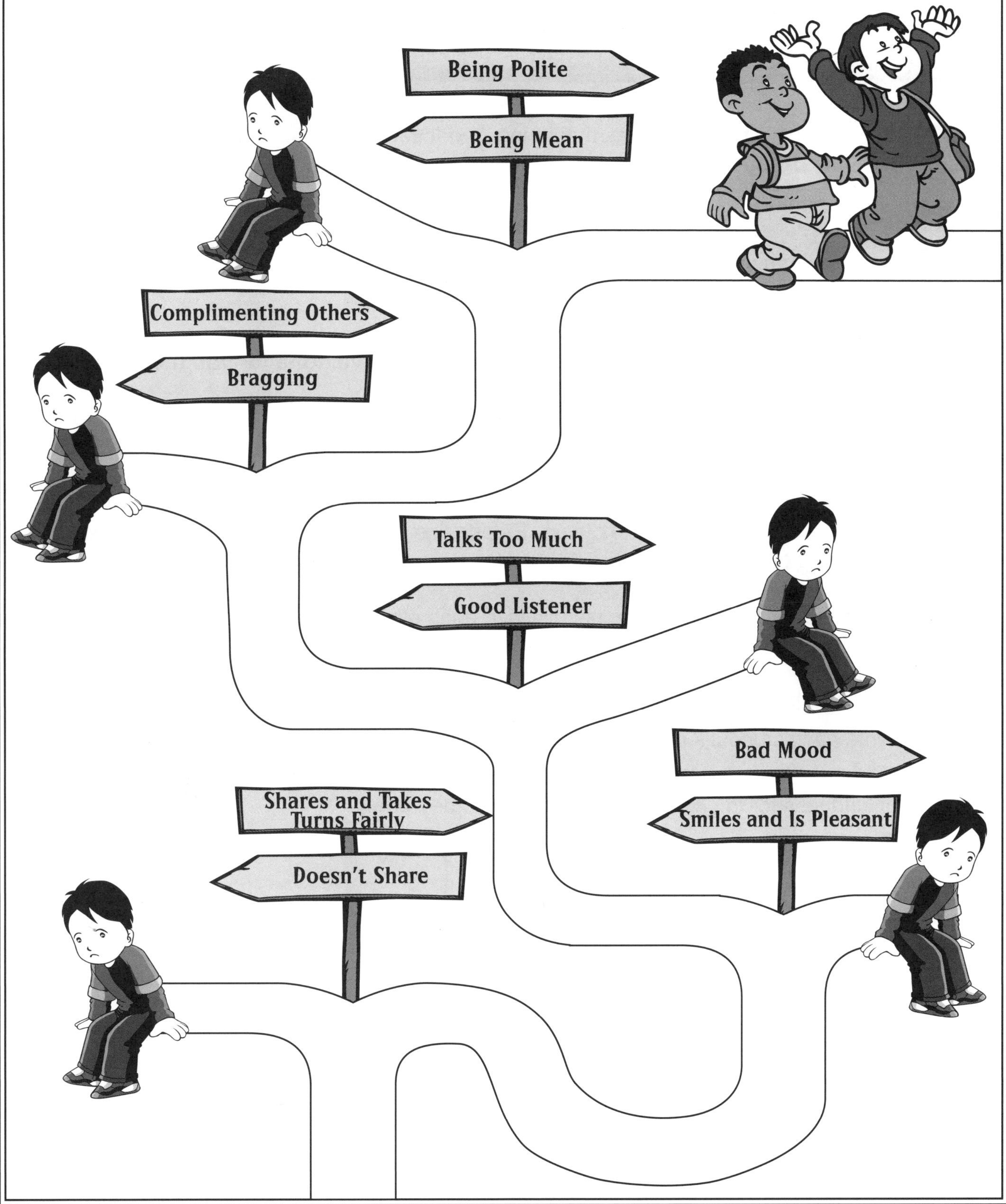

Activity 17 · Activity for LIVING · Friendship

Kind Acts of Caring

Overview: This activity emphasizes that being kind, caring, and nice is an important part of friendship.

Materials

✓ Paper and pen/pencil for each student

Procedures

1. Say: **Share kind, caring, or nice things that others have done for you that you appreciate.**

2. Ask: **How did it feel when others shared an act of kindness toward you?** Discuss.

3. Direct students to draw a large heart on a sheet of paper and list all the ways they can think of to be nice, kind, and caring to others. Emphasize that being kind, caring, and nice is an essential part of being a good friend.

4. Allow time for students to share their list with each other and to add additional items to their own list.

5. Assign the following *CARING CLASSMATE* activity:
   - ★ Write each student's name on a slip of paper and have each student draw a name.
   - ★ Then instruct each student to choose acts of kindness from their "heart list" to do the act of kindness for the classmate whose name they drew.
   - ★ Set a time frame for completing the acts of kindness – either by the end of the school day or week.
   - ★ At the end of the day/week, allow students to guess their "Caring Classmate" and tell why. Then ask the class, "Will the real "Caring Classmate" of ___ please stand up?"

Activity 18

Activity for LIVING

Friendship

When to Say 'No'

Overview: This activity focuses on the importance of saying 'no' to a friend in certain situations and provides strategies and support for making the right choice.

Materials

- ✓ Copy of the *When to Say 'No'* worksheet
- ✓ Copy of the *When to Say 'No'* posters

Procedure:

1. Ask: **What does the saying "Monkey See, Monkey Do" mean? Why do people go along with or copy what other people are doing?** (Bring in the concept of peer pressure.)

2. Ask: **Have you ever done something to go along with your friends and you got that *uh-oh* feeling? What does that *uh-oh* feeling mean?**

3. Ask: **We want to be able to say YES to our friends but could there be times when we should say NO to our friends? What are some situations when we should say NO? What risk do we run if we say NO to a friend? Is it worth it?**

4. Ask: **How do we say NO to a friend?** Review the different techniques given at the top of the *When to Say 'No'* worksheet. Add additional techniques of your own.

5. Share and discuss the *When to Say 'No'* posters.

6. Direct students to complete the friendship dilemmas on the *When to Say 'No'* worksheet.

When to Say 'No'

WORK SHEET

Directions: *Complete the following friendship dilemma situations. Use the "Ways to Say No" information to help you handle the situation.*

Friendship Dilemma: *Your friend forgot to do his homework and ask you if he can copy your homework so he won't get in trouble.*

What are you thinking?

____

How would you handle?

____

Friendship Dilemma: *Your friend is mad at Nancy and tells you not to talk to her anymore but Nancy is also a friend of yours that you enjoy talking to and spending time with.*

What are you thinking?

____

How would you handle?

____

Friendship Dilemma: *Your friend asks you to go in the teacher's desk and take some candy while she distracts the teacher.*

What are you thinking?

____

How would you handle?

____

WAYS TO SAY NO

JUST SAY NO -

"No, thanks."

"I don't want to."

MAKE AN EXCUSE -

"I can't. I have a test to study for."

SAY IT WITH DRAMA -

"Are you crazy!"

"No way! If I got caught I'd be grounded for the rest of my life!"

BETTER IDEA -

"Why don't we play video games instead."

OTHER SUGGESTIONS -

____

____

IF A FRIEND ask you to do something that breaks a rule, goes against what you know is right, or makes you feel uncomfortable you can,

JUST SAY NO!

Friends

are important…

but it's more important to

BE TRUE TO YOURSELF!

Know when to say YES

and when to say NO

to your friends!

THINK FOR YOURSELF!
Don't be controlled by your friends.

Friends may come and go but your

best

friend

is

yourself

who is with you for a lifetime.

PROBLEM SOLVING*

Problem Solving is an essential skill to success. Problems are and will be a part of everyday life now and in the future so it's important for children to learn the framework and skills to handle problems. Often our young people either turn to adults to "fix" their problems or they get mad or frustrated with the situation. Our goal is to teach the steps and provide a wide variety of strategies so children themselves can take responsibility for solving or managing the problems that arise.

This section includes the three steps to problem solving, managing our anger that may arise so that it does not escalate the problem, and then learning eight problem solving skills that can be utilized to solve problems. This section begins with a Problem Solving Pond visual that incorporates all the problem solving skills presented in this section. The Problem Solving Pond offers a creative approach to learning the basic three steps of problem solving as indicated by the three stepping stones, provides a detour for anger management (Anger Management Island), and then offers eight strategies for handling the problem as shown on the lily pads. **The activities in this section can be used independently to teach problem solving skills or can be used in its entirety utilizing the skills in the visual of the Problem Solving Pond Poster.**

If you are teaching all of the skills in this section, consider creating a booklet of the worksheets for each student to be used as a reminder and reinforcement of the skills shared.

** Strategies in the Problem Solving Section are adapted from Senn and Sitsch, (1999) Coping with Conflict: An Elementary Approach. Youthlight, Inc. Chapin, SC*

Problem Solving Pond
I need to calm down!
Take a deep breath, count to 10, & calm down
Draw or write about it
Tell someone
Listen to music or sing a song
Three Rules of Anger Management
1. Do not hurt yourself.
2. Do not hurt others.
3. Do not hurt property.
ANGER MANAGEMENT ISLAND
(Name) I feel ______ when you ______ Please ______
Heart Talk
Take Turns
Humor
Apologize
Give and Take
For BULLYING Problems, Visit BULLY-Free ISLAND
Problem Solving Pond
Share
Anger Management
Detour to Anger Management Island
Get Help
Stay Away
Ignore
SUCCESS LAND
Who? What? Why?
STEP ONE
WHAT IS THE PROBLEM?
Be a Fact Finder
STEP TWO
WHAT CAN I DO?
STEP THREE
TRY AN IDEA!

Activity 19

Activity for LIVING

Problem Solving

Problem Solving Pond

Poster and Overview

Overview: The Problem Solving Pond provides the visual to teach and reinforce the skills of problem solving.

Materials

- ✓ *Problem Solving Pond Poster* from the book can be copied as is or enlarged and/or color added and displayed for discussion. OR a 17"x11" full color *Problem Solving Pond* poster can be purchased through YouthLight (1-800-209-9774) to display in each class.
- ✓ Copy of the *Problem Solving Pond Role Play Cards*

Poster Explanation

The challenge of the Problem Solving Pond is to successfully help our frog friends get across the water to Success Land by using the problem solving stepping stones and problem solving lily pads to solve their problems. The poster focuses on the following concepts:

- ✭ **Three steps to problem solving** as shown on the three stepping stones of: What is the problem? What can I do? and Try an idea!
- ✭ **Problem solving strategies** as indicated by the lily pads: anger management (refers students to visit the anger management island), share, take turns, heart talk, apologize, give and take, humor, ignore, stay away, and get help. An additional lily pad, "For Bullying Problems, visit Bully Free Island" is added for bullying problems. See the section on Bullying Prevention for more information.
- ✭ **Guidelines and strategies for managing our anger** are provided on the Anger Management Island. Often anger can accompany problems and if the anger and frustration are not managed they can do more harm to the problem. Therefore students are referred to the Anger Management Island to follow the three rules of anger management (do not hurt yourself, others, or property) and to follow suggestions on the life preserver to calm or manage the anger.
- ✭ **Optional:** The **angry alligator** is included in the pond. You may choose to add a reference in your lessons of the importance of staying on the right path of the stepping stones and lily pads so you don't end up in the water with the alligator.

Variety of Uses of the Poster

- ✯ Share the poster as an **introduction or overview** to problem solving. You may choose to copy, enlarge and color, create as an overhead, or scan to display with LCD projector, promethean, smart board, etc. OR 17"x11" full color *Problem Solving Pond* posters can be purchased through YouthLight (1-800-209-9774).
- ✯ Display the poster for individual, group, or class as a **reference and visual reminder** of problem solving steps and strategies.
- ✯ Poster can be copied and **sent home for reinforcement** of skills introduced.
- ✯ Turn the poster into an **INTERACTIVE WALL MURAL** where students can cognitively, visually, and kinesthetically participate in the problem solving process. Here's how:
    - Paint the poster as a wall mural in a hallway or other targeted area that students have access.
    - On the floor underneath the wall mural make and tape down the three stepping stones spaced along the wall mural. This allows the students to step on each stepping stone as they follow the process. You may choose to add removable, laminated, construction paper, problem solving lily pads on top of the painted lily pads so the selected lily pad can be removed and placed on the floor for the student to continue their problem solving journey.
    - **Make available role play cards (see *Problem Solving Pond Role Play Cards*) so students can practice and/or "walk through" the problem solving process**.
    - Direct students to the Problem Solving Pond Wall Mural to assist when they have a real problem to solve.
    - Direct students to the Anger Management Island when struggling with anger issues.
- ✯ Start a **Problem Solvers Club** at your school. Participants can include those who have used good problem solving skills for a difficult problem, or participants may be a chosen group whose job it is to help others to use the problem solving framework to solve problems. Students can also be challenged to add new problem solving lily pads to the poster/wall mural as they find other problem solving strategies that work.

Problem Solving Pond
Role Play Cards

WORK SHEET

Directions: *Help our frog friends solve their problems. Refer to the Problem Solving Pond Poster for strategies and steps to solve problems.*

My friends and I always argue over who gets to go first when playing a game. What can I do?

I am trying to do my homework in the afternoons but my brother is making so much noise that I can't think. What can I do?

At recess when I was playing soccer, some of the others started laughing at the way I kicked the ball. What can I do?

My friend borrowed my markers without asking and it bothers me. What can I do?

When I sat in the back of the bus, some of the older kids started teasing me. What can I do?

I was in a bad mood this morning and said some mean things to my friend. Now she won't talk to me. What can I do?

Activity 20 | Activity for LIVING | Problem Solving

The Stepping Stones

Overview: This activity presents the following three steps in the problem solving process: What is the problem? What can I do? and Try an idea!

Materials

✓ 3 large circles for visuals of the stepping stones with the following information:

- ✯ Step 1: What is the problem? Be a fact finder.
- ✯ Step 2: What can I do?
- ✯ Step 3: Try an idea!

✓ Copy of *The Stepping Stones* worksheet

✓ Optional: Copy of the *Problem Solving Pond* poster

Procedures

1. Ask: **Do problems ever come up in our day? Give some examples.** (May include such examples as classmate borrows something without asking, classmate has their 'stuff' on your desk, being teased, arguing about whose turn it is or who goes first, cutting in line, etc.) **How do we handle the problems when they come up?** Use this opportunity to role play some appropriate and some inappropriate ways to handle problems. Compliment them on knowing the right way to handle problems. If the student shares that they would go to an adult for help, agree that there are times that we do need adults but there are many times that we can handle our problems on our own by using our good brain to be problem solvers. Share with the student that we will be learning the steps and strategies of problem solving so we can handle our problems well.

2. Hold up the first step to problem solving and share. Ask: **Why is it important to ask "What's the problem? What do you think it means by "Be a Fact Finder"?** Point out that there may be times that because we haven't gotten all of the facts we jump to the wrong conclusion about a problem and actually create a problem that wasn't there. In order to be a 'fact finder' we need to gather information by observation and asking questions. You may choose to use the visual of a detective whose job is to get the facts.

3. Share some examples of not getting the facts and jumping to the wrong conclusion. Examples may include: someone bumping into you and at first you think they did it on purpose but later realize it was an accident, or hearing through gossip that someone said something mean about you but later learned that it wasn't true, or friends seem to

be leaving you – telling secrets - but then you find out later they were planning a surprise birthday party for you.

4. Share the second and third stepping stone of "What can I do?" and "Try an idea!" Explain that once we get all of the facts about a problem then we need to choose an appropriate way to handle the problem and then try it.

5. **OPTIONAL:** If you are using the *Problem Solving Pond* poster as a visual, relate the idea of using the problem solving stepping stones and problem solving lily pads to safely get through the water to the other side to Success Land. Point out the angry alligator in the water and the importance of staying on track using the stepping stones and lily pads to stay away from the alligator.

6. Complete *The Stepping Stones* worksheet to reinforce the basics of problem solving and promote further discussion on how to gather the facts to determine the actual problem.

The Stepping Stones

WORK SHEET

Materials Needed: *crayons, scissors, and glue*

Directions: *Read each of the pieces of the puzzle and color the puzzle pieces that share good ways to solve problems. Next, cut out the colored puzzle pieces. Then put the pieces of the puzzle together inside the shape of the stepping stone and glue the pieces in place.*

Be a detective, ask questions (who? what? why?) and gather information to understand the problem.

Always blame the other person for the problem.

Be a good problem solver by trying different ideas to solve the problem.

Yell at the other person.

Get mad at the person and plan to get back at him or her.

If you try one way to solve a problem and it dosen't work - give up!

Don't jump to conclusions about the problem - get the facts.

Always get mad when you see a friend looking your way and laughing.

Take responsibility for being a problem solver.

Always wait for an adult to take care of all your problems.

Think of good ways to solve problems by asking yourself, "What can I do?"

Activity 21 | Activity for LIVING | Problem Solving

Anger Management Island

Overview: This activity reviews the damage our 'out of control anger' can do in problem solving and provides guidelines (rules) and suggestions for anger management.

Materials

- ✓ Visual of a life preserver – picture, replica, or actual life preserver
- ✓ Copy of the *Anger Management Island* worksheet
- ✓ Optional: copy of the *Problem Solving Pond* poster
- ✓ Optional: lifesaver candy for each student

Procedures

1. Ask: **What happens when we get angry? Do we always think straight and make good choices when we are angry?**

2. Ask: **If we have a problem and we choose to let our anger get out of control – will it make our problem better or worse?** Summarize that feeling angry is okay but our anger out of control is not okay. Relate anger to the visual of the volcano sharing that when a volcano is inactive and doesn't have the steam and heat there is no danger but when a volcano erupts then the hot lava and fire damages everything in its path.

3. Ask: **What are ways that we can calm our volcano or calm our anger?** Refer to the *Anger Management Island* worksheet or the *Problem Solving Pond* Poster and review the sign of the three rules of anger management located on the Anger Management Island. The three rules include: Do not hurt yourself, Do not hurt property, Do not hurt others. Explain each rule, giving examples.

4. Hold up your visual of a life preserver and ask: **What is the purpose of a life preserver?** Connect that calming our anger is like a life preserver. Share that we can save ourselves from making the problem worse by finding okay ways to calm our anger and be in control. Brainstorm okay ways to calm our anger. Use the guidelines of the anger rule sign on the worksheet.

5. Complete the *Anger Management Island* worksheet. You may choose to give students lifesaver candy to reinforce the concept.

6. **OPTIONAL:** If you are using the *Problem Solving Pond* as the problem solving framework, refer to the poster and explain that if your anger gets out of control regarding a problem then you need to detour to the Anger Management Island to calm you anger. On the Anger Management Island follow the rules of anger management sign and the suggestions on the life preserver so you can return to problem solving.

Anger Mangement Island

WORK SHEET

Directions: *On the life preserver, write suggestions of good ways to handle anger.*

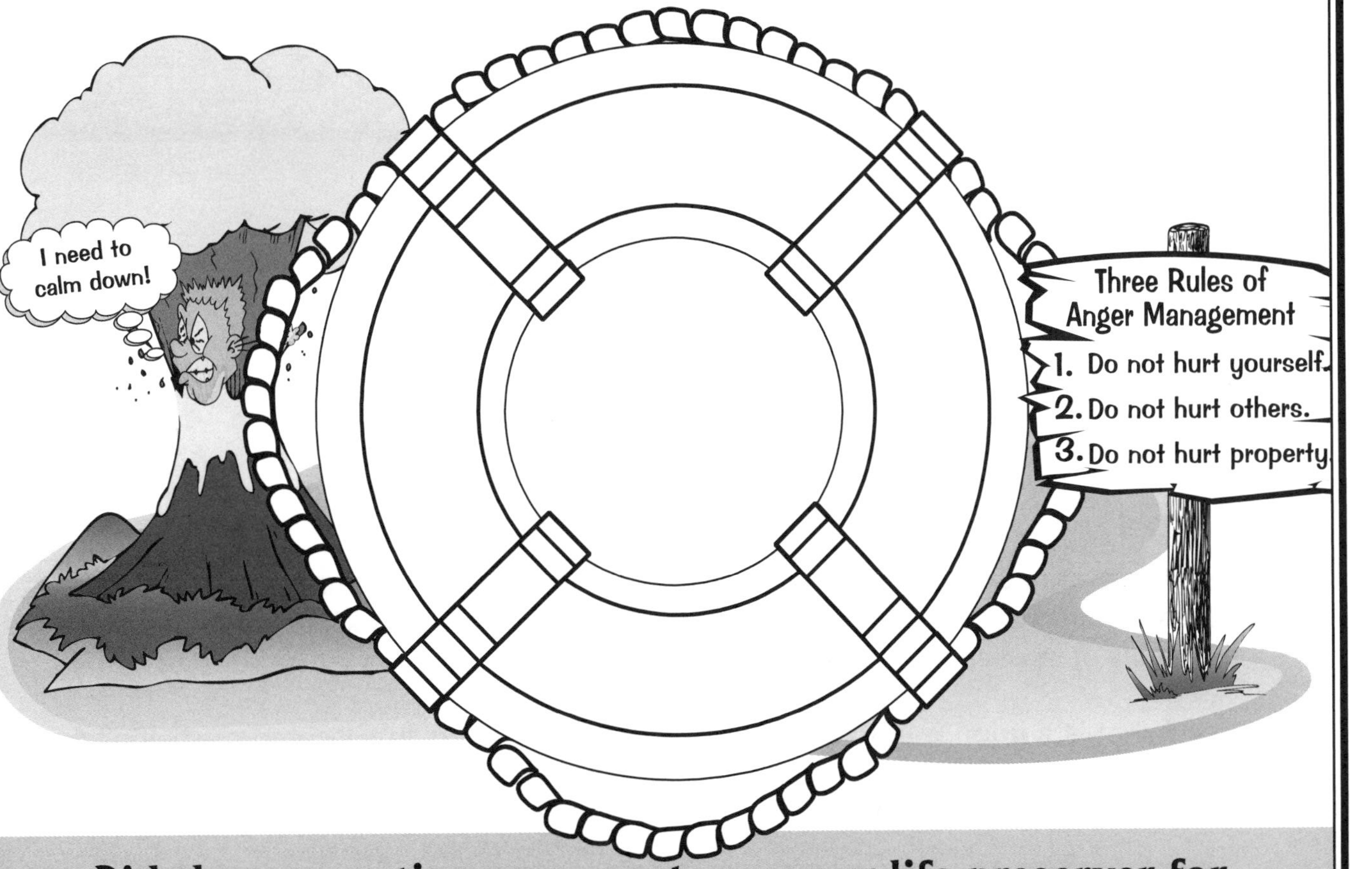

Did the suggestions you wrote on your life preserver for handling anger follow the rules of anger management?

Directions: *Answer the following.*

1. You feel angry when your friend won't let you join the game. How would you manage your anger?

    ____

    ____

2. You feel angry when Kevin bumped into your Science project you had worked hard to complete. Your project fell to the floor and broke into pieces. How would you manage your anger?

    ____

    ____

Activity 22 | Activity for LIVING | Problem Solving

Share

Overview: This activity explores the problem solving strategy of sharing.

Materials

- ✓ Copy of the picture book, "*Mine!*" By Kevin Luthardt
- ✓ Copy of the *Share* worksheet
- ✓ Optional: copy of the *Problem Solving Pond* poster

Procedures

1. Ask: **What are some ways you solve problems by sharing? Name some things that can be shared and things that cannot be shared** (include medicine or toothbrush as examples of what cannot be shared).

2. Ask: **What is a good way to share?** (Include such answers that incorporate being fair such as offering, letting the other person choose, one person can half it and the other person chooses which half).

3. Introduce the story "*Mine!*": **In our story today the two brothers have a problem sharing a gift from their grandmother. Let's read to find out how the boys felt about not sharing and the problems it caused and what they learn.**

4. Share the story. Take time to explore each picture, looking at the body language to guess the feelings and sharing what each may be thinking about the problem.

5. After reading the story, reinforce the words - MINE, YOURS, and OURS - and connect them to the problem solving strategy of Share.

6. **OPTIONAL:** If you are using the *Problem Solving Pond* as the problem solving framework, refer to the poster and point out the Problem Solving Lily Pad of SHARE. Explain that SHARING is one strategy that can be used to solve problems.

7. Complete the *Share* worksheet.

Share

WORK SHEET

BE A PROBLEM SOLVER... SHARE

When you share, both can use at the same time.

When I have a problem such as ______________________________

____

I could problem solve by using the **SHARE** strategy.

_ _

Directions: *For each situation, circle the 👍 to indicate things that can be* ***SHARED*** *and the 👎 for things that are not okay to SHARE.*

1. crayons
2. lollipop
3. prescription medicine
4. books
5. cards, games

Activity 23

Activity for LIVING

Problem Solving

Take Turns

Overview: This activity explores the problem solving strategy and methods of taking turns and reviews appropriate responses when having the first turn or not.

Materials

- ✓ Dice, coin, 3 different length straws or sticks
- ✓ Copy of the *Take Turns* worksheet
- ✓ Optional: copy of the *Problem Solving Pond* poster

Procedures

1. Ask: **What are some problems you can solve by taking turns? The problem solving strategies of sharing and taking turns are similar but different. What is the difference between sharing and taking turns?** (the difference is when you share, you can both use at the same time and when you take turns only one person can use or do at a time.)

2. Create the scene for a role play by saying: **Barry just got a new video game – it is a one player game. Two of Barry's neighborhood friends are over at his house when they see the new game. All are excited and want to play the game. They begin to argue over who gets to go first.** (Explain that one of the friends could have just offered to let the other go first and that would have solved the taking turns but if both or all want to go first you have to find a fair way to decide. Brainstorm with the students fair ways to decide who goes first).

3. Hold up a pair of dice and ask: **How can dice help decide who takes the first turn?** Invite two volunteers to come up and roll the dice to help decide who goes first with the highest roll going first. For the person that got the highest roll of the dice, turn to them and ask them if they should brag and say "I get to go first! I won!" then turn to the person who rolled the lowest and ask them if they should pout, get mad, or say, "That's not fair, I want to roll again". As a group determine appropriate things each could say with the roll of the dice.

4. Continue different role plays teaching different chance or luck strategies to help determine who goes first. Role play a flip of the coin, drawing straws, or rock/paper/scissors. Have the students practice saying polite things to each other as they may win or lose the flip of the coin, draw of the straw, or rock/paper/scissors.

5. **OPTIONAL:** If you are using the *Problem Solving Pond* as the problem solving framework, refer to the poster and point out the Problem Solving Lily Pad of TAKE TURNS. Explain that TAKING TURNS is one strategy that can be used to solve problems.

Take Turns

WORK SHEET

BE A PROBLEM SOLVER... TAKE TURNS

Find a fair way to decide who goes first, second, third...

When I have a problem such as ______________________________

____

I could problem solve by using the **TAKE TURNS** strategy.

Directions: *For each of the following, what would be fair to decide who has the first turn? Write a polite thing you could say if you did or did not get to go first. Write your answers.*

1. **Two friends both want to bat first at a neighborhood baseball game.**

   What would you do? ______________________________

   What would you say if you DID get to go first? ______________________________

   What would you say if you DID NOT get to go first? ______________________________

2. **Three students in class all want to borrow the same book from the class library.**

   What would you do? ______________________________

   What would you say if you DID get to go first? ______________________________

   What would you say if you DID NOT get to go first? ______________________________

3. **Your brother and you both want a turn on the snow sled. The sled only holds one person at a time.**

   What would you do? ______________________________

   What would you say if you DID get to go first? ______________________________

   What would you say if you DID NOT get to go first? ______________________________

Activity 24

Activity for LIVING

Problem Solving

Heart Talk

Overview: This activity uses the format of an "I" message to teach a caring way to discuss problems with friends.

Materials

- ✓ Board or chart paper and marker
- ✓ Copy of *Heart Talk* worksheet
- ✓ Optional: copy of the *Problem Solving Pond* poster

Procedures

1. Ask: **Do you think people listen better if you are mad and yell at them or if you are able to talk to them in a polite way?**

2. Share: **Problems do come up with our friends but yelling at them typically doesn't help the problem. It only makes it worse. There are also times when our friends may not realize they are doing something that is a problem for us and our yelling only creates a problem that wasn't there to begin with.**

3. Explain that Heart Talk is a caring way to tell someone that you have a problem with something they are doing. Share that Heart Talk has four steps:

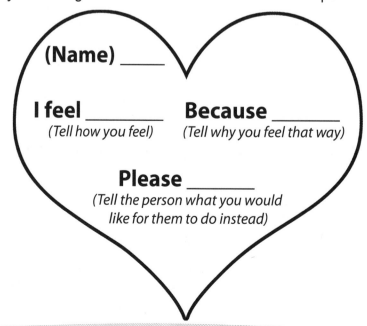

(Name) ____

I feel ______
(Tell how you feel)

Because ______
(Tell why you feel that way)

Please ______
(Tell the person what you would like for them to do instead)

4. Practice role playing with students having the student respond with a Heart Talk message. You may choose to put on the board or chart paper the beginning sentences to the Heart Talk message. Remind students that their tone of voice and body language also need to send a caring message.

5. **Caution** students that Heart Talk typically works in dealing with problems with friends or if the problem is created by accident. Heart Talk is usually not effective if someone is being mean or creating a problem on purpose. A different problem solving strategy would need to be used.

6. **OPTIONAL:** If you are using the *Problem Solving Pond* as the problem solving framework, refer to the poster and point out the Problem Solving Lily Pad of HEART TALK. Explain that HEART TALK is one strategy that can be used to solve problems.

Heart Talk

WORK SHEET

BE A PROBLEM SOLVER use... HEART TALK

Heart talk is a caring way to talk over a problem.

When I have a problem such as ______________________________

____

I could solve the problem in a caring way by using the **HEART TALK** strategy.

_ _

Directions: *Complete the Heart Talk Messages.*

______________ *(Name)*

I feel ________________ **because** ______________________________.

Please ______________ __________.

Jessie steps in front of you in line.

Charlie uses your marker without asking.

______________ *(Name)*

I feel ________________ **because** ______________________________.

Please ______________ __________.

Samantha, who you sit next to, always has her books and things over on your desk and it bothers you.

______________ *(Name)*

I feel ________________ **because** ______________________________.

Please ______________ __________.

Michael is making noises while he is working and it is bothering you.

______________ *(Name)*

I feel ________________ **because** ______________________________.

Please ______________ __________.

You share a room with your sister, Julia, who always leaves trash and other things on the floor. She never puts anything up. It bothers you.

______________ *(Name)*

I feel ________________ **because** ______________________________.

Please ______________ __________.

Activity 25

Activity for LIVING

Problem Solving

Apologize

Overview: This activity explores two types of apologies, the "my fault" and the "no fault" apology, and explores the two parts of an apology, say you're sorry and prove you're sorry.

Materials

- ✓ Copy of the story "*Sorry!*" By Trudy Ludwig
- ✓ Copy of the *Apologize* worksheet
- ✓ Optional: copy of the *Problem Solving Pond* poster

Procedures

1. Ask: **Does an apology, saying "I'm sorry", count if you don't really mean it?**

2. Share: **In our story today, Jack's friend Charlie knows how to get away with just about everything – just say "sorry" and grown-ups will always back down. Let's read and find out what happens when the person you've hurt knows you don't mean it.**

3. Discuss the story, including the following questions:
   - ✯ Jack said that 'being Charlie's friend wasn't easy'. What do you think he meant by that?
   - ✯ What did Leena mean when she said, "Sorry doesn't cut it!"?
   - ✯ How did Jack feel about what they did to Leena's science project? How did Charlie feel?
   - ✯ Mr. Marcus told the boys to "show Leena you're sorry by making right your wrong". What did the boys do to show they were sorry?
   - ✯ What do you think Jack learned in the story?

4. Share: **There are 2 kinds of an apology – the MY FAULT apology and the NO FAULT apology. With the MY FAULT apology we have done something wrong – sometimes by accident, sometimes on purpose, and sometimes we do the wrong thing and hurt others because we are not thinking. When we create a problem with another person we need to apologize. A true apology has 2 parts:**

Part 1: SAY YOU'RE SORRY - Use sincere words and body language (explain what you did wrong and how you feel about what you did).

Part 2: PROVE YOU'RE SORRY - Show that you are sorry by making right your wrong.

When we do make a mistake and cause a problem be ready to say "I'm sorry" and correct your wrong.

The second kind of an apology is a NO FAULT apology when you have a problem or argument with someone and you don't really know whose fault it is or who started it. That's when you can apologize by saying: "I'm sorry we have gotten into this argument. Let's find a way to work it out." Those words can be the first steps to ending the argument and solving the problem.

5. **OPTIONAL:** If you are using the *Problem Solving Pond* as the problem solving framework, refer to the poster and point out the Problem Solving Lily Pad of APOLOGIZE. Explain that APOLOGIZE is one strategy that can be used to solve problems.

6. Complete the Apologize worksheet.

Apologize

WORK SHEET

BE A PROBLEM SOLVER... APOLOGIZE

MY FAULT APOLOGY: *Use a "my fault apology" when you are responsible for saying or doing something wrong. Remember, there are two parts to the apology; saying you're sorry and proving you're sorry.*
"I'm sorry I __________. I feel __________. I will __________."

NO FAULT APOLOGY: *Use a "no fault apology" when both are arguing and you don't know who or how it started.* ***"I'm sorry that we got into this argument. Let's ________________."***

When I have a problem such as ____

____

I could problem solve by saying **I'M SORRY...**

_ _

Directions: *Write an apology for each of the situations below.*

By accident you bump into Henry in the hall. What would you say to apologize?

____

____

You are tired and don't want to be at school. A classmate asks you to help carry some books. You say, "I don't have to help you – leave me alone." What would you say to apologize?

____

____

When you were mad, you 'mess up' your friend's science project. What would you say to apologize?

____

____

After being together all weekend you and your best friend begin to argue over every little thing. What would you say to apologize?

____

____

You made fun of a classmate who was having trouble with their math. What would you say to apologize?

____

____

Activity 26

Activity for LIVING

Problem Solving

Give and Take

Overview: This activity explains the problem solving strategy of compromise.

Materials

- ✓ Approximately a 6' rope to demonstrate a 'tug of war'
- ✓ Copy of *Give and Take* worksheet
- ✓ Optional: copy of the *Problem Solving Pond* poster

Procedures

1. Hold up the rope and ask: **Who has ever played 'tug of war' before or seen it played?** Ask for a volunteer to join you to demonstrate the tugging in opposite directions. Ask: **What is the object of the game?** Summarize that in 'tug of war' there is a winner and a loser. Explain that problem solving is different. In problem solving we both want to be winners so we need to meet the other person in the middle to manage the problem. Demonstrate with the help of your volunteer that both bring the ends of the rope to the middle – both can then be declared a winner.

2. Ask: **What do you think we mean in problem solving when we say to both give in a little and meet the other person in the middle?**

3. Ask: **In what type of problem would the "Give and Take" strategy be helpful?**

4. Ask for volunteers to role play an example of the "Give and Take" strategy. Have two students hold opposite ends of the rope. Explain that they need to pretend they are siblings at home watching TV and start arguing over who gets to stretch out on the couch to watch TV. Have the students tug at their end as they each shout, "I want the couch… No, I want the couch". Then freeze the picture and have each student suggest a way they could give in a little and meet the other in the middle to solve the dilemma of the couch and TV. Then have them continue the role play sharing their "Give and Take" solution. (Perhaps they choose to share the couch by both sitting on the couch rather than one person getting to stretch out.)

5. **OPTIONAL:** If you are using the *Problem Solving Pond* as the problem solving framework, refer to the poster and point out the Problem Solving Lily Pad of GIVE AND TAKE. Explain that GIVE AND TAKE is one strategy that can be used to solve problems.

6. Complete the *Give and Take* worksheet, giving advice on how to give and take in a problem situation.

Give and Take

WORK SHEET

BE A PROBLEM SOLVER... GIVE AND TAKE

Meet the other person in the middle by each giving up something but also gaining something.

When I have a problem such as ______________________________

____

I could problem solve by using the **GIVE AND TAKE** strategy.

– –

Directions: *Give your advice below on the GIVE AND TAKE needed to manage the problem.*

Dear Problem Solver,

We have family night once a month and my brother and I get to choose the restaurant and movie for the family but we always seem to disagree. We end up fighting about which restaurant and movie. What is suppose to be a fun night ends up being miserable. What should we do?

Signed,
Miserable

Dear Miserable,

____

____

____

____

____

Signed,
Problem Solver

Dear Problem Solver,

A classmate and I have been assigned a Science project to complete. We have to write a report and make a visual or display related to the report. We both want to make the display and neither of us want to write the report. We seem to keep arguing over who gets to do the display. What should we do?

Signed,
Confused

Dear Confused,

____

____

____

____

____

Signed,
Problem Solver

Activity 27

Activity for LIVING

Problem Solving

Humor

Overview: This activity explores the right time and place for humor in dealing with problems.

Materials

- ✓ Copy of the *Humor* worksheet
- ✓ Optional: copy of the *Problem Solving Pond* poster

Procedures

1. Say: **Another problem solving strategy is HUMOR. What do you think HUMOR means?** Explain that humor means to add some laughter – to find the fun in it.

2. Say: **We don't need to get upset and take every problem so seriously, there are some problems that we just need to laugh off and keep going.**

3. Ask: **Do you think we should ever laugh at the other person or make fun of them? What do you think may happen if we did that?**

4. Say: **HUMOR and finding a way to laugh about your problem is a great strategy as long as you don't laugh at or make fun of the other person – that will only add to the problem.**

5. **OPTIONAL:** If you are using the *Problem Solving Pond* as the problem solving framework, refer to the poster and point out the Problem Solving Lily Pad of HUMOR. Explain that HUMOR is one strategy that can be used to solve problems.

6. Review the *Humor* worksheet. You may choose to role play the examples. Give each student a copy of the worksheet to complete and to save as a reinforcement of the skill.

Humor

WORK SHEET

BE A PROBLEM SOLVER use... HUMOR

At times, a little humor or laughter can help us deal with our problems. But make sure you don't ever laugh at or make fun of the other person.

When I have a problem such as ______________________________

____

I could problem solve by using **HUMOR**.

_ _

Directions: *Read the following and circle the best answer to handle the problem situation.*

1. You are walking down the hall and you trip. Someone laughs and says, "What - you haven't learned to walk yet? You could:
   A. Turn red in the face, with head down and walk away.
   B. Join in the laughing and say, "Yeah, I guess it did look pretty funny".
   C. Get mad and yell at the person to stop.

2. You wore your new glasses for the first time at school and a classmate laughs at you calling you four eyes. You could:
   A. Go tell the teacher.
   B. Say something mean back.
   C. Laugh and tell them you can see twice as good now.

3. You strike out at your time to bat at baseball. Your teammate teases you about how you swing the bat.
   A. You say, "Oh, it was just hot out here, I was just trying to stir up a breeze."
   B. You walk off in a huff.
   C. You throw the bat toward your teammate.

4. In a rush getting dressed you put on 2 different color socks. At school a classmate makes fun of you not being able to dress yourself.
   A. You can say, "Yeah, just wanted to be colorful today."
   B. You get embarrassed and your face turns red.
   C. You get mad and shove your classmate.

Activity 28

Activity for LIVING

Problem Solving

Ignore

Overview: This activity emphasizes the problem solving strategy of ignore. It teaches two steps in ignoring – don't react and get busy doing something else.

Materials

- ✓ Pair of earmuffs
- ✓ Copy of the *Ignore* worksheet
- ✓ Optional: copy of the *Problem Solving Pond* poster

Procedures

1. Display a pair of earmuffs and ask: **What does a pair of earmuffs block out?** (the cold)

2. Say: **Today we are going to pretend that the earmuffs can block out mean things someone may say to us. We can't control what others may say and do but we can control how we choose to handle it and we may choose to pretend we do not hear the mean things they are saying.**

3. Explain that there are 2 key points to effectively use the strategy of Ignore:
   - ✯ Don't React – say little or nothing.
   - ✯ Get Busy Doing Something Else (turn to a friend on the other side and talk with them, go sharpen a pencil, pretend to drop your book and get up to pick it up, walk away, etc.).

4. Model for them and then role play with students how to effectively block out or ignore the problem.

5. **OPTIONAL:** If you are using the *Problem Solving Pond* as the problem solving framework, refer to the poster and point out the Problem Solving Lily Pad of IGNORE. Explain that IGNORE is one strategy that can be used to solve problems.

6. Continue practicing this strategy by completing the *Ignore* worksheet.

Ignore

WORK SHEET

BE A PROBLEM SOLVER use... IGNORE

Choose not to react to the problem and get busy doing something else.

When I have a problem such as ________________________________

____

I could problem solve by choosing not to listen or react - to use the **IGNORE** strategy.

_ _

Directions: *Use the "ignore" strategy to problem solve the following situations. Answer the following.*

Situation: *A teammate starts bragging about how great he can play baseball and then he laughs and makes fun of how you can't seem to ever catch the ball.*

What to think to myself? ________________________________.

I can ignore by ________________________________.

Situation: *In the hallway a student starts laughing and pointing in your direction.*

What to think to myself? ________________________________.

I can ignore by ________________________________.

Situation: *As the graded test papers were being returned, a classmate saw your low grade and made a hurtful comment about how you're not very smart.*

What to think to myself? ________________________________.

I can ignore by ________________________________.

Activity 29

Activity for LIVING

Problem Solving

Stay Away

Overview: This activity shares the problem solving strategy of "stay away" when the situation is dangerous or frequently ends up as a problem.

Materials

- ✓ Copy of the *Stay Away* worksheet
- ✓ Optional: copy of the *Problem Solving Pond* poster

Procedures

1. Ask: **Do you think there are times that you need to stay away or avoid a problem? Give examples.**

2. Explain that if the situation is dangerous or frequently ends up as a problem then consider staying away or avoiding the situation.

3. Ask: **Should we stay away from or avoid every problem? How do we know which to stay away from and which to deal with?**

4. **OPTIONAL:** If you are using the *Problem Solving Pond* as the problem solving framework, refer to the poster and point out the Problem Solving Lily Pad of STAY AWAY. Explain that STAY AWAY is one strategy that can be used to solve problems.

5. Complete the *Stay Away* worksheet and then role play the situations.

Stay Away

WORK SHEET

BE A PROBLEM SOLVER... STAY AWAY or AVOID

If the situation is dangerous or frequently ends up as a problem, consider staying away or avoiding the situation.

When I have a problem such as ______________________________

____

I could problem solve by **STAYING AWAY**.

_ _

Directions: *Answer the following.*

I seem to be arguing a lot with a friend or classmate. What should I do?

____

____

We are playing at recess and everyday we end up fighting about the rules or how someone is playing the game. What should I do?

____

____

I sit at the back of the bus where the older kids sit. They always tease me. What should I do?

____

____

Directions: *List situations of your own that you may need to stay away from or avoid.*

1. ____

2. ____

3. ____

4. ____

Activity 30

Activity for LIVING

Problem Solving

Get Help

Overview: This activity helps to differentiate between handling problems independently and when to "get help".

Materials

- ✓ Copy of *Get Help* worksheet
- ✓ Optional: copy of the *Problem Solving Pond* poster

Procedures

1. Ask: **When you were very young who handled all of your problems? When you are an adult who will handle your problems?**

2. Summarize: **In most cases when we are adults we are the ones responsible for handling our own problems. So, if as an adult, our goal is to know good ways to solve problems how does that happen?** Reinforce with the students that learning now and practicing our problem solving skills is very important. Share that the skills we learn now can help us throughout life – the problems will change but the skills still apply.

3. Ask: **Are there some problems that are difficult that we need help to handle? Share some examples.**

4. Share: **The general guideline is if someone is about to be hurt you need to get help OR if you have a problem and you have tried many ways to settle the problem but have been unsuccessful then you need to get help from someone you trust.**

5. Ask: **Who are some people you can trust to help you deal with a problem?**

6. Ask: **When you become an adult and are handling your own problems will there still be some problems that you may need help with? As adults who do you turn to for help when you have a difficult problem?** (Review such answers as: the police, church, helping organizations…)

7. **OPTIONAL:** If you are using the *Problem Solving Pond* as the problem solving framework, refer to the poster and point out the Problem Solving Lily Pad of GET HELP. Explain that GET HELP is one strategy that can be used to solve problems. However, it would be important to try at least 3 or 4 other problem solving strategies on your own first and if you still have a problem then GET HELP. Try other strategies first unless the problem is an emergency and someone is being hurt – if it is an emergency, then use the GET HELP strategy first.

8. Complete the *Get Help* worksheet.

Get Help

WORK SHEET

BE A PROBLEM SOLVER... GET HELP when needed

If someone is about to be hurt or you have tried many ways to settle the problem unsuccessfully, go to a person you trust for help.

When I have a problem such as

I could problem solve by **GETTING HELP**.

Directions: *List examples of problems that are dangerous and you would need to GET HELP.*

List those you would go to for help:

HEALTHY CHOICES

It is important that we offer a foundation for our students in making healthy choices for themselves including saying 'no' to harmful drugs. This section includes field day type activities, skits, and posters to add to your healthy choice focus during the year.

Activity 31

Activity for LIVING

Healthy Choices

Recess Stations
Passport to Healthy Choices

Overview: The *Passport to Healthy Choices* provides a field day type activity where 6 stations are set up outdoors to include jump rope, friend compliment, sack race, jumping jacks, hula hoop, and making the responsible choice to say 'no'. The six stations are connected to the theme of "making healthy choices to stay drug free." Each student participating is given a passport where they can participate at each station to collect a stamp or sticker for their participation. This activity can typically be completed by a grade level in 30 minutes and can be offered during a grade level's extended recess time. Students are encouraged to go to ALL stations but can visit the stations in any order and can move from station to station when they are ready. Classroom teacher help is needed to take a few moments prior to the event to distribute the PASSPORTS and to review the procedures in visiting the stations (a teacher memo is included to explain procedures). Volunteers are also needed for each of the 6 stations. The intent of this activity is for students to experience and gain an understanding of healthy choices as students visit each station as well as to have a Passport as a reminder of the strategies for making healthy choices.

Materials

- ✓ Copy of the *Passport to Healthy Choices* for each participant - copy the 2 page passport on 1 sheet front and back
- ✓ Copy of the teacher memo for class teachers to explain procedures to students
- ✓ Adult volunteers (6-12), station signs, stamp/stickers for each station, and perhaps a desk/table at each station
- ✓ Equipment: 10 hula hoops, 10 jump ropes, 5 sacks

Preparation

- ★ Enlist the support of administration and faculty and schedule the event on the school calendar. The event can typically be offered during a grade level's recess time (20-30 minutes).
- ★ Secure adult volunteers (preferably 2 volunteers for each station) for the day/time of the event.
- ★ Advertise the upcoming *Passport to Healthy Choices* Recess event with posters and announcements days prior.

- ✯ Create station signs on posters to indicate the stations and gather the needed equipment as well as stamps/stamp pad or stickers to be used for the passports.
- ✯ Fold the *Passports to Healthy Choices* into fourths to create a booklet (fold so that the cover, *Passport to Healthy Choices*, is the front of the booklet and the station numbers are in order as you open the booklet with the "Winners Don't' Do Drugs" being the back cover.) Count out and distribute the booklets for each class along with the *Teacher Memo.*
- ✯ Ask the teacher's help to take a few moments to review with their students the event. See the *Teacher Memo* for event information.
- ✯ As the grade level or classes arrive you may welcome the students and direct them to visit the stations to complete their *Passport to Healthy Choices*.

Name ______________

Station 1: JUMP ROPE

Be Smart!
Don't Smoke!
Don't Take Harmful Drugs!

Jump Away From Drugs!

TEAM UP AGAINST DRUGS

Winners Don't Do Drugs!

Station 2: FRIENDS

Say something nice to a friend.

Report what you said to the volunteer at Station 2.

Friends Help Friends Stay Drug Free!

Station 3: SACK RACE

Drug Free... The Healthy Way To Be!

Join the race to GOOD HEALTH!

Station 4: EXERCISE

It is important to take care of your body:

* Eat good, nutritious food.
* Exercise each day.
* Drink plenty of water.
* Get a good night's rest.

Do 10 Jumping Jacks!

Station 5: HULA HOOP

I've got better things to do than drugs!

Don't go around in circles in your life!

Station 6: The RESPONSIBLE CHOICE

Read the ways to say NO to harmful drugs. Pick your favorite and tell the volunteer at Station 6.

- ❒ I want to stay healthy.
- ❒ I don't do drugs.
- ❒ I've got better things to do.
- ❒ No way!
- ❒ You've got to be kidding!
- ❒ I'm happy the way I am.

Teacher Memo
for Passport to Healthy Choices

To: Teachers
Re: Recess Event: *Passport to Healthy Choices*

Thank you for your continued support as we work together to help our students learn the importance of making healthy choices. Our upcoming *Passport to Healthy Choices* event is scheduled for ____. The *Passport to Healthy Choices* is a recess event that allows students to visit the 6 Stations to participate in a fun activity and to learn about making healthy choices and saying no to drugs. The focus of the stations is as follows:

Station 1: Students jump rope as they talk about the importance of "Jumping away from harmful drugs!"

Station 2: Students say something nice about a friend while stressing the importance of friends helping each other make good choices.

Station 3: Students participate in a sack race to promote the theme, "Join the race to Good Health."

Station 4: Students do jumping jacks and discuss the importance of taking care of their body through exercise, eating properly, and getting plenty of rest.

Station 5: Students play with the hula hoops but talk about healthy, better things to do rather than going around in circles with unhealthy choices/drugs.

Station 6: Students share ways they can say NO to harmful choices/drugs.

Distribute the passports to your students to review and explain the different stations.

Share that students may visit the stations in any order. There is no time limit for each station but encourage the student to keep moving on to different stations so they can visit all the stations during the recess time.

Share with the students that as they participate at each station they will get their passport stamped. Explain to students the concept of a passport and how passports are stamped as they visit different countries.

Encourage students to participate, enjoy, listen, and learn from the recess event. Explain that at the end of the event students will have a completed/stamped *Passport to Healthy Choices* that they can save, review, and display to remind them of making healthy choices.

Thank you for your help in making this event successful and meaningful for our students.

Activity 32

Activity for LIVING

Healthy Choices

Commercial
Healthy Choices... Priceless

Overview: This activity provides a short skit/commercial promoting the choice to be drug free.

Materials

- ✓ Items you choose to use in your skit such as video game, tickets, soccer ball
- ✓ Poster sign: "Being Drug Free is Priceless"
- ✓ 4 students to provide the skit

Skit

Student 1: *(Holds up a video game and says…)* **Video Game $285.**

Student 2: *(Holds up amusement park tickets and says…)* **Tickets to DisneyWorld $135.**

Student 3: *(Holds up a soccer ball and says…)* **Soccer ball $16.**

Student 4: *(Holds up the poster sign and says…)* **Being Drug Free is Priceless**

All Students: *(Other students join the 4th student and the students say in unison…)* **It doesn't cost anything to be drug-free. Make the right choice to say no to harmful drugs!**

Activity 33

Activity for LIVING

Healthy Choices

Skit - Just Say No!

Overview: This skit shares suggestions of ways to say NO to unhealthy choices.

Skit

(Need one person to introduce the skit and 3 students with speaking parts)

Introduction: **We know it's important to make healthy choices, therefore it's important to be prepared to say "no" if someone asks you to smoke, or take a drink, or tries to get you to do something you know is wrong. Here are some suggestions to saying no…**

Student 1: **Just say NO. No explanation needed. If "No" doesn't work the first time, then say it again stronger, "NO WAY!"**

Student 2: **Know the FACTS. Then, you can say, "No, it's unhealthy. I'm not interested."**

Student 3: **Have SOMETHING BETTER TO DO. You can say, "No thanks, I'm headed out to play basketball – do you want to join me?"**

Student 1: **When someone tries to pressure you to do something that is wrong you can just WALK AWAY.**

Student 2: **CHANGE THE SUBJECT. If someone says, "Hey, try this." You can say, "No, thanks. What did you think about that game last night?"**

Student 3: **AVOID situations or places that you feel could be trouble.**

All Students: *(in unison)* **Remember to say NO to drugs and YES to a healthy life.**

Activity 34

Activity for LIVING

Healthy Choices

Posters - Don't Do Drugs!

Overview: The posters provide a visual reinforcement of making the choice to say no to drugs.

Materials

✓ Copy of a set of posters for each classroom

Procedures

Posters can be copied and displayed around the room at the following strategic locations:

- ✯ "My Future is Bright Without Drugs" - Place by the light switch.
- ✯ "Time to Stay Healthy and Say No to Drugs" - Place by the clock.
- ✯ "Dump Drugs" - Place on the trashcan.
- ✯ "Wash Away Drugs" - Place by the sink.
- ✯ "Stay Sharp…Don't Do Drugs" - Place by the pencil sharpener.

MY FUTURE IS

BRIGHT

WITHOUT DRUGS

"TIME"

TO STAY HEALTHY

AND SAY "NO" TO DRUGS

DUMP
DRUGS

WASH AWAY DRUGS

STAY SHARP
DON'T DO
DRUGS

CHARACTER
Making the Home Connections with Table Talk

The development of good character is not an isolated skill to be taught in one area of a child's life. It is an effort of home, school, and community to instill in our young people the value of character. The development of good character touches our personal development for living, it impacts our success with academic development in learning, and good character is essential in the work force to be successful in our work.

Lessons, discussions, modeling, wall displays, skits, role-playing, puppet shows, awards, and highlighting historical figures of character are all creative ways to promote the development of good character. This section, **CHARACTER: MAKING THE HOME CONNECTIONS with TABLE TALK** adds another avenue to continue the talk, connecting **HOME** and **SCHOOL** for character development.

Introduction
Making the Home Connections with Table Talk

Overview: The *Character Table Talks* provide a set of questions for specific character traits. These questions were developed for home use to guide family discussions on character as school and home work together to instill the value of good character.

Materials

✓ Copy of the *Table Talk* reproducible that correlates to the character trait being addressed

Directions for Assembling

Fold the *Table Talk* in the middle and the ends at the top and bottom as indicated by the fold line so that the paper forms a triangle. The triangle forms a base so the *Table Talk* can be displayed on a table.

Options for Use

- You may choose to copy the *Table Talk* on white or colored paper and send home.
- You may choose to copy the *Table Talk* on cardstock (for sturdiness) and send home.
- You may choose to display the questions on the board and have the students write the questions on construction paper as they create their own *Table Talk* to send home.
- The *Table Talk* may also be displayed on the school website for parents to download, print, fold, and use.

Take time to review with your students how to use the *Table Talk* at home. Later, follow-up by allowing students to share about their home discussions.

Classroom teachers may choose to display a completed *Table Talk* to use in weekly class discussions.

Follow the directions on the *Table Talk* for use.

fold

Discuss: How do we show respect for our country? Review and discuss the words to the "Pledge of Allegiance" and our National Anthem, "The Star Spangled Banner."

Discuss: What does it mean to show respect for others? How does being respectful of others guide us in the right way to treat others?

(Include in your discussion how teasing, gossipping, pushing, shoving, or laughing at others in a mean way is not okay and does not show respect.)

RESPECT

fold

RESPECT

Character Table Talk Directions: At home, "Table Talk" discussions can be folded, placed in the center of the table at meals or other times so that each week discussions can reinforce good character. Thank you for working together to help our children develop good character.

Discuss: Our character word is RESPECT. Respect means to think well of, to honor, to care about, or have a good opinion of. Give examples of ways we show respect for ourselves?

Discuss: What does it mean to show respect for authority? Name some people in authority and give examples of how we are respectful.

fold

RESPONSIBLE

Discuss: How can we be responsible with our behavior and what we say and do? How can we be good problem solvers? What are some other examples of responsible actions?

Discuss: How does making a commitment and being dependable relate to being Responsible?

fold

RESPONSIBLE

Character Table Talk Directions: At home, "Table Talk" discussions can be folded, placed in the center of the table at meals or other times so that each week discussions can reinforce good character. Thank you for working together to help our children develop good character.

Discuss: Our character word is RESPONSIBLE. Being Responsible means to recognize and follow through with what is expected of one's self and things we need to do. What are some jobs or responsibilities you have at home?

Discuss: What are some ways that we can be responsible at school – in the classroom? On the playground? On the bus?

fold

fold

THANKFUL

Discuss: Share some things that people have said to you or done for you that you appreciate. Discuss ways that you can let others know that you are thankful and appreciative of what they say and do for you. Make a plan to show your appreciation.

Discuss: What are some things you can say and do for others that others would appreciate?

fold

THANKFUL

Character Table Talk Directions: At home, "Table Talk" discussions can be folded, placed in the center of the table at meals or other times so that each week discussions can reinforce good character. Thank you for working together to help our children develop good character.

Discuss: Our character word is THANKFUL. Being Thankful has two parts. One is being grateful for all that we have and what people say and do for us. The other part is taking the time to show our appreciation by telling others or writing a note. Make a list of things that you are thankful or grateful for.

Discuss: What does the following mean? "Rather than complain about what I do not have, I need to be thankful for the things that I do have."

fold

fold

CARING

Discuss: Empathy is an important word that relates to caring. Empathy is understanding and caring about another person's thoughts and feelings. It's like putting yourself in their place. Think back over your week and put yourself in someone else's place who may have had a difficult time. Discuss how you may have thought or felt if that were you. Share how you can help and show the person you care.

Discuss: What is your plan for this week to show others you care?

fold

CARING

Character Table Talk Directions: At home, "Table Talk" discussions can be folded, placed in the center of the table at meals or other times so that each week discussions can reinforce good character. Thank you for working together to help our children develop good character.

Discuss: Our character word is Caring. Caring means to show interest and concern for others – to be friendly and considerate. What are some ways you can show others you care?

Discuss: How do the following words relate to caring: being kind, sharing, and helping?

fold

fold

Discuss: What are some ways to be self-disciplined at home? At school?

Discuss: How do the following words relate to being self-disciplined: discipline (doing the things that *need* to be done – not just what you *want* to do), self-control (controlling your actions – your impulses and your anger), good judgment (considering the consequences to help us make a better choice)?

SELF-DISCIPLINED

fold

SELF-DISCIPLINED

Character Table Talk Directions: At home, "Table Talk" discussions can be folded, placed in the center of the table at meals or other times so that each week discussions can reinforce good character. Thank you for working together to help our children develop good character.

Discuss: Our character word is SELF-DISCIPLINED. Self-Discipline is you disciplining yourself or telling yourself to do the right thing without an adult telling or reminding you. Name some ways you already show your self-discipline.

Discuss: Why is being self-disciplined important?

fold

fold

COOPERATION

Discuss: How can you be cooperative with your family? Your friends? At school?

Discuss: Why is cooperation important?

fold

COOPERATION

Character Table Talk Directions: At home, "Table Talk" discussions can be folded, placed in the center of the table at meals or other times so that each week discussions can reinforce good character. Thank you for working together to help our children develop good character.

Discuss: Our character word is COOPERATION. Cooperation means working well together and getting along with others. Think about your week and share examples of *cooperation in action*.

Discuss: How do the following words help us to be cooperative: teamwork, positive attitude, compromise, being fair?

fold

fold

HONEST

Discuss: How do the words sincere and integrity relate to honesty?

Discuss: Are there times when being honest is difficult? Explain. What does the saying, „Honesty is the best policy" mean?

fold

HONEST

Character Table Talk Directions: At home, "Table Talk" discussions can be folded, placed in the center of the table at meals or other times so that each week discussions can reinforce good character. Thank you for working together to help our children develop good character.

Discuss: Our character word is HONESTY. Honesty means being truthful in our actions and words. What does that mean to be honest or truthful in our *actions* and our *words*? Why is honesty important? Give examples.

Discuss: What is a conscience and how does our conscience help us to be honest?

fold

-fold-

Discuss: Being a Good Citizen also involves caring about and helping others. What are some ways that you help others at school? In our community?

Discuss: Another part of being a Good Citizen is making a positive contribution to our world. What are some of your strengths and things you are good at that you can share with the world? What type of job or career are you interested in for your future?

GOOD CITIZEN

-fold-

GOOD CITIZEN

Character Table Talk Directions: At home, "Table Talk" discussions can be folded, placed in the center of the table at meals or other times so that each week discussions can reinforce good character. Thank you for working together to help our children develop good character.

Discuss: Our Character word is GOOD CITIZEN. A citizen is a person who is a member of a group. The group can be a classroom, school, or community. What are some ways that you can be a Good Citizen in your community? At school? At home?

Discuss: Part of being a Good Citizen is following the rules and laws. What rules and laws do you have to follow?

-fold-

fold

Discuss: Name some things that you do that take courage.

Discuss: Give examples of people throughout history and people you see and know today who show courage.

COURAGE

fold

COURAGE

Character Table Talk Directions: At home, "Table Talk" discussions can be folded, placed in the center of the table at meals or other times so that each week discussions can reinforce good character. Thank you for working together to help our children develop good character.

Discuss: Our character word is COURAGE. Courage means having the inner strength to handle difficult or hard situations. How does having courage help us in our day to day activities?

Discuss: How does being brave and having perseverance help us be courageous?

fold

BULLY PREVENTION

Bullying problems are in our schools today. Bullying can range from the more direct physical such as shoving, pushing, threatening, "in your face" type bullying to the more indirect, "behind your back" social bullying of exclusions, teasing, gossips, rumors, bossing, controlling, manipulation, and intimidation. Each of these types is harmful and damaging. Bullying can be defined as a pattern of repeated mean behavior that is intended to harm physically, emotionally, or socially and usually has an imbalance of power. The days of thinking that bullying is only that low self esteem, tough guy who just wants to beat up on people are gone. The bully or aggressor can also be thought of as having high self-esteem, social status and the image of being well liked. Bullying today is an integral part of our social system thus making it even more challenging.

Bullying, in this unit, is presented by the three roles that are a part of a bullying situation: the one doing the bullying (the aggressor) is termed as having BULLY BEHAVIOR, the TARGET/VICTIM as the one being bullied or hurt, and the BYSTANDER as the person standing by who sees or witnesses the bullying. The goal of this unit is multi-fold and incorporates the following beliefs:

- ✯ It is the thought that all people are guilty of having bully behavior at times and at different degrees. Therefore the term BULLY BEHAVIOR is used as opposed to BULLY as we encourage people to be aware and acknowledge their behavior and the damage it causes so they can work on changing their behavior.
- ✯ It is believed that over time and in different situations we play all three roles in the bullying problem: BULLY BEHAVIOR, TARGET/VICTIM, and the BYSTANDER.
- ✯ Because we play all three roles it is important to learn how to handle and what to do to help in each of these three roles. The activities in this section seek to help our students have a basis for knowing how to help in each of these roles.

The activities in this section can be used to teach and reinforce the Bully Free Island Poster or can be used independently to teach bully prevention.

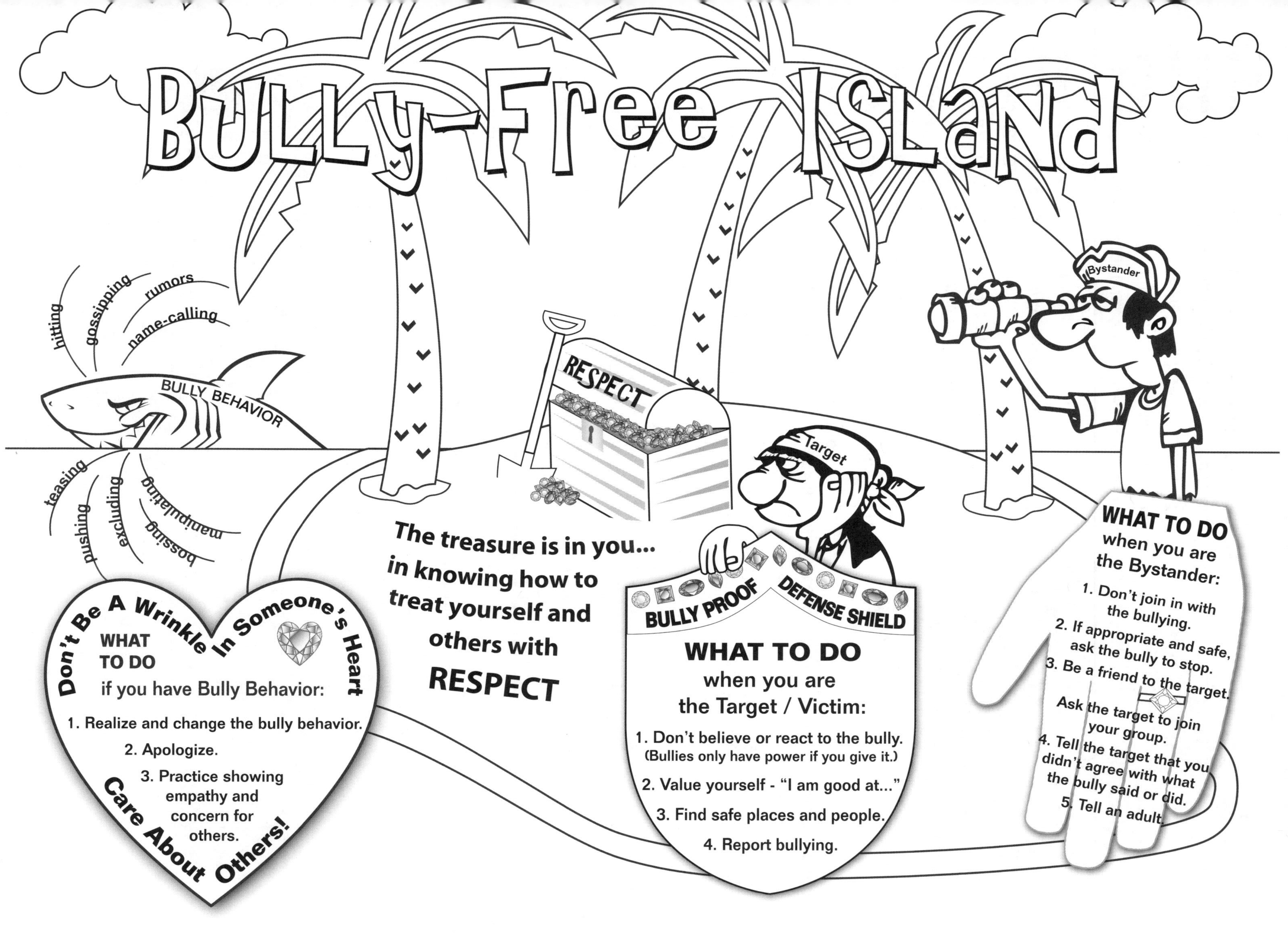
BULLY-FREE ISLAND
hitting
gossipping
rumors
name-calling
BULLY BEHAVIOR
teasing
pushing
excluding
manipulating
bossing
RESPECT
Target
Bystander
The treasure is in you... in knowing how to treat yourself and others with RESPECT
Don't Be A Wrinkle In Someone's Heart
WHAT TO DO
if you have Bully Behavior:
1. Realize and change the bully behavior.
2. Apologize.
3. Practice showing empathy and concern for others.
Care About Others!
BULLY PROOF DEFENSE SHIELD
WHAT TO DO
when you are the Target / Victim:
1. Don't believe or react to the bully. (Bullies only have power if you give it.)
2. Value yourself - "I am good at..."
3. Find safe places and people.
4. Report bullying.
WHAT TO DO
when you are the Bystander:
1. Don't join in with the bullying.
2. If appropriate and safe, ask the bully to stop.
3. Be a friend to the target.
Ask the target to join your group.
4. Tell the target that you didn't agree with what the bully said or did.
5. Tell an adult.

Activity 44

Activity for LIVING

Bully Prevention

Bully Free Island

Overview: The Bully Free Island poster encourages respect and provides an overview of the three roles of bullying and what to do in each role.

Materials

- ✓ *Bully Free Island* poster from the book can be copied as is, enlarged, and/or color added and displayed for discussion. OR a 17"x11" full color laminated posters can be purchased through YouthLight (1-800-209-9774) to display in each class.
- ✓ Copy and cut apart the *Bully Free Island Role Play Cards*

Poster Explanation

The underlying belief is that over time and in different situations we play all three roles in the bullying problem – the bully, the target, and the bystander. Therefore it is important to identify the role we are playing, and find a way to handle appropriately. The poster focuses on 4 concepts:

- ✯ The TREASURE CHEST provides the message of *the treasure is in you… in knowing how to treat yourself and others with Respect*. Respect for self and others is the theme to handling bully situations.
- ✯ The SHARK indicates different types of bullying both direct and indirect for an awareness of our behavior. The HEART shares ways of what to do when we have bully behavior. The symbol of the heart reminds us to care about others.
- ✯ The SHIELD shares ways to protect ourselves when we are the target. (It's important to share that we may all be a "target" at some time but we can stop ourselves from being a "victim" of bullying by how we choose to handle it.)
- ✯ The HELPING HAND encourages us to get involved and help others. A variety of ways to be a helping "bystander" are shared.

Variety of Uses of the Poster

- ✯ Share the poster as an **overview/introduction** to the problem of bullying. You may choose to copy/enlarge/color, create as overhead, or scan to display with LCD projector, promethean, smart board, etc. OR a 17"x11" full color laminated *Problem Solving Pond* posters can be purchased through YouthLight (1-800-209-9774).

★ Display the poster for individual, group or class as a reference and **visual reminder** as you explore the different roles of bullying and what to do.

★ Poster can be copied and **sent home for reinforcement** of skills introduced.

★ Turn the poster into an **INTERACTIVE WALL MURAL** where students can cognitively, visually, and kinesthetically participate in bully intervention/prevention strategies. Here's how:

- Paint the poster as a wall mural in a hallway or other targeted area that students have access.
- Adhere 5 sets of footprints on the floor in front of the mural. One set labeled "BULLY BEHAVIOR" placed on the floor below the shark/heart, one set labeled "TARGET" below the shield, and then three sets of footprints labeled "BYSTANDER" below the helping hand.
- Copy and cut apart the *Bully Free Island Role Play Cards*
- Individuals, groups, or small groups can go to the mural to role play bullying siutations. For individuals, draw a role play card of a bullying situation and then have the person stand on each of the footprints – bully behavior, target, bystander - and talk from that perspective on how they could find a good way to handle the situation. If you have a small group or class, have five students stand on the different sets of footprints, draw a role play card, and each take turns talking from that point of view on how to help. You can create your own bully situations or use "real situations" to work through bullying problems.
- The wall mural serves as a great visual for school-wide focus on Bully Prevention.

Bully Free Island
Role Play Cards

WORK SHEET

Directions: *Copy and cut apart the cards. Select a card and read the bully situation. Discuss the bully situation naming the bully behavior, target, and bystander. Review the thoughts and feelings of each. Next role play helpful ways to handle from each of the 3 perspectives – the bully behavior, the target, the bystander. You may choose to refer to the Bully Free Island poster for helpful information.*

In our group, Max likes to take charge and tell everyone else what to do. When John tried to share a suggestion, Max told him that was a lame suggestion and it wouldn't work. The others in the group were sitting there when all of this was said.

The teacher was at the door talking with another adult, while Brad was at the board working on a math problem. Brad kept making mistakes. Jackson whispered loudly, "Brad is so dumb, he can't even count the toes on his feet." The classmates all heard what Jackson said.

The new student was trying to find a group to play with at recess. She went up to one group of girls but got eye-rolls and hurtful comments saying she didn't belong in their group. Others were out on the playground and saw what was happening.

Angie and Caroline are good friends but Caroline didn't like Angie spending so much time with Sara because she was getting left out. Caroline started a bad rumor about Sara so Angie wouldn't like her anymore. She shared the rumor with the classmates.

Sam was sitting at our lunch table with Joel and some other friends. Joel opened a package of ketchup and accidentally / on purpose leaned over and squirted it on Sam and said, "Oh… my bad." And then started laughing. The others at the table saw what happened.

Nancy usually sits with a group of her friends at lunch. When she went to sit at the table today, Lyn rolled her eyes and turned her back to Nancy. The other friends sitting at the table saw what happened.

Activity 45

Activity for LIVING

Bully Prevention

Bully Behavior - Who Me?

Overview: This activity brings an awareness of the various types of bully behavior and provides encouragement to take ownership of our bully behavior and make a change for the positive.

Materials

- ✓ Copy of the *Bully Behavior – Who Me?* worksheet
- ✓ Copy of the *Bully Behavior – Who Me?* poster to display for reinforcement
- ✓ Optional: copy of the *Bully Free Island* poster

Procedures

1. Say: **Raise your hand if you are a bully**. (If someone does raise their hand, acknowledge with a head nod and continue.)

2. Say: **Describe a bully.**

3. Say: **Hitting, shoving, or punching is one way to describe a bully but there are also some other bully behaviors that we may all be guilty of such as: name calling, teasing, joining in by laughing, making fun of someone, spreading rumors or gossipping, excluding or leaving others out, bossing, controlling, manipulating, and intimidating.** (You may choose to go into detail as you share the behaviors – giving examples and describing a situation. Keep in mind the age of the student as to the examples and words you choose to share. If appropriate add cyber-bullying as an example). **These types of behaviors can be just as hurtful if not more so. Raise your hand now if you have ever had bully behavior.** Compliment students as they own up to their behavior and share that only when we realize our behaviors can we make a change for the better. (You may choose to use the term Bully Behavior to include both the direct and indirect forms of bullying. It is often easier to accept that we may have 'bully behavior' as opposed to being a 'bully'.)

4. Review and display the *Bully Behavior – Who Me?* poster

5. Give the definition of bullying as, "A pattern of repeated mean behavior that is intended to harm physically, emotionally, or socially and usually has an imbalance of power."

6. Ask: **Why do you think people bully – both the direct (physical) and indirect (social-emotional) hurt?** (Include in the discussion – for power, fear, to show-off, to fit in, to gain social status).

7. Ask: **What does our bullying do to others?**

8. Ask: **What can we do about this bullying behavior? How can we change?**

9. **Optional:** Refer to the Bully Free Island poster with the shark behaviors and the #1 on the heart.

10. Complete and review the *Bully Behavior – Who Me?* worksheet.

Bullying - Who Me?

WORK SHEET

Directions: *Put a check beside each statement that is an example of bullying.*

Bullying is repeated behavior that:

_____ 1. Calls people names and makes fun of them.

_____ 2. Makes fun of the way someone looks or something they may not do well.

_____ 3. Tells everyone else in your group what to do and does not care or listen to what others may want to do.

_____ 4. Won't allow others to sit with them at lunch even though there's room.

_____ 5. Bumps into a person and pushes them down on purpose.

_____ 6. Threatens you with their fist in your face to give him/her your lunch money.

_____ 7. Joins in and laughs with a person who is making fun of someone else.

_____ 8. Rolling their eyes at you when you walk up to join in the group.

_____ 9. Chooses to give "your friend" the "cold shoulder" because the popular girl told you not to talk to her anymore.

_____ 10. Repeats or spreads a bad rumor about someone.

_____ 11. Makes up an untrue rumor about someone to get back at them.

_____ 12. Tells someone they can't join your group.

_____ 13. Takes someone's personal belonging, plays "keep away" with the item, and does not give it back.

_____ 14. Threatens to tell everyone that __ is your boyfriend if you don't do what they say.

_____ 15. Calls someone names referring to their race or skin color.

_____ 16. Promises someone they can "hang out" with their popular group if they will do the group project for everyone and put their names on it.

_____ 17. A person being bossy, telling everyone where to sit.

_____ 18. A classmate being asked to sign a petition that says, "I agree to hate Sherrie and exclude her from all activities."

_____ 19. Trips the person in the hall to get back at them.

_____ 20. Writes a note, text, or sends an email making fun of someone.

Directions: *Read the following definition of bullying and then review your answers. Make changes if needed.*

Bullying: *"A pattern of repeated mean behavior that is intended to harm physically, emotionally, or socially, and usually has an imbalance of power."*

Directions: *All of the statements above are examples of bully behavior. Beside each example add the letter **"P"** for Physical Bullying, the letter **"E"** for Emotional Bullying, **"S"** for Social Bullying. (You may use more than one letter per behavior).*

BULLY BEHAVIOR WHO ME?

Bully Behavior is not just someone being mean and hurting others **PHYSICALLY** by

Intimidating

Shoving

Pushing

Threatening

Hitting

Bully Behavior is also being mean and hurting others **EMOTIONALLY** and **SOCIALLY** by

Teasing

Spreading Rumors

Gossipping

Bossing

Manipulating

Excluding or Leaving Others Out

CHECK YOUR BEHAVIOR!

Activity 46

Activity for LIVING

Bully Prevention

Bully Behavior- Don't Be a Wrinkle in Someone's Heart

Overview: This activity counteracts bully behavior by acknowledging its damage and by encouraging caring behavior.

Materials

✓ Construction paper heart for demonstration and/or a paper heart for each participant

✓ Copy of the poster, *Don't Be a Wrinkle in Someone's Heart*

✓ Optional: copy of the *Bully Free Island* poster

Procedures

1. Display a paper heart and ask: **What does a heart remind you of?** Focus on the heart being the symbol of care and love.

2. Ask the students to share examples of things people say or do that are intended to hurt others. Fold your paper heart once for each example shared. (Accept examples of both direct and indirect bullying such as hitting, punching, teasing, exclusions, rumors, gossip, bossing, etc.)

3. After the heart has been folded many times, attempt to unfold the wrinkled/folded heart and straighten it out removing all of the folds and wrinkles. Point out the impossible task of removing all the wrinkles from the heart.

4. Relate the impossibility of getting the wrinkles out of the heart to the impossibility of removing or "taking back" hurtful words or deeds once said or done – the hurt in the heart remains.

5. Share the following questions for thought:
   - **What have I said or done recently that hurt another person? What wrinkle have I put in someone's heart?**
   - **How did the person feel?**
   - **What do I need to work on or change to be a caring heart?**

6. **OPTIONAL:** If you are using the *Bully Free Island* poster refer to the heart with the reminder to 'not be a wrinkle in someone's heart'.

7. Display the *Don't Be a Wrinkle in Someone's Heart* poster

*Wrinkled/folded Heart Analogy – source unknown

Don't Be a Wrinkle in Someone's Heart

POSTER

Activity 47

Activity for LIVING

Bully Prevention

Bully Behavior

Don't Be a Banana Bruiser*

Overview: This activity emphasizes the hurt and damage of indirect/social bullying.

Materials

- ✓ Banana
- ✓ Optional: copy of the *Bully Free Island* poster

Procedures

1. Say: **Name some physical kinds of bullying**. (Review answers such as hitting, kicking, punching.) **What kind of marks may be left behind with the physical bullying?** (Review answers such as bruises, cuts, bloody nose.)

2. Say: **Name some examples of indirect or social bullying.** (Review answers such as teasing, exclusions, gossip, rumors, controlling, manipulation, add cyber-bullying if appropriate.) **What marks are left behind with the indirect or social bullying?**

3. To help the student understand the hurt of indirect or social bullying, display a banana and ask the student(s) to think of this banana as a person for a moment. Review the examples of indirect/social bullying and as you share each example press your thumb into the banana on the outside peel of the banana. After several examples have been shared, examine the banana to see if there are any marks on the outside of the peeling. No marks are noticeable at this time but peel the banana, examine, and you will find bruise marks on the inside left by the thumb imprints. Make the connection relating that indirect/social bullying doesn't leave marks on the outside of the body such as the physical bullying, but indirect/social bullying leaves bruises on the inside. Point out that this hurt can often do more damage than physical bullying.

4. OPTIONAL: Refer to the *Bully Free Island* poster focusing on the shark behaviors.

*Source unknown

Activity 48

Activity for LIVING

Bully Prevention

Bully Behavior

Let Empathy Guide Your Behavior

Overview: This activity promotes using empathy for understanding and to help guide toward caring behavior.

Materials

- ✓ Need 5 pairs of shoes for display and role playing.
- ✓ Role-play worksheet, *Let Empathy Guide Your Behavior*
- ✓ Optional: copy of the *Bully Free Island* poster

Procedures

1. Ask: **What do you think *empathy* means?**

2. Ask: **What do you think it means if someone said, "Try to understand other people by *standing in their shoes*"?**

3. Display a pair of shoes.

4. Lead a discussion of the definition of empathy to include empathy as the "ability to recognize and understand the thoughts or feelings of another person and their point of view." Give the following two guidelines that can help people have empathy:

   - ✯ Think of a time when you felt the same way as the other person.
   - ✯ Pretend to be the person you are trying to understand. Ask yourself: What would I be thinking? How would I be feeling?

5. Share: **Once you have empathy, let it guide your actions away from mean behaviors but instead toward caring behaviors.**

6. Introduce the role-playing activity by saying: **We have an opportunity to practice our empathy through role-playing.** Refer to the *Let Empathy Guide Your Behavior* role play worksheet. Choose from one of the following options for the role-play activity:

   - ✯ Have a volunteer come up and stand in a pair of shoes while you read one of the situations from the *Let Empathy Guide Your Behavior!* role-play worksheet and have the student respond through role play.

- ✯ You may choose to add to each pair of shoes, a role-play situation to be read.
- ✯ You may choose to divide a class into 3 groups with each group getting a pair of shoes to read and discuss the role-play and then share with the class.
- ✯ You may choose to copy the worksheet for each student and have them write ways to think, say, or do to help, not hurt, in each situation. Take turns role-playing for the group/class.

Encourage the student to follow the guidelines given in the sidebar of the worksheet.

7. After the worksheet/role-play exercise, ask: **If each of us were using our empathy, do you think there would be any type of bullying problems – physical, emotional, or social bullying? Why or why not?**

8. **OPTIONAL:** Refer to the BULLY FREE ISLAND focusing on the shark and heart.

Let Empathy Guide Your Behavior

WORK SHEET

Directions: *Walk in another person's shoes by reading the situation and using the empathy guidelines to help rather than hurt others. Write a helpful way to put your empathy into action.*

When Jessie, the new student, came over to our lunch table to join us, I rolled my eyes at her and said, "You are not welcome at our table."

Pretend you are Jessie...

- What would she be thinking?
- How would she feel?

What could you say or do instead that is caring?

____

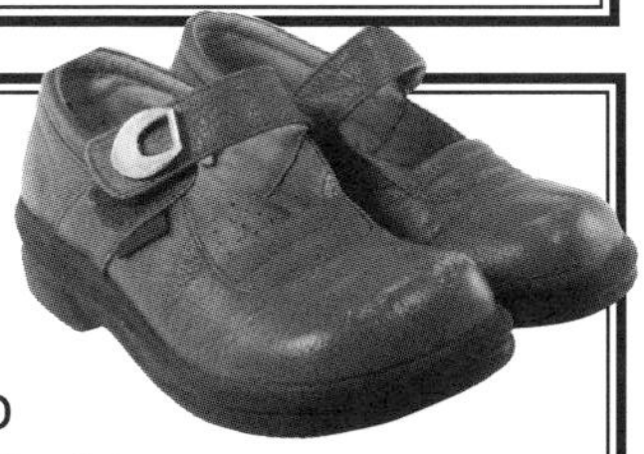

Hannah whispered to me that Whitney's grades were so low that she was going to have to repeat the grade. I didn't know if it was true or not but when I went to my next class I said to Misty, "Hey, did you hear that Whitney is being held back a grade?" When I shared the rumor, Misty wanted to talk to me more and included me in her popular group.

Pretend you are Whitney. If Whitney knew what was being said behind her back...

- What would she be thinking?
- How would she feel?

What could you say or do instead that is caring?

____

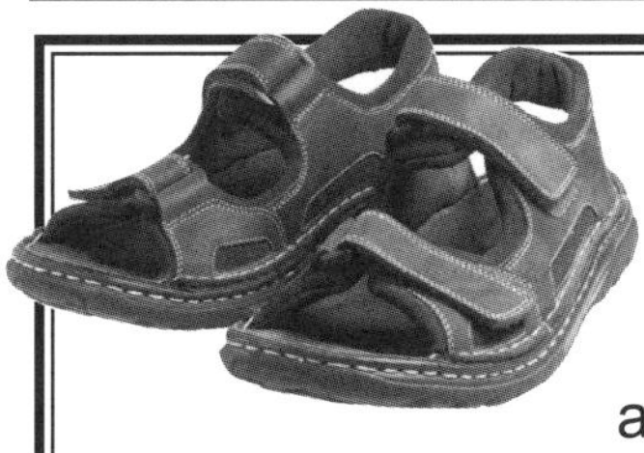

Larry is a math whiz but not as coordinated when it comes to playing sports. Out at recess he wanted to join our team to play kickball but I told him he couldn't play because he wasn't any good.

Pretend you are Larry...

- What would he be thinking?
- How would he feel?

What could you say or do instead that is caring?

____

Guidelines to Having Empathy for Others

STEP ONE

Think of a time when you felt the same way as the other person.

STEP TWO

Pretend to be the person you are trying to understand. Ask yourself:

What would I be thinking?

How would I be feeling if that were me?

Once you have empathy, let it guide your actions away from mean behaviors toward caring behaviors instead.

STEP THREE

Ask yourself:

What could I SAY and DO that is caring?

Activity 49 · Activity for LIVING · Bully Prevention

Bully Behavior
Apology From The Heart

Overview: This activity reviews the steps needed for a sincere apology.

Materials

- ✓ Copy of *Apology from the Heart* worksheet
- ✓ Optional: copy of the *Bully Free Island* poster

Procedures

1. Share: **There are countless stories of people who have made fun of others, spread rumors, and have been mean to people, who have had bully behavior, but years later totally regret how mean they were to others and wish they had not been mean. You have the opportunity now to review your behavior, to use your empathy in thinking about how others may feel about what you say and do, and you have the opportunity to apologize. No one is perfect, we all make mistakes at times in what we say and do but an apology can help correct our wrong – that is if we apologize from the heart. Let's look at what we may know about apologies. As I read each statement tell me if the statement is true or false and explain why.**

Apologies don't totally fix the problem, but they do help.
(TRUE: Once something mean has been said or done there is damage. An apology can start the healing but it doesn't totally fix the problem.)

The words "I'm sorry" are all a person needs to say to apologize.
(FALSE: It takes more than just two words. A person can communicate they are truly sorry by explaining what they are sorry about and then proving they are sorry.)

Once a person says, "I'm sorry" they can say or do the mean behavior again.
(FALSE: When we apologize it means that we have learned from our mistake and will not do it again.)

Apologies, if done correctly, can help heal the hurt.
(TRUE: The words of an apology are the first step in the healing, the second step is showing we are sorry by what we say and do.)

2. Ask: **Has someone said the words "I'm sorry" to you before but you didn't believe them? Or have you ever said "I'm Sorry" to another person but they still act like they are hurt or mad at you? Well, you can't control what other people believe but you can check yourself to see if you are coming across as sincere or that you really mean that you are sorry. Let's look at how to say, "I'm sorry" and mean it, in other words - to make an apology from the heart.**

3. Review the *Apology from the Heart* worksheet and point out THE 2 STEP APOLOGY, discuss the example, then complete the apology for the given situation – create others.

4. OPTIONAL: Refer to the heart on the *Bully Free Island* poster.

Apology From the Heart

WORK SHEET

Directions: *Review THE 2 STEP APOLOGY and discuss the example given. Read the next situation and complete the apology by filling in the information for Corrected Thought and The Apology.*

THE 2 STEP APOLOGY	1. **Use a full sentence, sharing what you are sorry about.** 2. **Show or prove that you are really sorry or do an act of kindness to make up for the wrong.**

Example:

Situation: Whitney was trying to show off for some "popular" friends and gave Amanda the cold shoulder at the lunch table because she didn't think it would look cool to be seen talking to Amanda.

Corrected Thought: Amanda has always been a good friend and I should never have treated her that way just to be accepted by some other girls.

THE APOLOGY

Step 1: Amanda, I am sorry that I was rude and didn't include you in the conversation at lunch today. That was wrong of me.

Step 2: Why don't we talk on the phone this afternoon and make plans to do something together this weekend?

Situation: Even though Brad was a good friend, Michael (wanting to 'fit in') laughed and joined in when the other guys were teasing Brad.

Corrected Thought: ____________________

____

THE APOLOGY

Step 1: ____________________

____

Step 2: ____________________

____

Activity 50 | Activity for LIVING | Bully Prevention

Target

Target Not Victim

Overview: This activity focuses on the difference between being a "target" and being a "victim" of bullying and provides encouragement and strategies to prevent becoming a victim.

Materials

- ✓ Need 6 copies of the Think Bubble on page 137 and add one of the following comments to each bubble:
  - ✯ My brain is the best weapon!
  - ✯ Just because they called me a name, doesn't make it true.
  - ✯ I believe in myself. Who I am is not defined by others.
  - ✯ I can find safe places and nicer people to be around.
  - ✯ There are more important things in this world to worry about.
  - ✯ I know I have value as a person, I excel in music and math.
- ✓ Copy of the *Target Not Victim* worksheet
- ✓ Optional: copy of the *Bully Free Island* poster

Procedures

1. Ask: **What do you think is the difference between a person being a *target* and a person being a *victim*?** (One of the definitions of *target* is "the aim of an attack by a hostile person or influence" and a definition of *victim* is a person who suffers from an adverse circumstance such as a hostile person or influence.)

2. Summarize: **The difference seems to be that a target is the aim of an attack and the victim is one who suffers from the attack.**

3. Ask: **When we get bullied by being teased, laughed at, gossipped about, or left out, is there any rule that says we have to suffer from what's happened?**

4. Share: **We have the power not to become a victim of bullying. All of us may be a target of bullying at times but we can prevent ourselves from being a victim of bullying by using helpful strategies so that the bullying does not negatively affect us.**

5. Display the completed *Think Bubbles* and discuss.

6. OPTIONAL: Refer to the *Bully Free Island* poster, reviewing the shield of "What To Do When You Are the Target/Victim."

7. As a class, group, or individual complete the *Target Not Victim* worksheet. (If you are working with a class you may choose to divide the class into 4/5 groups to complete the worksheet as a team and then have each team share their answers. Be aware of the dynamics of the group and closely monitor – you may choose to call on the typical bully behavior student to give suggestions on how the target doesn't have to believe the aggressor and suggestions of ways the target doesn't have to be negatively impacted.)

Target Not Victim

WORK SHEET

Directions: *Your brain is the best weapon, so come up with helpful ways the target can think about the following bully situations so they are not hurt by and become a victim of bullying.*

Situation: A person is called a name because of the color of their skin or the way they dress, or how they talk.

Helpful Target Thoughts: ______________________________

____

Situation: Other students won't let a person sit with them at lunch even though there is room.

Helpful Target Thoughts: ______________________________

____

Situation: Someone is spreading untrue rumors about someone.

Helpful Target Thoughts: ______________________________

____

Situation: Someone is teasing, making fun of, or laughing at another person because they cannot do something as well.

Helpful Target Thoughts: ______________________________

____

My brain is my best weapon!
I can find safe places and nicer people to be around.
Just because they called me a name, doesn't make it true.
There are more important things to worry about .
I believe in myself. Who I am is not defined by others.
I know I have value as a person, I excel in music and math.

Activity 51

Activity for LIVING

Bully Prevention

Target
The Shield*

Overview: This activity allows students to develop and practice their protective strategies of ways to "think, say, and do" when they are a target of bullying.

Materials

- ✓ Chart paper/board and markers
- ✓ Copy of the *Bully Free Island* Poster
- ✓ Armor or shield (plastic shields/armor may be purchased at area department stores or you can make one out of poster board covered with tinfoil).
- ✓ 5 sheets of paper wadded or balled up
- ✓ Copy of the *Target – The Shield* worksheet

Procedures

1. Refer to the Bully Free Island Poster. Ask: **Why do you think a Bully Proof Defense Shield is used for the 'what to do when you are the target…'?** Relate that we can choose to hold our shield up for protection so being teased, laughed at, gossiped about, or left out doesn't get to us and hurt us. Display your sample shield/armor as a visual of protection.

2. Say: **We can create our own pretend shield to protect us by how we choose to THINK, SAY, or DO in response to the social/emotional bullying.** On chart paper/board, divide the area into three columns and write the three heading words – THINK, SAY, DO. Brainstorm a list of helpful, safe, and acceptable ways to protect ourselves against bullying and add to the correct column. Include such items as;
   - ✯ valuing self
   - ✯ maintaining the power – just because they say it doesn't make it true
   - ✯ body language of confidence
   - ✯ find a different group of people to enjoy being with
   - ✯ use self-talk statements of "I can handle this!" or "I'm not going to react."
   - ✯ hold your head high and walk away

* adapted from D. Senn, 2008, *Bullying in the Girl's World*, Chapin, SC: YouthLight, Inc.

You can discuss the use of "comeback" statements but add caution that the statements should not be making fun of the bully/aggressor. This can only escalate the situation, and statements should be said with confidence, non-emotional, good eye contact, and then walk away to be effective. The following are some possible comeback statements, but take into consideration the age of the student – what may be okay for a 5th grader to say is not necessarily okay for a 1st grader to say. Possible statements are:

- ✯ "Are you talking to me?"
- ✯ "You're right, I agree."
- ✯ "I can't believe we used to be friends."
- ✯ "That's ridiculous – whatever."
- ✯ "The real you can't be this mean."
- ✯ "I hope no one is doing this to your little brother."

3. Refer to the *Target – The Shield* worksheet and have students personalize their protective shield by adding THINK, SAY, or DO statements and/or strategies to their shield that would protect.

4. Then, model for the students how they can use their defense shield to protect them. Hold your display shield/armor up and ask a student to throw a paper wad at you as they say a bullying statement. You may tell them a bullying statement to say to you so they just repeat it for role playing purposes. As the paper wad is thrown at you, deflect the paper wad with your shield as you share a THINK, SAY, or DO statement of protection.

5. Next, allow students to role-play being the target. Instruct them to hold the display shield/armor, tape their own personalized shield to the back so they can read information from it to respond in the role play. You need to take the role of the aggressor/bully as you throw paper wads/bully statements at the student (instruct the student to use the shield to protect them). Compliment the student as they share a helpful way to THINK, SAY, or DO in order to protect themselves. (Add a disclaimer that the bullying statements are only pretend statements for the benefit of our practicing our protection strategies.)

Target
The Shield

WORK SHEET

Directions: *Create your own protective shield from bullying by how you choose to THINK, SAY, or DO. List helpful, safe, acceptable ways to protect yourself against bullying and add to the shield under the THINK, SAY, or DO column.*

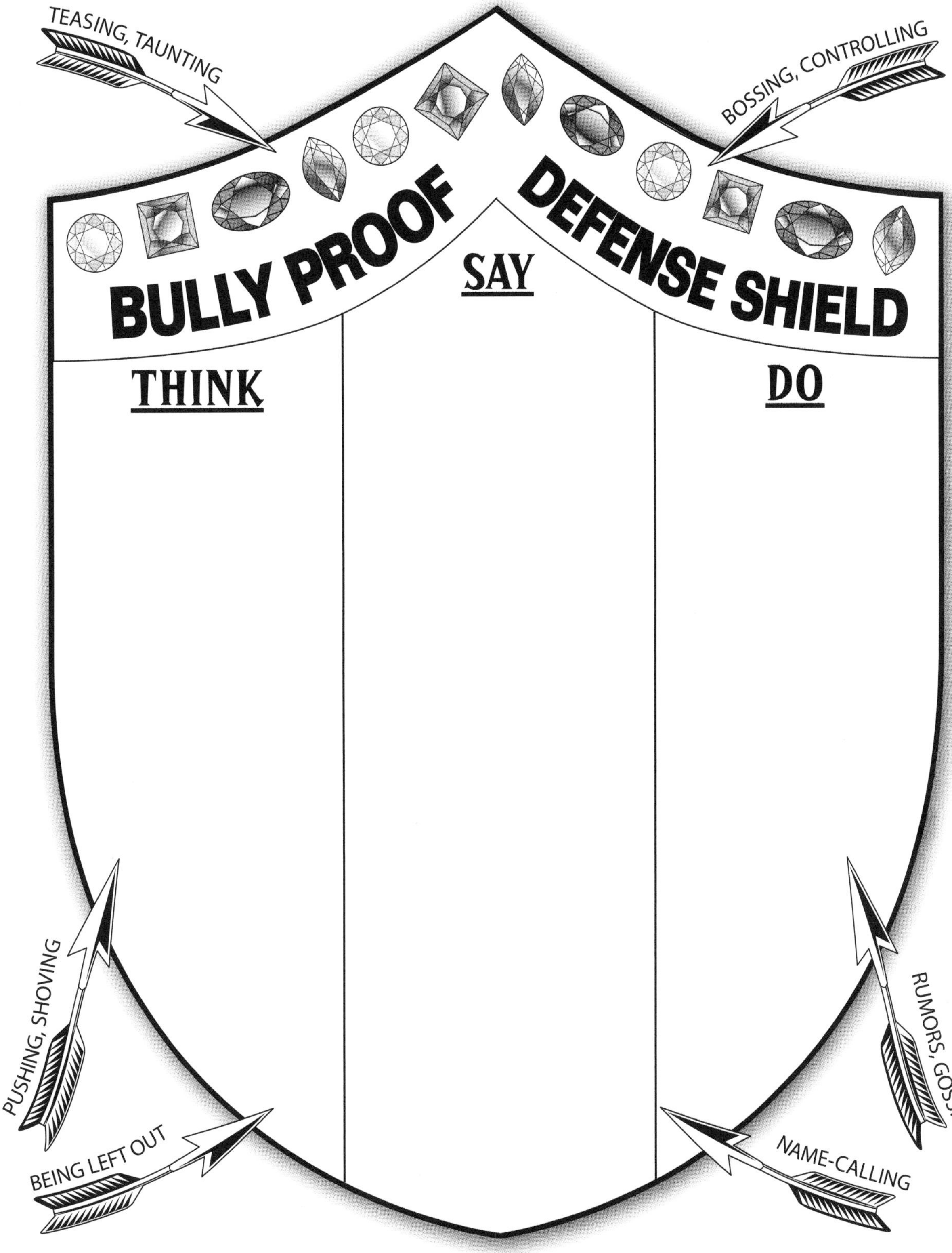

Activity 52

Activity for LIVING

Bully Prevention

Bystander
The Helping Hand

Overview: This activity is intended to motivate students to use their power to make a difference by becoming helping bystanders in bullying situations.

Materials

- ✓ Copy of *Bystander – The Helping Hand* worksheet
- ✓ Optional: copy of the *Bully Free Island* poster

Procedures

1. Ask: **What does it mean to be the "bystander" in a bully situation?** Clarify that the bystander is the one who witnesses or sees the bullying happening.

2. Discuss the following responses or reactions of bystanders that are *not helpful* in bullying situations:
   - ✯ The bystander could join in with the bullying by making fun of, laughing, or just by watching.
   - ✯ The bystander could do nothing, but then this sends the message that it's okay because you say nothing.
   - ✯ The bystander could think that bullying is normal and just happens and that it is not his/her place to get involved or help.
   - ✯ The bystander may be afraid to say something for fear that the bully would turn on them.
   - ✯ The bystander may choose not to help because it is a *popular* person doing the bullying and they don't want to get on *their bad side*.

3. Ask: **What are some ways that a bystander can *help* a bullying situation?** Include in the discussion that bystanders do have the power to make a difference in bullying situations. Bystanders help reduce the power of the bully/aggressor. If no one thinks what the bully says or does is funny or they choose not to follow everything the *popular* person says, then the bully/aggressor loses power and hopefully will find a better way to relate to people. Bystanders can also increase the power of the target when they let the target know that they don't agree with what the bully said or did.

4. Review the first part of the *Bystander – The Helping Hand* worksheet that provides questions to "help get your head on straight" about what's right and wrong in regards to bullying.

5. Ask: **What are some helpful ways to be a "bystander" in a bully situation?** (Caution students that standing up to the bully and telling them to stop isn't always the best approach. That approach only can work if as the bystander you have equal or greater power than the bully. If the bully is older or you are afraid they could turn on you, do not stand up to the bully but instead turn your efforts to helping and talking with the target.) See the helping hand section on the *Bystander – The Helping Hand* worksheet for a list of 5 helpful approaches. If time allows, role play with students the five helpful approaches listed on the helping hand.

6. OPTIONAL: Refer to the Bully Free Island poster and review the "What to Do when you are the BYSTANDER."

Bystander
The Helping Hand

WORK SHEET

Directions: *What are your beliefs about what is right and wrong about bullying? Just because people do it does it make it right? As a group, discuss the questions in "Get Your Head on Straight…" to help you build a belief system that takes other peoples' feelings into account.*

GET YOUR HEAD ON STRAIGHT…

Is it okay to do nothing and watch as someone else gets excluded or made fun of?

Is it okay not to let someone sit by you or join in the group?

Is it okay to make fun of someone and laugh at them?

Is it okay to talk bad about someone and spread rumors? What if someone else started it first - should you repeat the rumor?

Is it okay to ignore someone who is your friend just so you can be in the popular group?

Is it okay to boss someone around and say, "If you don't do it my way then I'm not going to be your friend?"

Is it okay to threaten or hit someone because you are mad?

Directions: *Review the Helping Hand for different ways to be a helpful bystander.*

WHAT TO DO when you are the Bystander:

1. Don't join in with the bullying.
2. If appropriate and safe, ask the bully to stop.
3. Be a friend to the target.

   Ask the target to join your group.
4. Tell the target that you didn't agree with what the bully said or did.
5. Tell an adult.

The Bystander has the Power to Make a Difference!

Activity 53

Activity for LIVING

Bully Prevention

Bystander
What Can I Say to the Bully?

Overview: This activity focuses on helpful statements/phrases a bystander can say to the bully (when it is safe and appropriate) to ask the bully to stop.

Materials

- ✓ Copy of the *Bully Free Island* poster
- ✓ Copy of *Bystander – What Can I Say to the Bully?* worksheet

Procedures

1. Share: **As a bystander in bullying situations we need to get involved and make a difference by helping others. Our bystander helping hand on the *Bully Free Island* poster shares 5 ways to help. Our lesson today will focus on #2 - " If appropriate and safe, tell the bully to stop." What do you think is meant by "if appropriate and safe?" Are there times that it may not be safe to tell a bully to stop?** (Reinforce that there are many ways to be a helpful bystander and that telling a bully to stop is only one way. However if the bully is older, has more power than you, or you are afraid that the bully may turn on you – DO NOT tell the bully to stop. Instead you can focus on other ways to help the target.

2. Ask: **Are there times that as a bystander it is safe or appropriate to ask a bully to stop? Explain.** Include in the discussion that it may be safe and appropriate if the bully is a friend of yours, perhaps someone younger, or you feel that they would listen to you.

3. Share: **There may be times that we do feel that it is safe and appropriate and we want to say something to the bully to help the target but we don't always know the exact words to use. Let's look at the *Bystander – What Can I Say to the Bully?* worksheet to review possible ideas of what to say.**

4. Use the role-play activity to put the words into action!

Bystander
What Can I Say to the Bully?

WORK SHEET

Directions: *There may be times as a bystander when we have equal or greater power than the bully/aggressor. We may want to say something to the bully to help the target/situation but we don't always know the exact words to use. Review the sentences below for possible words a bystander can use in talking to the bully/aggressor. Put a check by the sentences that you could use and then add some sentences of your own. (Caution: never turn around and bully the bully – don't make fun of them or try to hurt their feelings as a way to help. This never helps but can only make the situation worse.)*

AS A BYSTANDER I CAN HELP BY SAYING…

ROLE-PLAY ACTIVITY: *Practice putting your words into action! First brainstorm a list of typical hurtful statements that a bully/aggressor may use. Then role-play the various bully statements by having volunteers use their selected phrases/statements to help the bully situation.*

Activity 54

Activity for LIVING

Bully Prevention

Bystander

What Can I Say to the Target?

Overview: This activity focuses on what a bystander can do or say to the target to offer support and help in a bullying situation.

Materials

- ✓ Need 2 card strips, write one of the following statements on each strip:
  - ✯ Be a friend to the target – ask them to join your group.
  - ✯ Tell the target that you didn't agree with what the bully said or did.
- ✓ Copy of the *Bystander – What Can I Say to the Target?* worksheet
- ✓ Optional: copy of the *Bully Free Island* poster

Procedures

1. Share: **As a bystander we have the power to make a difference by choosing to help in a bullying situation. There are several ways to help. If it is safe and appropriate (if the bully is a friend of ours, perhaps someone younger, or we feel that they would listen to us) then we may choose to talk to the bully about what they are doing and how it hurts. As a bystander we may choose to go and get help. Or as a bystander, we may choose to talk with the target. Letting the target know you care and that they are important and appreciated can give them the confidence not to let the bully situation bother them. Today's activity focuses on what to say to the target to help.**
2. Hold up the card strip and read: **"Be a friend to the target – ask them to join your group."** Explain that as you see that a person is the target of bullying – motion, yell, or walk by to ask the target to come, go… anything to help get them away from the bully situation safely. Tell the students that if they feel the situation is unsafe, don't stop in front of the bully but keep walking as you ask the target to join you.
3. Hold up the second card strip and read: **"Tell the target that you didn't agree with what the bully said or did."** Explain that this approach involves talking with the target later and letting them know what you saw/heard earlier and that what the bully said or did was wrong.
4. Refer to the *Bystander – What Can I Say to the Target?* worksheet. The worksheet is divided into the two approaches. Discuss and role-play the given situations that address these two areas and then create more of your own.
5. **OPTIONAL:** Refer to the *Bully Free Island* poster to reinforce how to be a helping BYSTANDER.
6. Challenge the student(s) to be there for each other, helping in those difficult, bullying situations. Remind the student that a kind word from a peer can go a long way in helping.

Bystander
What Can I Say to the Target?

WORK SHEET

Directions: *Read, role-play, and discuss each role-play focusing on what the bystander can do and say to help the target. Create additional role-plays of your own.*

Role-Plays for "Be a friend to the target - ask them to join your group."

- ★ Out at recess, you see that Larry is being made fun of by some of the other classmates. You and your friend walk closer to Larry and say, "Hey Larry, want to join us over on the soccer field?" You turn and keep walking toward the soccer field as Larry joins you.
- ★ In the hallway at school, you are at your locker and can see Melissa not far from you with her head down. The girls next to her are giggling and pointing at her. You walk closer and say, "Melissa, I'm headed to the media center to start our research for the social studies project. Do you want to come?" Melissa smiles and joins you.
- ★ Write a role-play of your own: ______________________________

____

____

____

Role-Plays for "Tell the target that you didn't agree with what the bully said or did."

- ★ On the bus, you hear Brad, one of your classmates, being teased by some of the older students. You feel bad for Brad but are too afraid to say anything to the older students. When you get to class, you go up to Brad and say, "Brad, I heard what those older students on the bus said to you this morning and I want you to know they shouldn't have said that mean stuff to you – you're a nice person."
- ★ In the lunchroom you see Elizabeth, a friend from class, get the cold shoulder from the girls at her table. They are whispering and laughing as they dart their eyes at Elizabeth. You can tell Elizabeth is embarrassed and hurt. At recess, you find Elizabeth and say, "Elizabeth, you are such a good friend, don't let those girls from the cafeteria bother you. You are so nice and kind to everyone."
- ★ Write a role-play of your own: ______________________________

____

____

Activities for LEARNING

Academic Development

We can make a difference in the lives of children!

FOCUSING

Activity 55 · Activity for LEARNING · Focusing

Tuned-In
What Does It Look Like?

Overview: This activity promotes good listening behavior.

Materials

✓ Copy of the *Tuned-In, What Does It Look Like?* poster

Procedures

1. Ask: **In order to learn, what is your job as a student?** (summarize answers such as: to listen, to complete class work and homework, etc.)

2. Share: **Today we are going to talk about the importance of LISTENING in order to learn. We are going to do a role reversal – I need you to pretend to be the teacher and I will pretend to be the student as we role play about being a good listener in the class.**

3. ROLE PLAY ACTIVITY:

   Explain: **I will ask for different volunteers to come to the front of the room to be the teacher. When you are the teacher you need to pretend to be teaching and you need to watch my listening behavior. After you have briefly observed my behavior, you need to first point out the unhelpful behavior that interferes with being a good listener and then second, suggest what I could do differently to be a better listener. As the teacher you can either share your answers or you may call on others in the class to help.**

4. As the student pretends to play the role of the teacher and is teaching, you need to first demonstrate a poor listening behavior. After each demonstration, prompt the student by asking, **"Am I showing good listening behavior…what suggestions do you have for me?** Replay again, but this time show the corrected listening behavior. Use the following listening problems to role-play:

   ☆ ***Listening Behavior: Eyes Focused***
   First, demonstrate poor listening behavior. Look everywhere around the room except at the teacher. Discuss. Then, replay with eyes focused on the teacher. Reinforce the importance of eyes looking at the teacher – share that typically 'your brain and thinking follows your eyes and what you're looking at'. Add that head nods while looking at someone also send the message of good listening.

- ✯ ***Listening Behavior: Body Settled***
  First, demonstrate excessive movement. Fidget and move all around in your seat – may choose to play with a toy or your pencil eraser, etc. Discuss. Then, replay with body settled and listening. Explain that excessive movement can distract yourself and others. To avoid excessive movement, get plenty of sleep at night – sometimes we are fidgety in order to stay awake, eat nutritious food – no sugar overloads, and take advantage of breaks in the day – enjoy recess and other activities.

- ✯ ***Listening Behavior: Good Posture***
  First, demonstrate poor listening posture. Slump in your desk with head down. Discuss. Then, replay showing good listening posture with body sitting up at the desk and head up. Explain that sitting up straight allows for good breathing which helps us to be alert.

- ✯ ***Listening Behavior: Participate*** *(Prompt your 'teacher' to ask you a question…)*
  First, demonstrate poor participation. When the 'teacher' asks you a question, don't raise your hand but turn and look at everyone else or just stare into space. Discuss. Then, replay being involved and raising hand to participate. Explain that raising our hand to answer questions keeps us listening, involved, and a part of the lesson.

5. Review the poster *Tuned-In, What Does It Look Like?* and post for a visual reminder of good listening.

Tuned-In
What Does It Look LIke?

POSTER

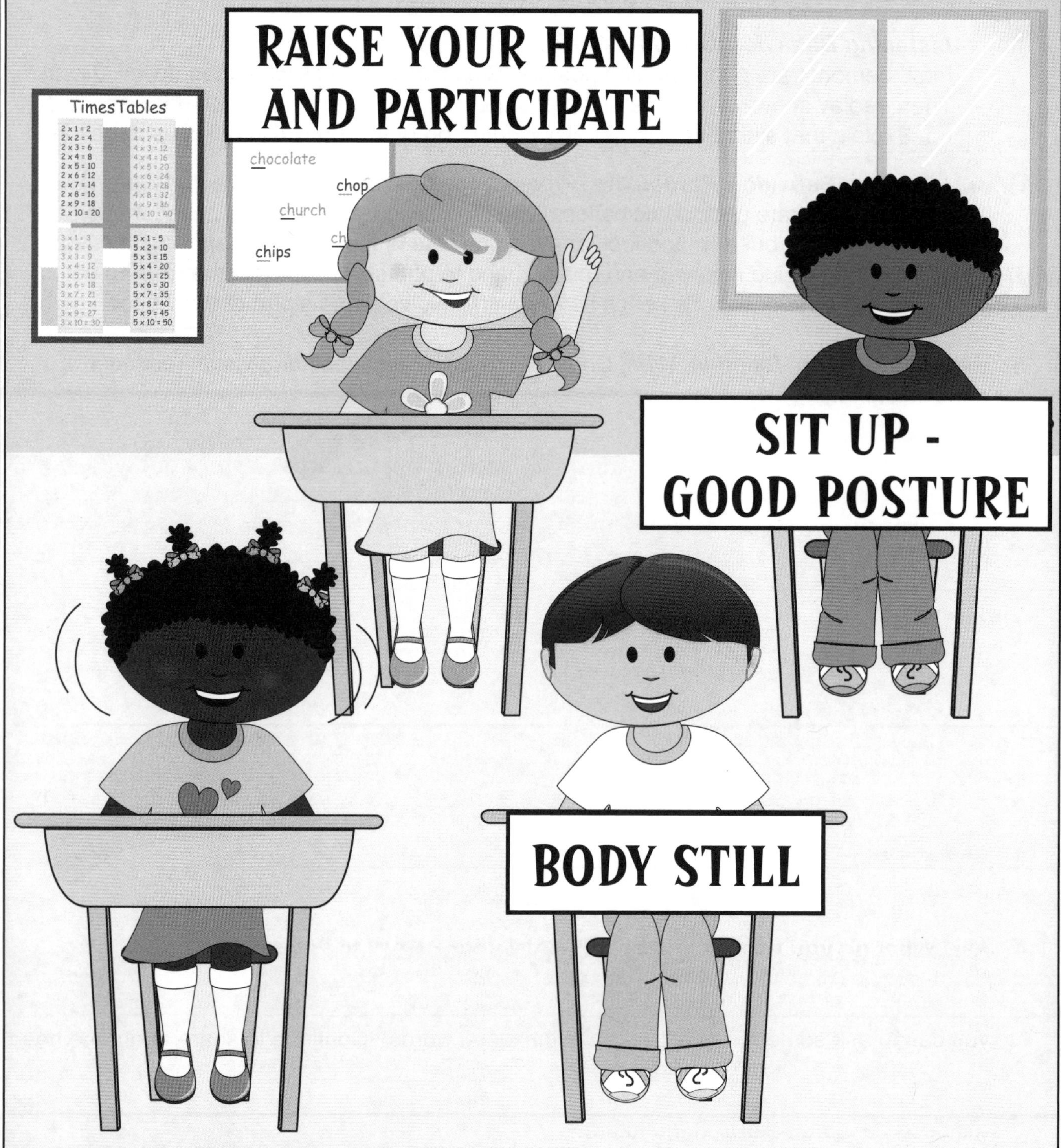

Activity 56 · Activity for LEARNING · Focusing

Train Your Brain

Overview: This activity promotes the importance of training your brain to stay focused and connected to listening and learning.

Materials

- ✓ Several small rewards such as candy or stickers
- ✓ Copy of the *Train Your Brain* worksheet

Procedures

1. Ask: **Have you ever read all the words in a paragraph or part of a story but when you had finished you didn't remember anything you had actually read? You can go through the motions of reading but if your brain is not plugged in or connected, you won't be successful. What do you have to do to not only read the words but also to know what it says?**

2. Continue talking on about general class behavior and the importance of listening and focusing. STOP in the middle of talking, go up to someone and ask them to repeat the last 3 words you just said. If they get it right give them a piece of candy or small reward, if they do not get it right say, "That's okay – keep listening…" Return to your summary talk about the importance of listening but continue to STOP several times asking different students to check the last 3 words for listening. If correct, share the extrinsic reward of stickers/candy.

3. Share: **Sitting in class listening to a lesson is not always as entertaining as being at a movie or playing a video game but it is important to TRAIN your BRAIN to listen.**

4. Ask: **What do you think it means to TRAIN your BRAIN to listen?** (Include in your discussion/talk the importance of disciplining your brain to focus, listen, and learn even though there may be distractions or even if it isn't easy. (Don't forget to STOP as much as you can to ask someone to repeat back the last 3 words). Continue to share about the need to get in the habit of making ourselves look, pay attention to, focus on, avoid distractions, concentrate, and process what is being taught. If we work on it now and TRAIN ourselves it will become more natural in the future.

5. Ask: **In class, some of you received a small reward of candy when you listened well and were able to repeat back the last 3 words. Did you listen in a different way when you knew you may have to repeat back the last 3 words? Explain.** Include in your discussion that you may have been more intense and more focused in how you were listening. Share that it is this type of listening that is needed in class.

6. Ask: **What is the reward when your brain is focused on the lesson and you are listening?** Stress how this reward is more valuable than candy because it is a part of your education, learning, and life that will help you achieve goals.

7. Complete the *Train Your Brain* worksheet, discussing different strategies to train the brain.

Train Your Brain

WORK SHEET

Directions: *Copy and cut apart the strategies below. Ask students to draw a card and lead a discussion on what this strategy means and how it would help TRAIN YOUR BRAIN to be a good listener.*

Don't just

HEAR

the words...

LISTEN

PICTURE IT!

DISCIPLINE

YOURSELF

to

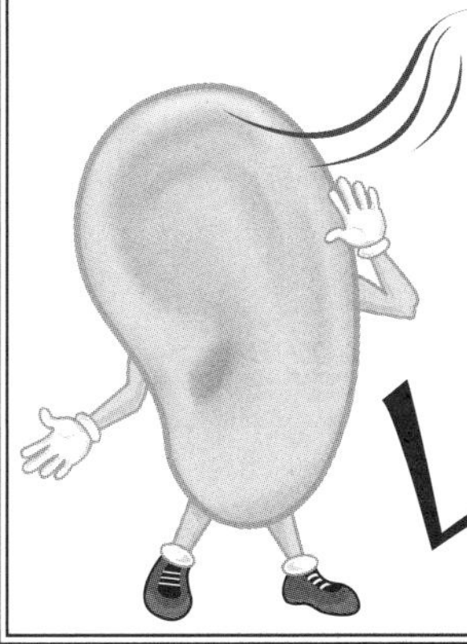

LISTEN

Use

Focusing Power

THE REWARDS OF GOOD LISTENING ARE PRICELESS.

Activity 57

Activity for LEARNING

Focusing

Where's the Self-Control Button?

Overview: This activity emphasizes the importance of self-control in order to stay focused on learning. Helpful strategies for self-control are provided.

Materials

- ✓ Dice
- ✓ Copy of the *Where's the Self-Control Button?* worksheet

Procedures

1. Ask: **What does Self-Control mean?**

2. Ask: **How does using our self-control help us with our learning?**

3. Ask: **Is it always easy to use our self-control in the classroom, during learning? Explain.** Bring into the discussion that at times we can get distracted by other students, our mind may wander and we start to daydream, or perhaps we may get distracted and react to a classmate bothering us.

4. Share the benefit of having a self-control button we could 'push' to engage our self-control so we could refocus on learning. Propose the idea of creating a pretend button we could push – let students brainstorm where their pretend button may be (perhaps their nose, elbow, tug of the ear, etc.). Share the importance of matching the pretend push of the button to the thinking strategy to help with self-control.

5. Review the Self-Control strategies on the *Where's the Self-Control Button?* worksheet. Relate the importance of using self-control in the learning environment.

Where's the Self-Control Button?

WORK SHEET

Directions: *Take turns rolling the dice and leading a discussion about the strategy for self-control that correlates to the number of the rolled dice. Include in the discussion:*

- ***WHEN would the Self-Control strategy be most helpful?***
- ***HOW or WHY would the Self-Control strategy be helpful?***

1. Turn eyes away from the distraction.
2. Focus eyes on the teacher or speaker.
3. Press the "mute" button.
4. Tell yourself to refocus on learning.
5. Take a deep breath and calm down.
6. Move away from or ignore.

Directions: *Review the situations below and choose a helpful self-control strategy. Fill in your answer.*

1. The teacher was reviewing for the Social Studies test when a classmate catches your attention and starts making funny faces and laughing. What self-control strategy would you use?

   ____

2. A classmate is sharing her book report but your mind starts to wander thinking about what you're going to do at recess. What self-control strategy would you use?

   ____

3. During seatwork time, 2 classmates behind you start to whisper as they pull something out of their desk. What self-control strategy would you use?

   ____

4. When getting your math workbook out to begin math, one of your classmates make a cutting remark to you about how you're dumb in math. What self-control strategy would you use?

   ____

5. Part of the group was completing seatwork while others that had finished could pair up and discuss the story. There was a lot of noise in the room and you were tempted to just write answers down to be finished so you could join in the talking. What self-control strategy would you use?

   ____

Activity 58

Activity for LEARNING

Focusing

Action Outcomes
Use Your Crystal Ball

Overview: This activity examines how we often can predict or guess the outcome for an action, therefore we can use our prediction powers to help us make good choices for learning.

Materials

- ✓ Whistle, balloon
- ✓ Copy of the *Action Outcomes – Use Your Crystal Ball* worksheet

Procedures

1. Ask: **Do you agree that everything we do, our actions, have outcomes or consequences? Explain.**

2. Hold the whistle up and ask: **If I hold this whistle up to my mouth and blow air into it what do you think will happen?** After you blow the whistle, turn to the person who shared what would happen and ask: **How did you know that would happen?** (reinforce the answer about having done that before – based on previous experience) **Do you have special powers?**

3. Hold a balloon up and ask: **If I hold this balloon up to my mouth and blow air into it what will be the outcome?** After you inflate the balloon, turn to the person who shared the answer and ask: **How did you know that? Do you have special powers? Can you see into the future?**

4. If you would like to add another example for fun, you may choose to ask the students what will happen when you let go of the inflated balloon. Process.

5. Summarize the lesson by saying: **For every ACTION (what we do) there is an OUTCOME (consequence). Many times we can guess or predict what may happen. Our ability to guess or predict outcomes is like having special powers to see into the future.**

6. Ask: **If we know the outcome do you think that could help us make a better choice about what we do – our actions?**

7. Inflate the balloon again but this time tie a knot. Hold the inflated balloon and suggest that we pretend this is our crystal ball that we can look into for our special powers to guess or predict the future or the outcome of our actions. Ask for volunteers to take turns holding the balloon/crystal ball to predict the outcomes of the actions on the *Action Outcome – Use Your Crystal Ball* worksheet.

*adapted from "Understanding Consequences" lesson in *Puzzle Pieces: A Classroom Guidance Connection* by Sitsch and Senn.

Action Outcomes
Use Your Crystal Ball

WORK SHEET

Directions: *For each situation below, predict or guess the OUTCOME (consequence) for the given ACTION. Use an inflated balloon to pretend to be your crystal ball to "see into the future."*

Action: What if you started daydreaming in class while the teacher was reviewing for the Social Studies test?

Outcome: What would happen? ______________________________

Is that a helpful action – something you should do or not? Explain

____

Action: What if you watched TV all afternoon and didn't do your homework?

Outcome: What would happen? ______________________________

Is that a helpful action – something you should do or not? Explain

____

Action: What if you rushed through your class work so you could have free time?

Outcome: What would happen? ______________________________

Is that a helpful action – something you should do or not? Explain

____

Action: What if you thought the math was too hard so you gave up and quit trying?

Outcome: What would happen? ______________________________

Is that a helpful action – something you should do or not? Explain

____

ORGANIZATION

Activity 59

Activity for LEARNING

Organization

What's Your System?

Overview: This activity focuses on the importance of organization and provides a TAKE 3 TO ORGANIZE system to help.

Materials

- ✓ Desk and/or book bag with books, notebooks, paper, and a math paper
- ✓ Copy of *What's Your System?* worksheet

Procedures

1. Preparation: disorganize a desk/book bag with papers crumpled and stuffed in the desk/ book bag with books out of order, etc. Take a math paper and crumple and stuff it in the desk/book bag.

2. Ask for a volunteer to find the specific math paper in the desk. You may choose to time the student. After the student has found the paper, process with them how it felt as they were looking for the math paper…did they have to think more, worry about finding it, did it take longer to locate the paper?

3. Ask the students to share different ways the desk/book bag could be organized. Organize the desk/book bag and put the math paper in a folder marked *math* or in a three ringed binder under the *math section.* Now ask for a volunteer to locate the math paper in the organized desk/book bag. You may choose to time the student and compare with the previous time. Process how it felt as they were looking for the Math paper… were they more confident that it could be found, at ease – not worried about locating it?

4. Review the TAKE 3 TO ORGANIZE listed on the *What's Your System?* worksheet and direct students to complete the 'What's Your Plan?' section.

What's Your System?

WORK SHEET

Directions: *Review the TAKE 3 TO ORGANIZE then complete the "What's Your Plan?"*

TAKE 3 TO ORGANIZE

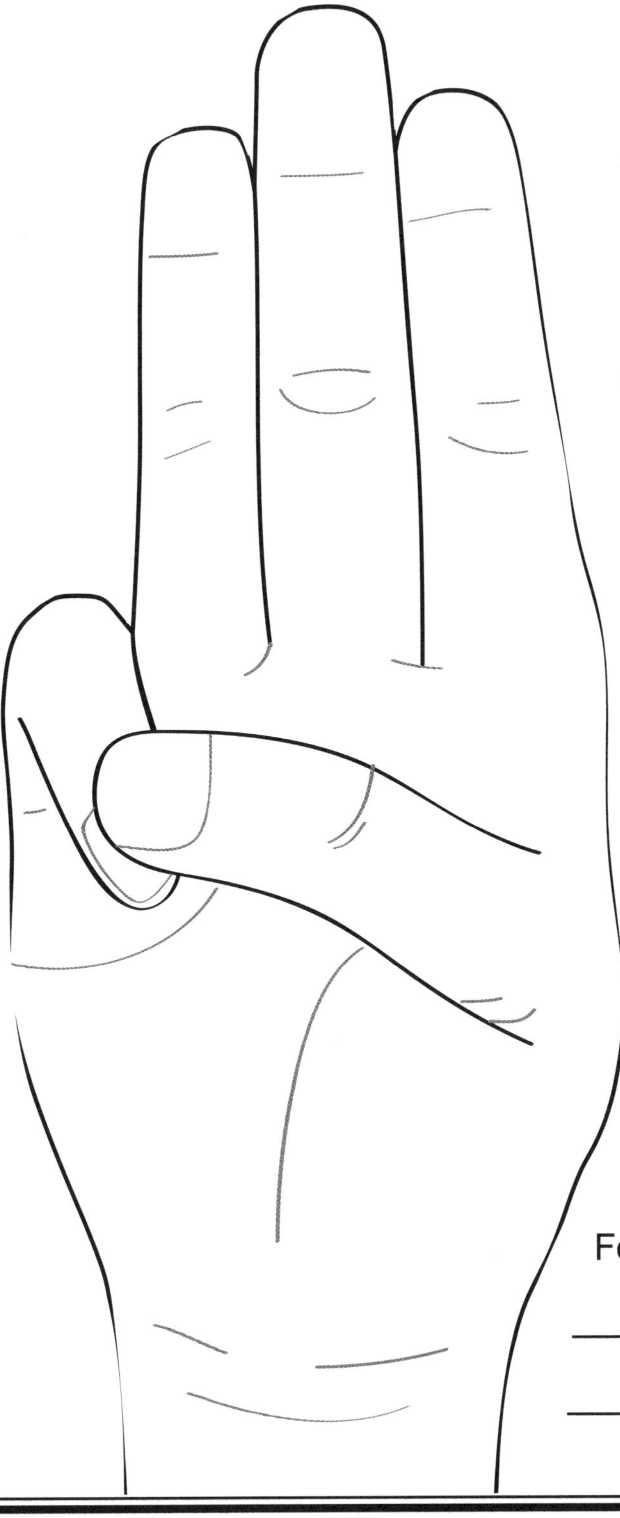

1. **Trash Out**
2. **Papers in Order**
   - **homework papers, signed papers, study guides...**
3. **Materials Needed**
   - **pencils, paper, eraser, books...**

WHAT'S YOUR PLAN?

For my desk area, I plan to ____________

____

____

For my book bag, I plan to ____________

____

____

For my home study area, I plan to ________

____

____

Activity 60

Activity for LEARNING

Organization

The List Maker

Overview: This activity emphasizes the importance of writing down homework assignments.

Materials

✓ Copy of *The List Maker* worksheet

Procedures

1. Ask: **When have you seen people make a list before? What type?** (ex. grocery list, 'to do' list). **When have you made a list?** (ex. Christmas list, chore list, homework list).

2. Ask for a volunteer to play a list game, explain the following: **I will give you a list of instructions that I ask you to follow. Are you ready?**
   - **Say your first and last name out loud.**
   - **What is 2+2?**
   - **Raise your right hand**
   - **Say and remember the following words: three, bed, arm, and seven.**
   - **Hop three times.**
   - **Clap your hands.**
   - **Say a word that rhymes with 'cat'.**
   - **What is your favorite movie?**
   - **Touch the top of your head.**
   - **Touch your feet.**
   - **Turn around three times.**
   - **Put your hands by your side.**
   - **What are the words I asked you to remember?**

   The correct words the student was asked to remember were 'three, bed, arm, and seven'. Typically the student cannot remember the words. Ask: **Why do you think it is difficult to remember the words?** Point out there were other activities to do that took brain power and perhaps distracted from remembering. **If I had told you to remember the words and had asked you to tell me the words immediately would you have been able to do that? When given a homework assignment to do, have you ever said or thought to yourself that you would remember but when you got home later that day you had trouble remembering the page number or other details?** Relate how your day can distract you from remembering all of the details of your homework assignment. Come to the conclusion that it is best to write down the homework assignment so it can be remembered correctly.

3. Complete *The List Maker* worksheet

The List Maker

WORK SHEET

My plan for writing down my homework assignment each day is to:

Be an Excuse Buster!

Directions: *If you started to use the following excuse for not writing down your homework assignment, tell what you would do instead.*

1. I don't have to write down my assignment, I'll remember… but I chose to ________

   ____.

2. The teacher didn't give us time to write it down… but I chose to ________________

   ____.

3. I didn't have time to write it down, I had to finish my class work… but I chose to ___

   ____.

4. I didn't have any paper to write down my assignment… but I chose to ____________

   ____.

5. I couldn't find my pencil… but I chose to ________________________________

   ____.

Activity 61

Activity for LEARNING

Organization

Over the Long Haul

Overview: This activity focuses on the importance of planning ahead for long range assignments.

Materials

- ✓ Copy of the *Over the Long Haul* pictures
- ✓ Copy of the *Over the Long Haul* chart

Procedures

1. Display the first picture from the next page and say: **I'm sure this has never happened to you but... explain what is going on in the picture.** Conclude that the student is just beginning to read his book the night before the book report is due. Ask: **Do you think the teacher just assigned the book report that day to be due the next day? How do you think he feels being on page 2 with the report due tomorrow? How could he have avoided this problem?**

2. Display the second picture and say: **Explain what is happening in this picture? Do you think it is always easy for a parent to go out to the store at that moment? Explain.**

3. Say: **Name some homework assignments that are not always due the next day but may be due several weeks later.** Include such assignments as book reports, projects, studying for major test.

4. Hold up the "Plan Ahead" sign. Discuss the message in the sign. Ask: **What are some helpful ways you have found to plan ahead for those long range assignments?**

5. Review the *Over the Long Haul* chart as a guide to dividing the long range assignments into smaller parts and setting deadlines along the way in order to accomplish the long range assignment.

Over the Long Haul

WORK SHEET

Directions: *Copy and cut apart each picture. Use in your discussion as instructed on the previous page.*

PLAN AHEAD

Over the Long Haul

WORK SHEET

Directions: *Write down your long-range project and due date. Then, divide the long-range project into smaller steps and list below. Assign a date to have each step completed. As you complete each step, circle "yes" to keep track of your progress.*

Name ______________________ **Date** ______________

Long-Range Project: ______________________

Due Date: ______________

	Date to be Completed	Circle "YES" when Completed
STEP 1: ______________________		YES
STEP 2: ______________________		YES
STEP 3: ______________________		YES
STEP 4: ______________________		YES
STEP 5: ______________________		YES
Project Completed:		YES

STUDY TIPS

Activity 62

Activity for LEARNING

Study Tips

Brain Storage and Retrieval

Overview: This activity differentiates between short and long-term memory and focuses on techniques for long term memory information.

Materials

- ✓ Board or chart paper/marker
- ✓ Pad and pencil for each group
- ✓ Copy of the *Brain Storage and Retrieval* worksheet

Procedures

1. Share: **Learning is about remembering or storing information so you can retrieve it later. There are two types of memory: Short-Term Memory and Long-Term Memory.**

2. Share: **I need to divide our group or class into 5 smaller groups. Remember the number I assign you so you will know which group to go to.** Proceed to go through the class assigning a number 1, 2, 3, 4, or 5 to a student. Say: **How many of you remember your number?** Direct all of the number 1's to go to a specific area and circle up, the number 2's to a different area, etc. Explain: **Now that we are divided into groups and ready for our activity would you have to necessarily remember your number anymore? This is an example of Short-Term Memory where you only needed to keep it in your head a short amount of time and don't need to remember it later.**

3. Explain: **A different type of memory that we use is Long-Term Memory. Long-Term Memory is for things we learn that we need to keep in our memory for an extended time, such as our phone number or address. How many of you know your phone number and address? Good. Think about how you learned your phone number and address. Take 4 minutes to share with others in your group how you learned it.** After 4 minutes, call time and have groups share their answers.

4. Ask: **What are some other things that we need to have in our Long-Term Memory?** Make a list on the board or chart paper. Include such items as our ABC order, multiplication facts, facts for a test. For each item ask: **Why does this need to be in the long-term memory and when/why would we need to retrieve it later?** (relate to how even as adults, for ex., use multiplication in our everyday shopping to calculate the best deals, in our careers, in our future learning, etc.)

5. Hand each group paper and pencil and have them brainstorm creative techniques to put each of the items the group listed on the board or chart paper into Long-Term Memory. In other words, what are some ways people learn their ABC order, their multiplication facts, etc? Allow 8 minutes to work and then have the groups share.

6. Hand each student a copy of *Brain Storage for Long-Term Memory* worksheet. Review the top section of the page adding any additional ideas brainstormed by the group. Then direct students to apply their Long-Term Memory techniques to the day to day learning by completing the second section of the worksheet.

Brain Storage and Retrieval

WORK SHEET

Directions: *Choose different topics/areas you are presently studying and apply a Long-Term Memory Technique to learn the information.*

1. To learn ______________________________

____

____

I will use the Long-Term Memory Technique of

____

____

____

2. To learn ______________________________

____

____

I will use the Long-Term Memory Technique of

____

____

____

3. To learn ______________________________

____

____

I will use the Long-Term Memory Technique of

____

____

____

LONG TERM MEMORY TECHNIQUES

- **Practice Makes Perfect**
  Repetition.
- **Picture It!**
  Connect the information to a visual or picture.
- **Creative Review**
  Use puppets or drawings to review the information.
- **Give it Rhythm**
  Make up a rhyme or song for the information.
- **Silly Sentence or Name**
  You can use the first letter of each word you are trying to remember and make a silly sentence or name. Ex. ROY G. BIV stands for the colors of the rainbow: Red, Orange, Yellow, Green, Blue, Indigo, Violet.
- ______________________

  ____

  ____
- ______________________

  ____

  ____

Activity 62 | Activity for LEARNING | Study Tips

Which Way Do I Learn?

Overview: This activity identifies the three learning styles with examples and applications to everyday learning.

Materials

✓ Copy of the *Which Way Do I Learn?* worksheet

Procedures

1. Ask: **What does it mean to learn by listening?**

2. Ask: **What does it mean to learn by looking?**

3. Ask: **What does it mean to learn by doing?**

4. Say: **We can learn in all three ways – listening, looking, and doing.** Refer students to the top of the *Which Way Do I Learn?* worksheet and review the three learning styles and the examples of each. After reviewing, ask students to share which way they think they learn best?

5. Complete *Which Way Do I Learn?* worksheet. Share answers and ask the students how they can study differently in the future to help them with their learning?

Which Way Do I Learn?

WORK SHEET

We learn by LISTENING (Auditory Learner)	We learn by LOOKING (Visual Learner)	We learn by DOING (Kinesthetic Learner)
Hearing the information.	*Creating visuals or pictures in our mind.*	*By being involved in the activity.*

Directions: *Put an A.B. or C. beside each example to indicate learning by:*

A. Listening ***B. Looking*** ***C. Doing***

_____ 1. Sit near the front of the class to see the board.

_____ 2. Sit in the class where I can hear well and focus on what the teacher is saying.

_____ 3. Use puppets or act out to retell the important information.

_____ 4. Practice the information by writing with sidewalk chalk or shaving cream on a table.

_____ 5. Create a song, rhyme, or rap to help remember the facts.

_____ 6. Add pictures and charts to class notes to help remember the information.

_____ 7. Create flash cards to help study.

_____ 8. Record important information on a tape recorder and play it back later.

_____ 9. Pretend to write the information in the air.

_____ 10. Reread information aloud.

Directions: *If you were studying the following, list some examples of ways that may help you learn. Use examples above or some of your own.*

1. If I were learning about the American Revolution, I could ____________________________.

2. If I were learning my math facts, I could ____.

3. If I were learning vocabulary words for a reading story, I could ______________________.

4. If I were learning spelling words for a spelling test, I could _________________________.

5. If I were learning about the water cycle in science, I could ___________________________.

Activity 64

Activity for LEARNING

Study Tips

The Right Way to Answer a Question

Overview: This activity reinforces the importance of listening to learn and shares an effective approach to ask questions for understanding.

Procedures

1. Begin by sharing the following story:

   Once upon a time when the teacher was teaching a new skill in math there was one student, Rachel, who was not listening but was daydreaming during the lesson. Rachel's eyes gazed out the window when all other students were looking at the board and following along. After the teacher had introduced and explained the new skill, she then passed out a math sheet for each student to practice the skill she had just introduced. As the paper was set on Rachel's desk she awoke out of her daydream, looked at the sheet, and realized she had no idea how to do the problems. Rachel raised her hand and said to the teacher, "I don't understand." Rachel thought this would be the perfect way to get the extra attention and have the teacher personally explain it to her. After all, her teacher was so nice and always willing and wanting to help her students learn. But to Rachel's surprise, the teacher was not happy with her. The teacher explained that in order for her to be willing to help her Rachel first needed to do her job of listening and that she had noticed that Rachel was not paying attention but looking out the window during the lesson. Rachel felt bad that she hadn't done what she was supposed to and she didn't like disappointing her teacher or herself.

2. Ask the students: **When the teacher is teaching, what is your job as a student?** Listening. **Describe good listening – what does it look like?** Eyes looking, head nods, blocking out distractions… **Are there times that even when you listen well you may still not understand something?** Yes, and asking questions is a part of learning.

3. Explain: **Most of the time teachers are able to tell which students are listening and which are not, but even the most amazing teachers can make mistakes. So, to make sure that your teacher does not confuse you with someone who was not listening, make sure to ask your questions in the "right" way. Here is a tip on the "right" way to ask a question.**

Include in your question the part you DO understand or repeat back what you heard the person say, but then share the part you DON'T understand or where you are confused.

4. By doing this you let the person know that you did listen and you are trying. For example:

   - ✭ "I heard you say… but I got lost on this part…"
   - ✭ "I understand this … but not this…"
   - ✭ "I understood when you explained this… but can you help me with this…?"

Activity 65

Activity for LEARNING

Study Tips

I Can Do This On My Own

Overview: This activity encourages students to transition from being a dependent to an independent worker in assuming responsibility for their work.

Materials

✓ Copy of the *I Can Do This On My Own* poster

Procedures

1. Share: **Perhaps you have heard or said the following: "Mom, how do you spell____?" or "I can't think about what to write, will you help me?" or "I don't understand this, will you explain it?"**

2. Ask: **What does it mean to work independently on your school work?** Summarize as taking responsibility to complete your work and not to depend on someone else for the answers or to direct what to do next.

3. Ask: **Becoming an independent student can be challenging, why?** Include in the discussion how when we are very young there is always someone else there taking care of us and doing for us. As we grow older we take on that responsibility of doing and learning on our own. The transition can be difficult, especially when things are hard for us, but when we assume responsibility and complete our work, even though it is hard, we build confidence in our abilities and become more independent.

4. Review the *I Can Do This On My Own* poster and then brainstorm with the students to fill in the blanks with the following situations below:

    Instead of asking someone how to spell a word, you can __________________.

    Instead of asking if your math subtraction problem is correct, you can _________.

    Instead of asking how to do your homework, you can____________________.

    Instead of saying, "I don't know what to write about," you can ______________.

    Instead of waiting for a parent to tell you it is homework time, you can ________.

I Can Do This On My Own

POSTER

When Problems Arise:

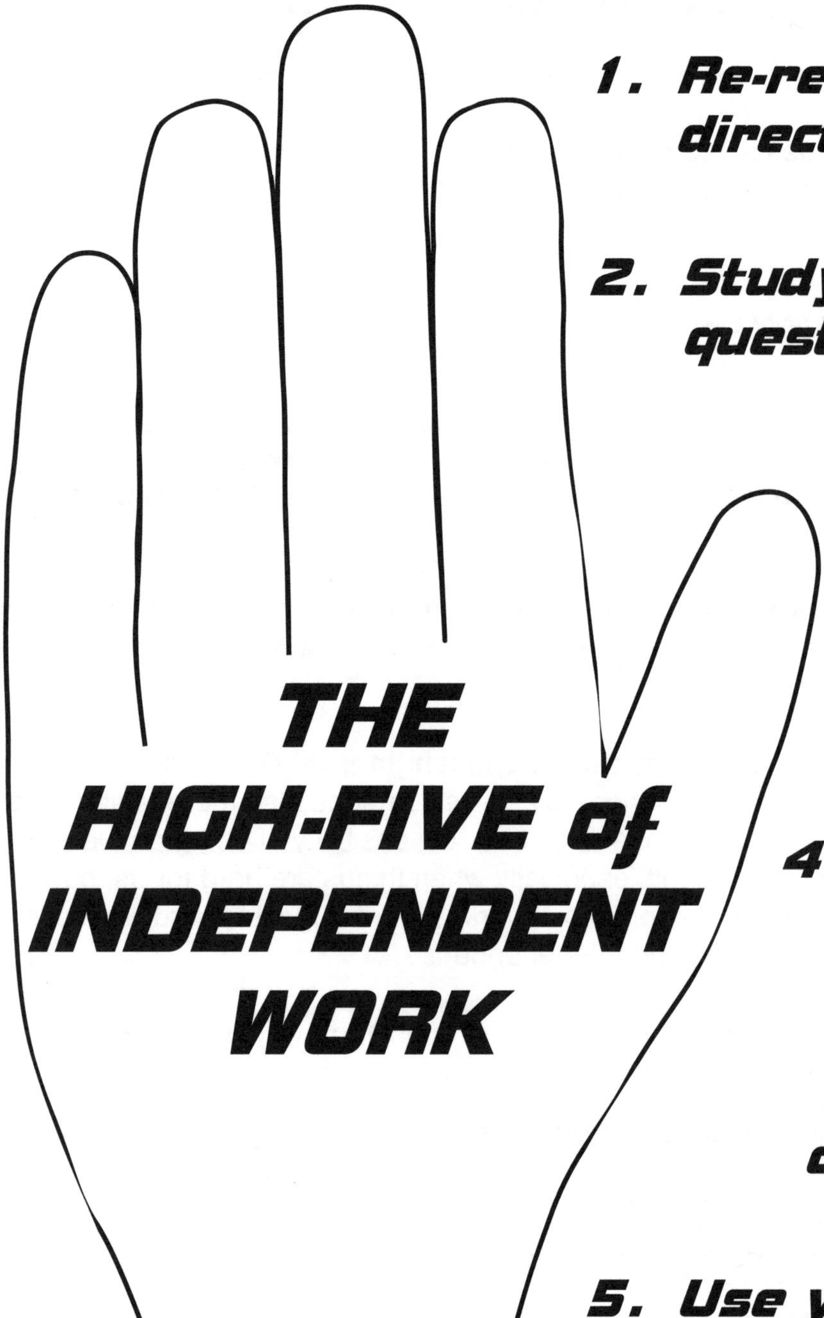

1. Re-read the directions.
2. Study the sample question/answer.
3. Listen well in class and ask questions.
4. Take your best educated guess, then follow-up in class to check/correct.
5. Use your resources: dictionary, computer, textbook.

Activity 66

Activity for LEARNING

Study Tips

And 'Yes'

Success Takes Hard Work

Overview: This activity focuses on the importance of hard work for success.

Materials

✓ Written on the board or paper strip, "Genius is 1% inspiration and 99% perspiration"

Procedures

1. Ask: **How many of you learned to walk when you were a baby? I don't know if you actually remember it but perhaps you have seen pictures or videos. When first learning to walk do babies go from the crawling position to standing up straight and walking perfectly or are babies' first steps wobbly and full of falls? Have you ever seen a baby quit trying to walk because they were not successful at first? Learning new things – failing and succeeding will always be a part of life.**

2. Ask: **How do the following words relate to SUCCESS?**
   - **Frustration**
   - **Failure**
   - **Try Again**
   - **Work**

3. Display the saying and ask: **Thomas Edison, a famous inventor, once said "Genius is 1% inspiration and 99% perspiration." What do you think it means?**

4. Ask: **Is there a different feeling between trying something that's easy and succeeding as opposed to trying something hard that you have to work at and succeeding? Do you feel a greater sense of satisfaction when you have to work hard at something?**

5. Brainstorm and/or role play a 'pep talk' that you may give yourself to help when the task is difficult.

HOMEWORK

Activity 67

Activity for LEARNING

Homework

Top Secret
Homework and Your Future

Overview: This activity presents four homework study skills and relates these skills to the valuable life long skills of: organized and uses time management skills, responsible, self-reliant and independent, and self-disciplined.

Materials

- ✓ Items to dress up a student as a Secret Agent (coat, old cell phone for a transmitter, etc.)
- ✓ Display the following words: ORGANIZED and USES TIME MANAGEMENT SKILLS, RESPONSIBLE, SELF-RELIANT and INDEPENDENT, and SELF-DISIPLINED.
- ✓ Copy of the "Study Tips Mission Report"

Summary of Activity

The intent of this activity is to present the 'Homework Study Tips' in a fun, creative way. You will need several student volunteers who are willing to take turns dressing up as Secret Agent 100 (1 Double 0) and to stand or sit up front as you read his/her mission report. At the end of each Study Tip Mission Report prompt the student to select the correct life skill (from the skills listed) that was learned on the mission and lead a class discussion. Change to a different student to play the role of the Secret Agent for each new Study Tip Mission Report. Read with 'drama' each mission report to add excitement to the lesson.

Procedures

1. Introduction, share: **Our Secret Agent 100 (1 Double 0) has successfully completed his mission: HOMEWORK AND YOUR FUTURE. During his mission he collected Study Tips to help with daily homework and while doing so learned valuable life skills that can help later in life. Listen to our briefing today and see if you can match the valuable life skill to Secret Agent 100's (1 Double 0's) Study Tip. The life skills you have to choose from are: ORGANIZED AND USES TIME MANAGEMENT SKILLS, RESPONSIBLE, SELF-RELIANT and INDEPENDENT, SELF-DISCIPLINED** (display the words). **I need a volunteer to come up front to pretend to be our Secret Agent 100 (1 Double O).** Give the student the props to help them "dress" for the part and ask them to stand or sit up front. **Let's give a warm welcome to our Secret Agent 100 (1 Double 0) . Come on down… Now let's all listen to the mission report…**

2. Read each of the Study Tips Mission Reports. After each report is read then ask your volunteer to connect the study tip to the life skill learned. Prompt the student to give explanations or to call on classmates to discuss.

3. Change to a different student volunteer to play the role of the Secret Agent for each new Study Tip Mission Report read and discussed.

4. Summarize the Study Tips. For reinforcement, ask the students to complete their own *Homework Mission Plan*. Review and display the four life skills discussed and encourage the student to include all four study tips in their homework plan. Begin their plan with…

My Homework Mission Plan will include ______________________.

Top Secret:
Study Tips Mission Report

WORK SHEET

Study Tip #1:
The report indicates that our Secret Agent, to prepare for his mission, located the perfect place to do his homework. It was quiet, contained a table and chair, and best of all it was away from his arch enemy – the TV Monster. He had previously been lured into the clutches of the TV Monster as he sat dazed in front of the TV watching one show after another. After he watched one TV show he would see the next advertised and then felt he HAD to watch that one also… and then another… and another. It did not have a happy ending… his homework had been left undone because of too much TV. Secret Agent 100 had learned his lesson to resist the temptation to watch TV before homework and he found a homework study area away from the TV. Secret Agent 100 learned the valuable life skill of ______________________ Mission Accomplished! (Self-Disciplined)

Study Tip #2:
The report indicates that our Secret Agent decided what homework subject to do first, second, and third. Our Secret Agent discovered that if you plan to do your hardest subject first when you have more energy and save the easiest assignment for last, the homework goes faster. Our Secret Agent also learned that using a timer to "guesstimate" how much each subject should take and then challenging himself to stick to the time set, helped him stay focused. However, the timer backfired once when he began rushing through the assignment, not doing a good job, just to beat the clock. He reminded himself 'that a job worth doing, is worth doing RIGHT" and he had no more problems with the use of the timer backfiring. Secret Agent 100 learned the valuable life skill of ______________________ Mission Accomplished! (Organized and Uses Time Management Skills).

Study Tip #3:
The report indicates how our Secret Agent learned to accomplish his mission of homework each day. He knew what his task was and didn't wait for headquarters to remind him of what needed to be done. To help with this task, our secret agent got a monthly calendar, listed all of his activities including scheduling a time each day to complete homework. When his undercover secret code alarm wrist watch signaled his time for homework, he went straight to his homework area, sat down, and completed his homework. Secret Agent 100 learned the valuable life skill of ______________________Mission Accomplished! (Responsible).

Study Tip #4
The report indicates that our Secret Agent was in the middle of his homework mission when the mission got tough – I mean really tough! His first thought was to call Headquarters for emergency help but on second thought he chose to work through the problem himself. He re-focused on the problem, re-read his directions, and then tried his best. And yes!! he was successful! He felt proud knowing that he had used his ability to be successful. Secret Agent 100 learned the valuable life skill of ______________________ Mission Accomplished! (Self-Reliant and Independent).

Activity 68

Activity for LEARNING

Homework

Help... I'm Going Under!

Overview: This activity provides strategies to help when a student is feeling overwhelmed with homework/work.

Materials

- ✓ Copy and cut out the life preservers on *Help! I'm Going Under* worksheet
- ✓ Optional: For more visual affect, you may choose to use larger life preservers with the information attached – plastic life preservers or inflatable swim rings can be used

Procedures

1. Ask: **What helps a person who is having trouble swimming when they begin to go under or drown? Explain that people often "throw them a line" or "life preserver" to help them stay afloat and bring them to safety.**

2. Ask: **Have you ever felt overwhelmed and "drowning in homework"? Explain.**

3. Say: **Let's look at our life preservers** (shared on the next page) **to see if the suggestions can help "save us" when we are overwhelmed with work.**

Help! I'm Going Under

WORK SHEET

Directions: *Copy and cut apart the life preservers. Students can select a life preserver and lead a discussion on how the suggestion can help us when we feel overwhelmed with our work. Add your own suggestion to the blank life preserver.*

I can take it one step at a time and organize what to do first, second, third...
I will set time limits for each task.
I need a chart to schedule my activities.
I will take short breaks between each job to clear the brain.
I will use positive thoughts of: "I can handle this!"
I can ________________ ________________ ________________

Activity 69

Activity for LEARNING

Homework

It's Greek To Me

Overview: This activity focuses on 'what to do' to help when a student is having difficulty understanding the homework.

Materials

✓ Copy of *It's Greek To Me* worksheet

Procedures

1. Ask: **Have you ever stood beside someone speaking a foreign language that you don't understand or perhaps visited a foreign country that speaks a different language? How does it feel when you don't understand the language that others seem to understand? If you were in a foreign country and didn't speak the language what might you take with you to help?** (translation book)

2. Say: **There may be times when our homework may feel like a foreign subject. Perhaps those around us understand but we don't. We need to have our translation book or code book of suggestions to help when we don't understand.**

3. Refer students to the *It's Greek to Me* worksheet for the code for suggestions of what to do when we don't understand our work.

Answer Box to the suggestions from the *It's Greek To Me* worksheet

1. Re-read the information.
2. Review the examples.
3. Take a short break and clear your head.
4. Call a friend for help.
5. Ask an adult.
6. Talk to the teacher.

It's Greek To Me

WORK SHEET

Directions: *Crack the code in order to find suggestions on what to do to help when you are having trouble understanding the homework.*

KEY to the CODE:

A	B	C	D	E	F	G	H	I	J	K	L	M
Z	Y	X	W	V	U	T	S	R	Q	P	O	N

N	O	P	Q	R	S	T	U	V	W	X	Y	Z
M	L	K	J	I	H	G	F	E	D	C	B	A

1. I V - I V Z W   G S V

   R M U L I N Z G R L M .

2. I V E R V D   G S V   V C Z N K O V H .

3. G Z P V   Z   H S L I G   Y I V Z P

   Z M W   X O V Z I   B L F I   S V Z W .

4. X Z O O   Z   U I R V M W   U L I

   S V O K .

5. Z H P   Z M   Z W F O G .

6. G Z O P   G L   G S V   G V Z X S V I .

Activity 70

Activity for LEARNING

Homework

Homework Incentives

Overview: This activity focuses on the importance of homework and provides homework signs and an incentive board.

Materials

- ✓ Copy of the 2 *Homework Signs*
- ✓ Copy of the *Homework Incentive Board* and dice

Procedures

1. Ask: **Why is homework an important part of learning?**

2. Say: **Homework is WORK. It may not always be something that comes easy or that we get excited about or can't wait to do but we know that it is important for our education. We need to do our homework and do our best job.**

3. The following 2 pages provide homework signs that can be copied, colored, and used by students to focus on homework.

4. The third page is an incentive board to be used as an incentive for homework completion. Our goal is for students to develop an intrinsic motivation to complete homework but at times a small incentive can help develop the habit. If you are using the incentive board, make sure to pair the incentive with statements/questions of "I was impressed with how well you focused on your homework." "How does it feel to get all of you work complete?" "Did it take long once you began?" in order to help move from the extrinsic to the intrinsic motivation.

fold

DO NOT DISTURB! LEARNING IN PROGRESS...

fold

DO NOT DISTURB! LEARNING IN PROGRESS...

fold

fold

HOMEWORK TIME. WORK BEFORE PLAY!

fold

HOMEWORK TIME. WORK BEFORE PLAY!

fold

Homework Incentive Board

WORK SHEET

Materials Needed: *Completed Homework Incentive Board, dice*

Directions for Creating Your Homework Incentive Board: *Develop your own homework incentive board for a job well done in completing homework. Create your board by adding to each of the squares a small reward or compliment for homework completion. Discuss appropriate rewards and compliments with the adult for agreement. You may include such rewards /compliments as:* ***choose a sticker, 15 minutes of game time with Mom or Dad, free pass to stay up 10 minutes beyond bed time, give yourself a pat on the back for a job well done, great job!*** *You may choose to write a reward more than once on the card but include a variety.*

Directions for Use: *When you have been successful and completed your homework, roll the dice. Then compare the roll of the dice with the square on your board and receive your reward/compliment. Remember that the true reward however, is in a job well done!*

Homework Incentive Board

 ________ ________ ________	 ________ ________ ________
 ________ ________ ________	 ________ ________ ________
 ________ ________ ________	 ________ ________ ________

Activity 71 | Activity for LEARNING | Homework

Caution:
Roadblocks to Homework Success

Overview: This activity brings an awareness of things that interfere with homework success and allows for brainstorming ways to effectively avoid or deal with the problem.

Materials

✓ Copy and cut out each sign (you may choose to enlarge the signs and copy on cardstock)

Procedures

1. Explain: **There are roadblocks or things that get in the way of our being successful with our homework. Review the *Caution: Roadblocks to Homework Success* signs and discuss how to effectively avoid or deal with the problem.**

2. You may choose to divide the students in pairs or groups to discuss a sign and present to others. They may choose to role play (showing the 'wrong' and 'right' way), choose to share their answers, or choose to lead a class discussion on each topic. Guide the students while working to create positive ways to think, or positive things to say or do to avoid or deal with the caution sign. An example to suggest for dealing with the "Caution: Speeding" may be to create a 'quality control exit checklist' for their homework to check for speeding.

Activity 71

Activity for LEARNING

Homework

Caution:

Roadblocks to Homework Success

CAUTION:
Blaming Others

"The teacher didn't tell us how to do it."

CAUTION:
Procrastinating

"I'll do it later."

CAUTION:
Speeding

"I'll just put something down to say I'm done."

CAUTION:
Exceeding the Time Limit

"I've got to make sure it's perfect."

Staring out the window rather than working.

TEST TAKING TIPS

Activity 72

Activity for LEARNING

Test Taking Tips

Tune-In to Key Words

Overview: This activity focuses on tuning in to key words said by the teacher and in the directions to help do your best on the test.

Materials

- ✓ Copy of the poster, *Pay Attention When You Hear…*
- ✓ Board and chart paper/marker

Procedures

1. Say: **Teachers often give us clues as to the most important information to study that may be on a test. What are some of these clues that we need to tune into?** Review the poster, *Pay Attention When You Hear…*

2. Ask: Have you ever 'messed up' a section on a test because you did not read the directions correctly? What are some typical errors we make by not reading the directions carefully?

3. List on board or chart paper key words in directions that we need to tune into. Include such words as:
   - ✯ Write in complete sentences.
   - ✯ Use correct punctuation.
   - ✯ Reduce to lowest terms.
   - ✯ Check your spelling.
   - ✯ Circle all answers that are correct.

Pay Attention When You Hear

Activity 73

Activity for LEARNING

Test Taking Tips

De-Stress for the Test

Overview: This activity reviews three steps to reduce test stress: be prepared, relax with deep breathing and exercise, and positive thinking.

Materials

- ✓ Inflatable beach ball with color sections
- ✓ Marker
- ✓ Copy of the *De-Stress for the Test* worksheet

Preparation

Using a marker, write one of the following questions on each section of the beach ball:

- ✭ How do you prepare for a Math test?
- ✭ How do you prepare for a Spelling test?
- ✭ How do you prepare for a Social Studies or Science test?
- ✭ How do you prepare for a Reading test or English test?

Procedures

1. Ask: **What are the different thoughts or reactions students have when there is a major test?** Summarize that the reaction can range from not caring to stressed and worried about the test. Share that our goal is to be in the middle of the range – in other words we need to be stressed enough about the test to prepare, care, and do our best but not to the extent that it negatively interferes with being able to think or focus on the test.

2. Share: **Today we will focus on reducing our stress about tests so that we can think and focus to do our best. There are three major steps to reduce stress:**

   STEP ONE: BE PREPARED

   STEP TWO: RELAX WITH DEEP BREATHING AND EXERCISE

   STEP THREE: POSITIVE THINKING

3. Hold up the beach ball and share that we are first going to talk about **STEP ONE: BE PREPARED** for the test. Show that there are questions on the sections of the beach ball asking how to prepare for different types of tests. Explain that the ball will be tossed to someone to catch and that they need to answer the question in the section that the pointer finger on their right hand is on. Begin tossing and having students share their answers and lead discussions on how to prepare for the different tests – Math, Social Studies/Science, Reading/English, Spelling.

4. Next share that we are going to practice the **STEP TWO: RELAX WITH DEEP BREATHING AND EXERCISE**. Have the students practice Step Two by pretending the following:
   - ✯ Take a deep breath, make a wish, and pretend to blow out the candles on your birthday cake.
   - ✯ Gently roll your head around as if watching a butterfly flutter above your head.
   - ✯ Shake your hand as if you are shaking a tambourine – switch hands with the tambourine.
   - ✯ Smile big as you would if you just found out that you made a 100 on your test. (Continue smiling and returning to a regular face with the following prompts: Smile big as you would if your teacher wrote a compliment note on your paper for your good work…Smile big as you would if your parents told you how proud they are of you.)

5. Finally, practice **STEP THREE: POSITIVE THINKING**. Ask students to brainstorm positive thoughts that would help us relax and do our best on the test.

6. Review the *De-Stress for the Test* worksheet/poster, allowing students to complete the worksheet and then encouraging the student to use the poster as a reminder.

De-Stress for the Test

WORK SHEET

STEP 1: BE PREPARED

List ways to prepare for a:

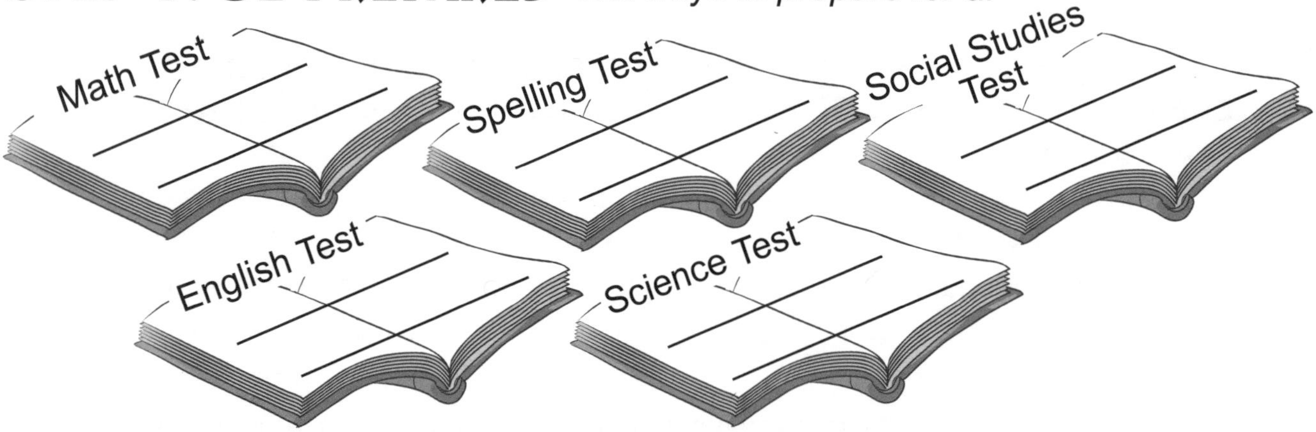

STEP 2: RELAX with DEEP BREATHS and EXERCISE

- **Take a deep breath, make a wish, and pretend to blow out your birthday candles.**
- **Gently roll you head as you pretend to watch a beautiful butterfly above your head.**
- **Shake your hands pretending to shake a tambourine, switch hands.**
- **Practice smiling big!**

STEP 3: POSITIVE THINKING

List encouraging thoughts:

POSITIVE ATTITUDE

Activity 74

Activity for LEARNING

Positive Attitude

Overcoming Obstacles

Overview: This activity includes inspirational stories of others who have persevered to overcome obstacles in their life and encourages students to continue working hard to overcome their obstacles.

Materials

- ✓ Index cards with one of the following sentences written on each card: "I quit!" "This is too hard!" "This doesn't make sense to me, I give up!"
- ✓ Story "*Wilma Unlimited*" by Kathleen Krull
- ✓ Copy of *Perseverance Pays Off...*

Procedures

1. Distribute the index cards to student volunteers and ask them to read out loud to the class/group the sentence on their card. Ask the class/group if they have ever said or had those thoughts about learning. Discuss when and why we may have had those thoughts.

2. Introduce the story "*Wilma Unlimited*" by sharing that Wilma faced a difficult obstacle – listen to find out what the obstacle is and how she handled it. Share the story.

   (Story Summary: "*Wilma Unlimited*" is a true story of Wilma Rudolph who was struck with polio at an early age and was crippled with the diagnosis of never being able to walk. She proved everyone wrong and with her determination and hard work she not only walked but became an Olympic gold medalist in 1960 in Track and Field and became known as the 'fastest woman in the world'.)

3. Discuss the story including how our problems and struggles may seem minor compared to Wilma's problem. Ask: **How do you think Wilma may have responded to the statements on the cards we shared earlier?** Review each of the statements and brainstorm a different way to look at or overcome the obstacle.

4. Read aloud *Perseverance Pays Off...* for other examples of well-known Americans who persevered to overcome obstacles in their life.

Perseverance Pays Off...

WORK SHEET

J.K. Rowling

Author of Harry Potter

J.K.Rowling, author of the Harry Potter books, was rejected by twelve publishing companies before being published. Since then she has written and published a total of seven books and continued with Warner Brothers purchasing the film rights to her books to create the Harry Potter Movie Series. Her life story is a "rags to riches" story where she moved from being on welfare to multi-millionaire status within five years.

Michael Jordan

Professional Basketball Player

Michael Jordan who is famous for his ability to play professional basketball for the Chicago Bulls was cut from his high school basketball team.

Walt Disney

Originator of Disneyland

Walt Disney began his career as a cartoon artist but his first company Laugh-O-Grams went bankrupt. He started over and reached success with many accomplishments: he created the first full length animated film; among the first to present color programming to television; and created our famous theme park – Disneyland.

Abraham Lincoln

The 16th President of the United States

Abraham Lincoln had success and was a great leader of our country who helped shape our history but Abraham Lincoln also met many failures and difficulties in life that he had to overcome. He lost eight elections through the years, his business failed, his sweetheart died, he had a nervous breakdown before he achieved success as the 16th president of the United States.

Activity 75 · Activity for LEARNING · Positive Attitude

And Why Do I Have to Learn This?

Overview: This activity connects today's learning to the future.

Materials

- ✓ Individually wrapped starburst candy for each student
- ✓ Copy of *And Why Do I Have to Learn This?* worksheet

Procedures

1. Ask: **Have you ever asked yourself, "Why I am going to school?" The first answer that comes to mind may be, "because Mom or Dad say I have to..." or "the law says I have to..." But beyond those answers – why**?

2. Share: **Let's pretend we have just stepped into a time machine and we have been jet ported into the future 15 years from now. We'll need some starburst to burst into the future...** Distribute to each student a wrapped starburst candy and a *And Why Do I Have to Learn This?* Worksheet. Begin a count down from 10-1 with the 1 signaling to unwrap and eat their candy as they think ahead to their future. Prompt with such thought provoking questions as, "What do you see yourself doing? What are the day to day jobs you do around your home? What career or job do you have?

3. Direct and allow time for students to complete their *And Why Do I Have to Learn This?* Worksheet. Either have students share their answers to the whole group or have the students gather in groups by the color of their candy wrapper to discuss and share.

And Why Do I Have to Learn This?

WORK SHEET

You have blasted off into your future 15 years from now... what career or job are you now doing?

____

How did going to school help you get your job?

____

Directions: *Pretend you are in your future. Read each item below and decide what subject in school – MATH, LANGUAGE ARTS, SCIENCE, or SOCIAL STUDIES, helped you be successful at the task listed. Write your answer in the space provided.*

______________1. You are at the Grocery store deciding the best deal, either "Buy one at $1.25 and get the second one free OR "Buy one for $.75?

______________ 2. Looking at the newspaper to know what is going on in the community?

______________3. Planning a vacation to another country and gathering information about the country's customs, their dress, their language, etc.

______________4. Deciding whether you can afford the new computer that is on sale for 15% off the price.

______________ 5. Driving a car and following the road signs.

______________ 6. Baking a cake following your grandmother's special recipe.

______________ 7. Knowing the best time to plant and care for a garden – need to consider temperature, rainfall/watering, using fertilizer...

______________ 8. Completing a job application in which they ask you to write about yourself and how your strengths make you the best person for the job.

______________ 9. Knowing the importance of recycling to live green and help our planet.

Close your eyes, count from 3 to 1 backwards and return to the present day and time. Now, get busy learning all that you can today because it is your life, your future!

Activity 76

Activity for LEARNING

Positive Attitude

I Think I Can... I Know I Can

Overview: This activity promotes the power of positive thinking and how our feelings and actions are related to our thoughts.

Materials

- ✓ Visual of a train with an engine, train car, and a caboose (May choose to enlarge the train graphic on the following page).
- ✓ Optional: "*The Little Engine That Could*" by Watty Piper
- ✓ Copy of *I Think I Can…I Know I Can!* worksheet

Procedures

1. Ask: **Do you recall a story that perhaps you read earlier in your childhood, "*The Little Engine That Could*?"** Either summarize the story or read the story aloud. Focus on the thought that it is our positive thinking or ATTITUDE that helps us achieve success.

2. Provide a visual of a train with an engine, a train car, and a caboose. Explain that there are three main words in the definition of Attitude and they are: THINK, FEEL, and ACT. Write the word THINK on the engine and relate that the power to our attitude is how we choose to *think* about a situation. Next write FEEL on the train car and relate that how we choose to THINK about a situation will determine how we feel about the situation. Next write ACT on the caboose and relate that how we choose to think will affect how we feel and how we feel will affect how we act. Point out that the train car (feelings) and caboose (actions) are both being pulled by the train engine or how we THINK about a situation.

3. Given the following situation: "you're having difficulty with your homework" first review with the student how you may THINK, FEEL and ACT if your train was on the wrong track and then review with your train on the right track. An example is given below.
   Train on the WRONG track:
   THINK: ***"This is too hard, I'll never understand this!"***
   FEEL: ***frustrated, discouraged***
   ACT: ***giving up, quitting***
   Train on the RIGHT track:
   THINK: ***"This is hard but I can handle this!"***
   FEEL: ***hopeful***
   ACT: ***Re-read directions. Review notes in order to understand and complete the homework.***

4. Complete the *I Think I Can…I Know I Can!* worksheet together or individually.

I Think I Can... I Know I Can

WORK SHEET

Directions: *For the given situations, write on each train engine, train car, and caboose a positive way to THINK, FEEL, and ACT. For the last one write your own difficult situation you may have had to deal with recently and write a positive way you could Think, Feel, and Act.*

SITUATION:
I'll never get this book read for my book report.

SITUATION:
This math is too hard for me.

SITUATION:
I don't know what to write about for my story.

SITUATION:
I'm too tired to listen to the lesson.

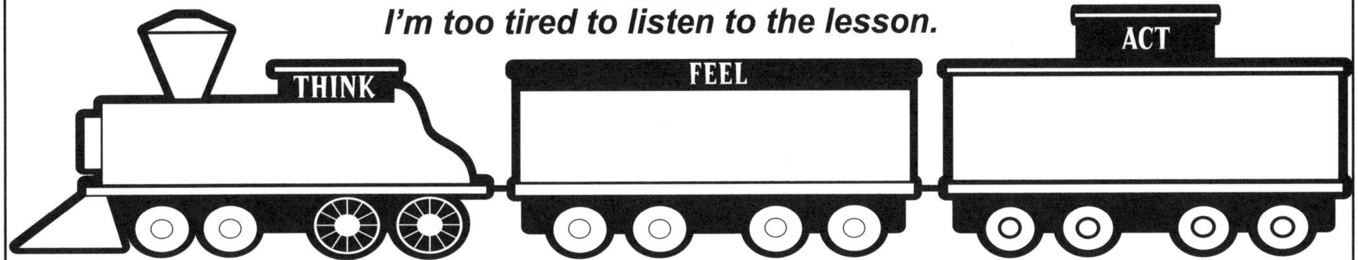

SITUATION:

____

Activity 77 | Activity for LEARNING | Positive Attitude

Taking Pride in a Job Well Done

Overview: This activity identifies that the job of a successful student is comprised of many parts or skills and that brain power, patience, and perseverance are often needed to put this puzzle of skills together.

Materials

✓ Copy on cardstock the *Taking Pride In A Job Well Done* worksheet

Procedures

1. Ask: **What makes it a job well done? The end results? Or what you did along the way?** Give time for discussions and explanations of their thoughts. Emphasize that taking time to do a job well and the feeling of pride is more important than taking short cuts just to say a job is complete.

2. Share that typically a job well done is a composite of many smaller steps that were needed in order to reach job success. Relate the smaller steps or pieces to a puzzle in which each puzzle piece is important and needed to give the whole picture. Continue the analogy sharing that putting together a puzzle also takes brain power, patience, and perseverance.

3. Brainstorm together the parts/skills that it takes to be a SUPER STUDENT. Include such skills as: listening in class, completing class work, completing homework, asking questions when needed, studying, being prepared, asking questions when needed, etc. Relate how brain power, patience, and perseverance are needed in each of the parts/skills shared.

4. Direct students to complete the *Taking Pride in a Job Well Done* worksheet as they complete their own puzzle of a SUPER STUDENT.

5. Optional: Students may create additional puzzles of “HOMEWORK SUPERSTAR” or “STAR LISTENER” or “STAR PARTICIPANT as they break down the skills/puzzle pieces needed for each.

Taking Pride in a Job Well Done

WORK SHEET

Directions: *Create your own puzzle of the pieces it takes to be a SUPER STUDENT. Brainstorm the different skills needed to be a SUPER STUDENT. Next, draw puzzle lines on the star dividing the star into puzzle pieces. Then, write a skill on each puzzle piece. Cut apart and put back together your puzzle of success. As you work on your puzzle remind yourself of the skills needed to be a successful student.*

SUPER STAR STUDENT

Activities for

THE WORLD of WORK

Career Development

We can make a difference in the lives of children!

CAREER AWARENESS

Career awareness is the start to career education for the elementary age student. It is here that the child begins to discover the variety of jobs available; to make a connection between school and work; to dream, play, and imagine him/her self in an occupation; and to develop the work-readiness skills to be successful. For the elementary child, their dreams of career choice may change many times through the years as their skills, experiences, and interests change but it is here that they begin to realize the multitude of possibilities and the foundations to exploring, connecting, and making good choices.

The activities in the **Career Awareness Section** provide a relation between present interests and possible future careers; reviews careers of family, friends, and those around us; provides discussion for ways to pursue helping others through volunteering; connects the present habits and skills to future success; and emphasizes the importance of good character now and in the future.

Activity 78

Activity for WORLD OF WORK

Career Awareness

Connecting Your Interest to Future Careers

Overview: This activity reviews how a student's present interest could relate to a future career.

Materials

- ✓ Board or chart paper and markers
- ✓ *Connecting Your Interest to Future Careers* worksheet
- ✓ Drawing paper and material for each student

Procedures

1. Ask: **What does it mean to have a hobby or special interest?** Ask students to give you examples of different hobbies or interests they have or students their age may have. List these on the board or chart paper. Connect their answers to possible future careers – see *Connecting Your Interest to Future Careers* Worksheet for examples.

2. Next, distribute to each student the *Connecting Your Interest to Future Careers* worksheet. Ask the student to turn the sheet over and on the back draw themselves enjoying a hobby or special interest they may have.

3. Have each student share their completed picture with the class and encourage the class to brainstorm what future careers might relate to that interest. Students may refer to the *Connecting Your Interest to Future Careers* worksheet for career possibilities. (Give examples broadening beyond the obvious). As different interests and careers are discussed, students may choose to add these interests and careers to the bottom of their worksheet.

4. Encourage students to continue exploring different hobbies and interests as they get older. Share that their interests and hobbies may change many times or some may remain the same. Explain to students that our interests and hobbies can be an important piece of the puzzle in choosing a career that we like when we are older.

Connecting Your Interests with Future Careers

WORK SHEET

Directions: *Consider the following possible careers for your future that may relate to your present interests and likes. Add additional careers and interests of your own.*

1. If you like **ART**… you may like using art to design houses, clothing, magazine ads, movie sets, draw cartoons, arrange flowers, or take photos for magazines and books.

2. If you like **MATH**… you may consider becoming an accountant, a computer programmer, an engineer or a statistician.

3. If you like the **OUTDOORS**… you may want to consider a career in landscape architecture, forestry, archeology, construction work, marine biology, or commercial fishing.

4. If you like **ANIMALS**… you may consider a job as a veterinarian, a groomer, an animal trainer, an animal shelter worker, or a pet store clerk.

5. If you like being **SOCIAL**… you may want to be a teacher, a lawyer, a customer service representative, a receptionist, a hotel manager, or a convention planner.

6. If you like to **PROTECT AND KEEP OTHERS SAFE**… you may choose a career as a police officer, a forensic scientist, a detective, an investigator, a parole officer, or a security guard.

7. If you like ________________, you may choose a career as a ________

   ____.

8. If you like ________________, you may choose a career as a ________

   ____.

9. If you like ________________, you may choose a career as a ________

   ____.

10. If you like ________________, you may choose a career as a ________

    ____.

Activity 79

Activity for WORLD OF WORK

Career Awareness

Jobs of Family and Friends

Overview: This activity allows the student to practice their interviewing, writing and presenting skills while learning about careers in their family as well as the careers of classmates' families.

Materials

✓ Copy of the *Job Interview Sheet* for each student

Procedures

1. For this activity information is gathered and then presented as a job SHOW AND TELL. Allow each student in the group or class to interview a family member or friend and to present their information to the class or group. All students may have the same due date or may be assigned different days to interview and present their information. Review the *Job Interview Sheet* with the students so they are prepared. Share interview tips such as:
   - good eye contact
   - clear voice when asking questions
   - head nods to show you are being a good listener
   - repeat back their answer to make sure you understand
   - thank the person for their time to participate in the interview

   Notes may need to be taken during the interview and then the final draft written on the interview sheet.

2. Create a wall or bulletin board space to display the interview page and any pictures pertaining to the job shared.

Job Interview

WORK SHEET

1. WHAT IS THE TITLE OF YOUR JOB?

2. WHAT ARE 3 ACTIVITIES YOU DO AT YOUR JOB?

3. DO YOU WORK WITH PEOPLE, THINGS, OR BOTH?

4. DO YOU WORK MAINLY INSIDE OR OUTSIDE?

5. WHAT DO YOU LIKE BEST ABOUT YOUR JOB?

6. WHICH SCHOOL SUBJECTS ARE IMPORTANT TO LEARN TO BE PREPARED FOR A JOB LIKE YOURS?

7. DO YOU HAVE ANY PICTURES ABOUT YOUR JOB THAT I MAY TAKE TO SCHOOL TO SHARE?

Activity 80 | Activity for WORLD OF WORK | Career Awareness

Careers All Around Us

Overview: This activity promotes the realization of the many jobs that are associated with a single everyday item and the interdependence and importance of each job.

Materials

- ✓ Reference is made to different items around the room (book, desk, lights, bookshelf, etc.)
- ✓ Board or chart paper and marker
- ✓ Copy of *Careers All Around Us* Worksheet for each group

Procedures

1. Hold up a "book" from the room. Ask the students to help brainstorm all of the people's jobs that are associated with the book. You may choose to list these on chart paper or board. Include such jobs as: author; illustrator; publisher; jobs at the printing company; jobs involved in making and selling of paper (loggers cut the trees and then send to a pulp yard); jobs that make the cardboard boxes for the shipping of the books; delivery trucks, salespeople, accountants ...and so forth.

2. **GAME:** For a class lesson, divide the class into groups and designate for each group an object from the room such as: a desk, an apple, the rug, the lights, bookshelf, the window... Have a set time for each group to brainstorm a list of all jobs associated with their object. Next have each group present their list to the class. A point is earned for the group for each correct item the group shares. Then other groups can suggest additional jobs associated with the item not listed by the original group and can then earn a point for their group/team; however, if the job the group shares was named by the team then the group losses a point (this encourages the importance of listening and focusing on other's presentations).

3. Ask: **Did you realize all of the jobs that can be connected to one simple item?** Share the reality that we may take everyday items for granted but when we examine all of the jobs that are needed to provide that item it is amazing to realize how we need each other and what they do to make our world happen.

4. Write the word “interdependence” on the board or chart paper and discuss its’ meaning. The dictionary defines interdependence as depending on (counting on) each other and one another. Ask the students to share examples of interdependence of how we depend on other people’s jobs in our world, such as: the *farmer* depends on a factory to produce the equipment to work on the farm and transportation service to export his product.

5. Ask: **In your family what do you depend on other people’s jobs to help you with?** (answers may include stores for food and clothing, trash/garbage pickup, to build or fix things at our house).

6. Ask: **Out of all the jobs shared today, are there any jobs that interest you?** Emphasize the importance of each and every job in our nation.

Careers All Around Us

WORK SHEET

Directions: *Label your object on the space provided. Next brainstorm and list all the possible jobs connected to this object.*

OBJECT: ____

1.	2.
3.	4.
5.	6.
7.	8.
9.	10.
11.	12.
13.	14.
15.	16.
17.	18.
19.	20.

Activity 81

Activity for WORLD OF WORK

Career Awareness

You Can Be a Volunteer… Service Learning Continues

Overview: This activity promotes the importance of volunteering and helping others as a life-long job.

Materials

- ✓ Copy of *You Can Be a Volunteer…Service Learning Continues* worksheet
- ✓ Crayons/markers and pencil

Procedures

1. Ask: **When there is a natural disaster like a hurricane, what do people do to help?** (allow time for various answers including what adults may do – volunteer rescue workers and Red Cross workers and other adults who help clear roads, take care of people in need, help provide food, clothing, shelter, etc. - as well as what children do to help – may collect canned foods, clothing and school supplies to send, or may write notes or cards of support.)

2. Ask: **When a family loses their home to fire what do people do to help? When a family doesn't have food or perhaps clothes or toys for their children for the holidays, what do people do to help?**

3. Ask: **What are the benefits for the person receiving the help? What are the benefits for the person giving the help?**

4. Ask: **What is a volunteer?** (Include in your answer that a volunteer is a person who performs a service or helps others willingly and without pay.)

5. Ask: **Are volunteers needed in our community? In our world? Why or why not?**

6. Ask: **What are some ways you can volunteer or help at home now?** (Include such answers as taking out the trash, sweeping the porch, reading to a younger brother or sister, etc.)

7. Ask: **What are some ways you can volunteer or help at school now?** (Include such examples as helping out in the classroom or in the media center or picking up trash in the hallways or by being an office helper, etc. Your school may have a specific school job program that you can relate to as volunteering their help.)

8. Ask: **What are some ways you can volunteer in the community now?** (Include examples such as: helping a neighbor rake their lawn, picking up trash in the neighborhood, planting flowers in a community area, collecting canned foods, visiting in a nursing home, etc.). Point out that volunteering now can give them experience in possible future careers.

9. Ask: **What are some ways you can volunteer in the future as an adult?** (Explain that in addition to their regular job they can also volunteer at different jobs like a volunteer firefighter, or at a hospital, at an animal shelter, or library, or at a school, or you can choose to help different helping organizations or support needs as they arise.)

10. Distribute the *You Can Be A Volunteer...Service Learning Continues* worksheet and discuss the different pictures of ways to volunteer. Allow time for the students to color all the ways they may want to volunteer and to add a picture of any additional ways to volunteer that they may consider.

You Can Be a Volunteer...
Service Learning Continues

WORK SHEET

Directions: *Review the different possibilities of ways you can volunteer. Color all of the ways you may want to be a volunteer now and when you are an adult. Add a picture of your own.*

Cancer Awareness

Library

Animal Shelter

Food Pantry

Church

Red Cross

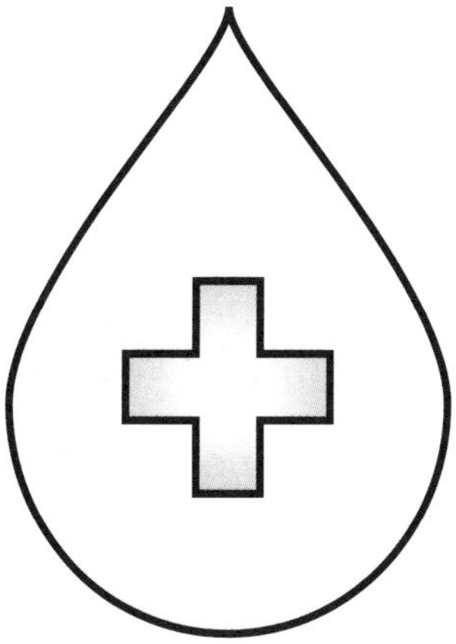

Add a picture
of your own way to volunteer and help.

Activity 82

Activity for WORLD OF WORK

Career Awareness

Making a Habit of Good Habits

Overview: This activity emphasizes the importance of establishing good habits for success now and in future careers.

Materials

✓ Copy of *Making a Habit of Good Habits* worksheet

Procedures

1. Ask: **What is a habit?** (Habit can be defined as an automatic behavior pattern that is developed through frequent repetition. Expand a discussion by asking what is meant by "automatic" and "developed through frequent repetition".)

2. Ask: **What are some examples of good habits needed for job success?** (Include examples such as being punctual, being prepared, being respectful, being focused, etc.)

3. Share the following thought questions and discuss what habit would be important:

   ✯ **Imagine a construction worker showing up for work with no tools. What would happen? What good habit does he/she need?** (Be prepared)

   ✯ **Imagine a firefighter moving slowly when heading to a fire. What would happen? What good habit does he/she need?** (Be efficient)

   ✯ **Imagine a pilot showing up for a flight an hour after the scheduled take off time. What would happen? What good habit does he/she need?** (Be punctual – on time)

   ✯ **Imagine a traffic cop daydreaming when at a busy intersection directing traffic. What would happen? What good habit does he/she need?** (Be focused)

   ✯ **Imagine a lawyer being rude in the courtroom to the Judge. What would happen? What good habit does he/she need? (**Be respectful or Be self-disciplined)

4. Have the class or group brainstorm together other good habits. Write these on the board or newsprint. (Examples of good habits to include are: be organized, be honest, be a good listener, be compassionate, be self-disciplined, etc.) Either as a group or in pairs assign a good habit to create a what would happen question that would negatively effect the person's career. Give the beginning sentence of:

   Imagine a ______________________________. What would happen? __________.

5. Come to the conclusion that good habits are important to job success. Refer back to the definition that habits are formed through frequent repetition – behaviors that are repeated. Ask how we can form good habits now that will help us in our future job. Distribute the *Making a Habit of Good Habits* worksheet for students to complete. Review the directions and complete a few examples together.

Making a Habit of Good Habits

WORK SHEET

Directions: *For the following good habits, write about how you can practice that good habit now so that it becomes a part of you.*

1. **I can develop the good habit of being ORGANIZED by**

____

2. **I can develop the good habit of being PREPARED by** ___________________________

____

3. **I can have the good habit of being PUNCTUAL by**

____

4. **I can develop the good habit of being FOCUSED by** ______________________________

____

5. **I can develop the good habit of being RESPECTFUL by**

____

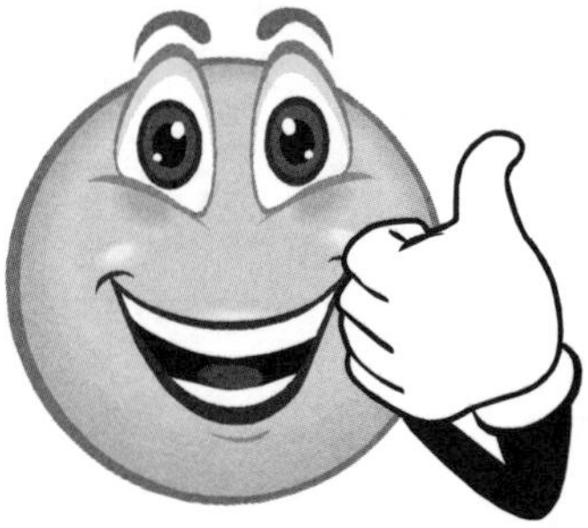

6. **I can develop the good habit of being HONEST by**

____

Add an additional good habit that would be important to develop:

7. **I can develop the good habit of being** ____________________________

by ____

GOOD HABITS ARE IMPORTANT NOW AND IN OUR FUTURE.

Activity 83

Activity for WORLD OF WORK

Career Awareness

Character Counts in Careers

Overview: This activity focuses on the importance of good character traits for success now and in future careers.

Materials

- ✓ Dice
- ✓ *Character Counts in Careers* game board - enlarged

Procedures

1. Enlarge the *Character Counts in Careers* game board and display. Discuss the character words, what they are and of how character traits are important for success now and in our future career.

2. Allow students to take turns rolling the dice. Correlate the roll of the dice with the character word on the game board. Ask the student to share what the character word means and then name a career and tell why the character trait would be important to be successful at the job.

3. Then ask students to share what future career they may be interested in and share what character traits would be especially important for success in that career.

Character Counts in Careers

WORK SHEET

Directions: *Roll the dice and tell the meaning of the character word. Then name a career that the character trait would be important to be successful at the job and explain why.*

CHARACTER COUNTS	
 Responsible	 Respectful
 Caring	 Cooperative
 Honest	 Self-Disciplined

What future career are you interested in?

____

What character traits would be especially important for success in this career?

____

____

CAREER VILLAGE

The **Career Village Section** provides a visual of the possibilities of career opportunities. The U.S. Department of Education defines sixteen career clusters and then continues the discussion with career pathways within each cluster. Our Career Village has at least one occupation represented from each of the sixteen career clusters. The Career Village Activities provide information and opportunities to discuss a wide variety of jobs within that career cluster. The purpose of the Career Village is to broaden the child's understanding of job opportunities beyond what they see their parents doing for a living or what they are exposed to in their daily interactions but provides a greater understanding of the wide variety of jobs that are out there and are necessary to 'make the world work'. If we can help our children learn about the broad range of careers, they will have more information when it comes time to choose their career.

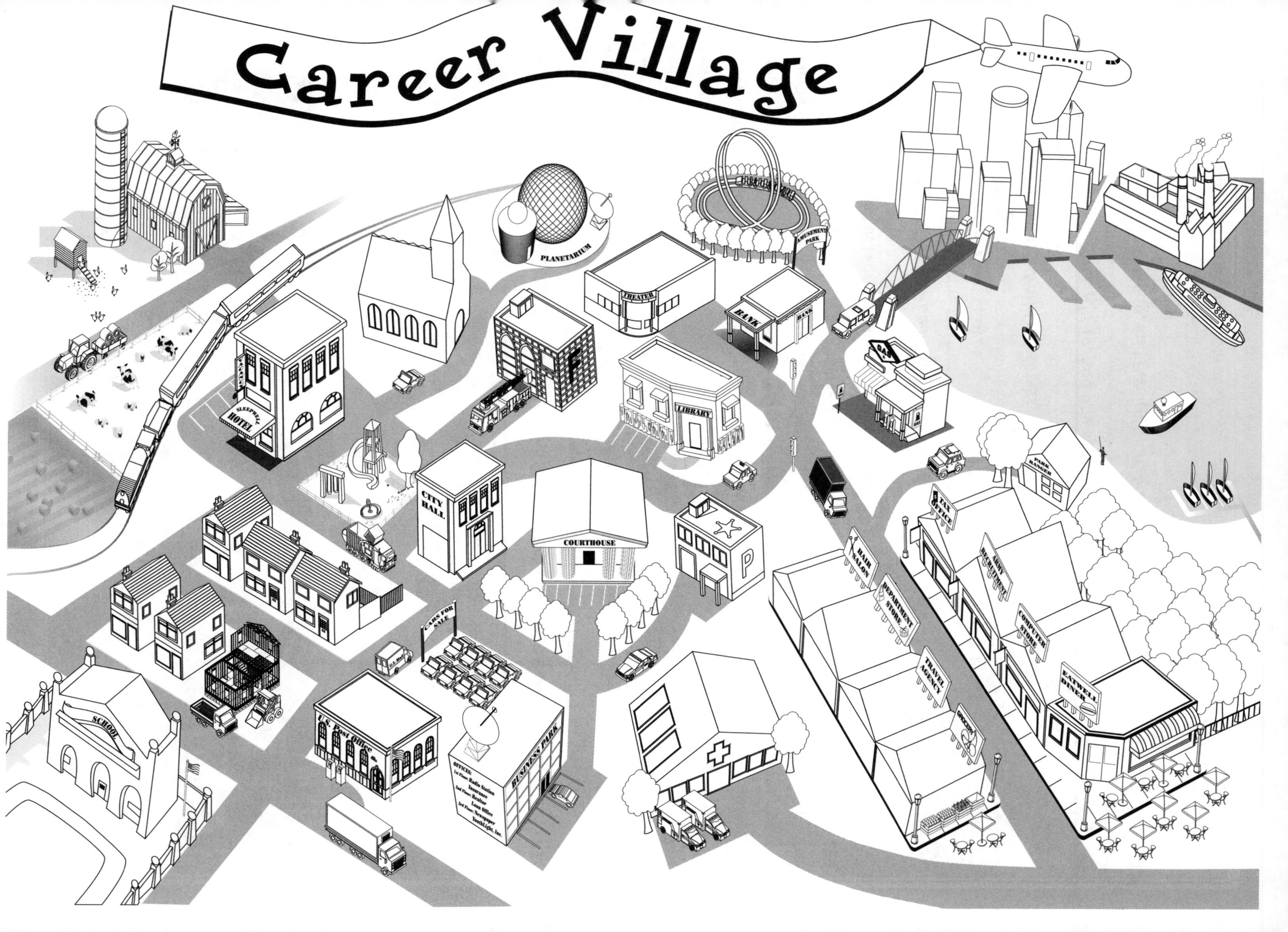
Career Village
PLANETARIUM
AMUSEMENT PARK
THEATER
BANK
BANK
GAS
SLEEPWELL HOTEL
LIBRARY
CITY HALL
COURTHOUSE
P
PARK RANGER
TAX OFFICE
ARMY RECRUITMENT
HAIR SALON
DEPARTMENT STORE
COMPUTER STORE
TRAVEL AGENCY
EATWELL DINER
GROCERY
SCHOOL
CARS FOR SALE
U.S. Post Office
BUSINESS PARK
OFFICES:
1st Floor: Radio Station
Insurance
2nd Floor: Realtor
Loan Office
3rd Floor: Newspaper
TeenRight, Inc.

Activity 84

Activity for WORLD OF WORK

Career Village

Career Village

Poster and Overview

Overview: The purpose of the Career Village is to provide a visual of job possibilities. At least one job is represented in the village from each of the sixteen career clusters defined by the U.S. Department of Education.

Materials

- ✓ Career Village poster from the book can be copied as is or enlarged and/or color added and displayed for discussion. OR 17"x11" full color laminated posters can be purchased through Youthlight (1-800-209-9774) to display in each class.
- ✓ Student activity and worksheet pages for each career cluster as well as the Career Village can be copied for each students' use and reference in career cluster discussions.

Career Village Explanation

The **Career Village Section** promotes career awareness and exploration by providing a visual of the possibilities of career opportunities as well as discussion questions, activities, and worksheet pages. The U.S. Department of Education defines sixteen career clusters and then continues the discussion with career pathways within each cluster. The Career Village has at least one occupation represented from each of the sixteen career clusters and provides a varied geographical area of community, rural, and metropolitan to enhance discussions. This section provides information, discussions, activities, and worksheets to promote an understanding of the various jobs available and the jobs needed to "make the world work."

Recommended Use of the Career Village and Activities

Each career cluster in this section has four pages related to that career cluster. As you present your lesson, you may choose one of these options:

- ✯ You can copy the four pages for each of the clusters and the Career Village poster to create a student booklet in order to provide a reinforcement, summary, and visual for the students to use and take with them.
- ✯ Or you can choose specific pages to copy and use with the students.
- ✯ Or you can transmit the career activity and worksheet pages electronically for a class to discuss and complete together.

The following gives a brief explanation of the four pages for each career cluster:

Page 1: The title page lists the career cluster and provides a graphic. Use as a coloring sheet and/or introduction page for the career cluster in the student booklet.

Page 2: The lesson activity is formatted as a series of questions (printed in bold type) for discussion. Present the questions as a career detective who is asking questions and getting the facts about the different jobs in the Career Village. You may choose to reference the detective or you may choose to dress up with a detective coat, hat, and magnifying glass to explore the jobs. Consider using a magnifying glass or one of the images below on the poster over the job(s) you are focusing on for the lesson.

Directions: Copy the small magnifying glass to use with the coloring page (pg. 232) or the large one to use with the Career Village poster (sold separately). Cut out the center of the magnifying glass. Place the magnifying glass over an image on your Career Village that you are discussing.

Page 3: Copy the student activity page for each student to complete or scan electronically to display for the class to complete together.

Page 4: Copy the student worksheet for each student to complete. Each worksheet uses the following format:

- ✯ Listing examples of jobs in the career cluster
- ✯ Answering questions about a selected job from that cluster to gain a better understanding
- ✯ Circling important character traits related to the selected job. A prior discussion of character traits, their meaning, and how character is important to job success would be important. Use the following definitions to help understand the character traits:

- RESPONSIBLE – being dependable, reliable, trustworthy
- RESPECTFUL – having high regard for, looking up to, following the rules
- HONEST – truthful, trustworthy, upright
- CARING – kind, thoughtful, compassionate, considerate
- COOPERATIVE – teamwork, helpful, supportive, positive attitude
- GOOD CITIZEN – community oriented, helping others
- SELF-DISICPLINED – self-controlled, disciplined, self-motivated
- COURAGEOUS – brave, overcoming obstacles

✭ Circling subjects in school today that can help with future career success. Include in the discussion how what students are learning now lays the foundation for what they will need in their future.

Additional Recommendations for Use of the Career Village and Activities

✭ Career Village posters can be displayed for individuals, groups, or a class as a **reference and visual reminder** in exploring future career opportunities. You may choose to copy/enlarge/color, create as overhead, or scan to display with LCD projector, promethean, smart board, etc. OR a 17"x11" full color laminated Problem Solving Pond posters can be purchased through YouthLight (1-800-209-9774).

✭ Turn the poster into a painted **WALL MURAL** in a hallway or other targeted area that students have access – provides a great visual and reinforcement of career opportunities.

✭ As you discuss each career cluster, locate a job from that career cluster represented in the Career Village. Discuss **additional jobs that could be added to the Career Village** and draw them in the picture or create a new Career Village of your own.

✭ Use the 16 career cluster activities throughout the year as part of a **Career emphasis with a different career cluster focused on** each day, or each week, or each month, etc.

✭ Create a **student booklet** for each student of the 16 career clusters. Include the poster and then for each career cluster include the title page, activity sheet, and worksheet. As the career clusters are discussed, students can complete and add information in their booklet and use as a reference in the future.

✭ Discuss a career cluster school-wide during morning announcements, TV broadcast, or assembly programs and follow-up with discussions and completing activity and worksheets in the classroom.

✭ In addition to the activities given in this section, **create career questions/activities of your own** that reference the Career Village, for example:

- Choose an everyday item such as a carton of milk or tennis shoes and trace back the item through the Career Village listing all of the jobs that are connected to the item.
- Choose a building in the Career Village and list all of the jobs that are in that building as well as the jobs that may come in contact with the jobs in the building. Choose a building such as the school, hospital, county court house…

I'm Running for President!

COLORING SHEET

Activity 85

Activity for WORLD OF WORK

Career Village

I'm Running for President!

Government and Public Administration

Overview of the Cluster: This activity focuses on the career cluster of Government and Public Administration which helps shape and protect the future of our cities, states, and country. Jobs in this cluster include areas of governance; national security; foreign service; revenue and taxation; government regulation; and public management and administration.

Materials

- ✓ Copy of the Career Village poster
- ✓ Copy of the *I'm Running for President!* Activity and Worksheet

Procedures

1. Ask: **What is a detective? How do detectives go about doing their job?** Include that detectives gather information and get the facts by asking questions, listening, observing, and investigating.
2. Invite the students to be a detective and to investigate the career cluster of Government and Public Administration. (For added effect you may use different props of a detective such as a hat, coat, and magnifying glass). Ask the following questions:
   - ✯ **What are some jobs in the career cluster of Government and Public Administration?** Sample jobs in this cluster include president, mayor, governor, congressional aide, house representative, senator, secretary of state, lt. governor, diplomat, lobbyist, legislative assistant, election supervisor, ambassador, census clerk, chief of vital statistics, child support officer, border inspector, Internal Revenue Service investigator, postal worker, city manager and members of the military such as Army, Navy, Marine Corps, Air Force, or Coast Guard.
   - ✯ **Where would you find a job from this career cluster in our CAREER VILLAGE?** In our Career Village, jobs from this career cluster may be found at CITY HALL (ex. mayor, city manager, office personnel for planning and development…), the POST OFFICE, and the ARMY RECRUITEMENT OFFICE. Expand your discussion to other possibilities.
   - ✯ **Choose a job in the CAREER VILLAGE from this career cluster and answer the following:**
     - **What would be the job responsibilities?**
     - **What skills would you need to do the job?**
     - **What academic subjects would help you prepare for this type of job?**
     - **What other jobs in the community would this person be working with?**
     - **How many people would have this type of job in a community – one, a few, many?**
     - **What jobs from this career cluster, not shown in our Career Village, could be found in a community? You may choose to add it to your career village.**

I'm Running for President!
Government and Public Administration

ACTIVITY SHEET

Directions: *Fill in the blank with the correct job. Choose from the following: child support officer, mayor, Internal Revenue Service investigators, chief of vital statistics, Census clerks, diplomat, President*

1. The ____________________ of the United States is the head of state and government and is the highest political official in the United States.

2. An elected person who is in charge of a city, village, or town is the ________________________.

3. A ________________ is a person who represents a government in talking with other countries and governments. It is important for this person to be polite and to handle conflicts or problems well.

4. ______________________ help count and gather information about the population every 10 years for the purpose of economic planning.

5. If you needed to get a copy of your birth certificate you would need to talk to the ____.

6. A ____________________reviews, investigates cases, and upholds the child support laws.

7. ____ check on people and situations who break the law in paying government taxes.

Directions: *Below the correct uniform, write the government job that serves and protects our country. Choose from the Army, Navy, Marine Corps, Air Force, Coast Guard.*

______________ ______________ ______________ ______________ ______________

I'm Running for President!
Government and Public Administration

WORK SHEET

List examples of jobs in the area of Government and Public Administration

Circle one job above and answer the following about that job

	YES	NO
1. Work alone?		
2. Work with people?		
3. Work inside?		
4. Work outside?		
5. Work during the day?		
6. Work during the night?		
7. Work on week days (Monday-Friday)?		
8. Work on weekends (Friday, Saturday, Sunday)?		
9. Does this job require a uniform?		
10. Does this job involve traveling?		
11. Do you need education or training beyond high school?		
If "yes," what:		
12. Will this job be needed in the future?		
13. What is the salary range for this job? Low, average, high?		

Circle the character traits that are especially important with this job

RESPONSIBLE	*RESPECTFUL*	*HONEST*	*SELF-DISCIPLINED*
COOPERATIVE	*GOOD CITIZEN*	*CARING*	*COURAGEOUS*

Circle the subjects in school that would help you with this job

READING	*MATH*	*SOCIAL STUDIES*	*ART*	*HEALTH*
SCIENCE	*MUSIC*	*COMPUTER*	*PHYSICAL EDUCATION*	

OTHER: ______________________________

Money, Money, Money

COLORING SHEET

Activity 86

Activity for WORLD OF WORK

Career Village

Money, Money, Money

Finance

Overview of the Cluster: This activity focuses on the career cluster of Finance which deals with money and helps plan, manage, and invest money. Jobs in this cluster include areas of banking; business financial management; financial and investment planning; and insurance services.

Materials

- ✓ Copy of the Career Village poster
- ✓ Copy of the *Money, Money, Money* Activity and Worksheet

Procedures

1. Ask: **What is a detective? How do detectives go about doing their job?** Include that detectives gather information and get the facts by asking questions, listening, observing, and investigating.
2. Invite the students to be a detective and to investigate the career cluster of Finance. (For added effect you may use different props of a detective such as a hat, coat, and magnifying glass). Ask the following questions:
   - ✯ **What are some jobs in the career cluster of Finance?** Sample jobs in this Cluster include bank teller, accountant, auditor, cashier, economist, personal financial advisor, financial manager, tax preparer, investment advisor, loan officer, debt counselor, and insurance appraiser.
   - ✯ **Where would you find a job from this career cluster in our CAREER VILLAGE?** In our Career Village, jobs from this cluster may be found at the BANK, BUSINESS PARK (Insurance office, Loan office), TAX PREPARER, CITY HALL and the COUNTY COURTHOUSE (billing and collecting city and county taxes). Other finance jobs may be found throughout the community such as the bookkeeper at the SCHOOL or district office, at businesses such as the HOTEL, THEATER, AMUSEMENT PARK, and RETAIL STORES, as well as managing the money on the FARM. Don't forget to include finance jobs that may be found in the METROPOLITAN AREA, the FACTORY, and on a CRUISE SHIP.
   - ✯ **Choose a job in the CAREER VILLAGE from this career cluster and answer the following:**
     - **What would be the job responsibilities?**
     - **What skills would you need to do the job?**
     - **What academic subjects would help you prepare for this type of job?**
     - **What other jobs in the community would this person be working with?**
     - **How many people would have this type of job in a community – one, a few, many?**
     - **What jobs from this career cluster, not shown in our Career Village, could be found in a community? You may choose to add it to your career village.**

Money, Money, Money
Finance

ACTIVITY SHEET

Directions: *Find the hidden picture by coloring the spaces green for the jobs from the Finance Career Cluster whose main job deals with money.*

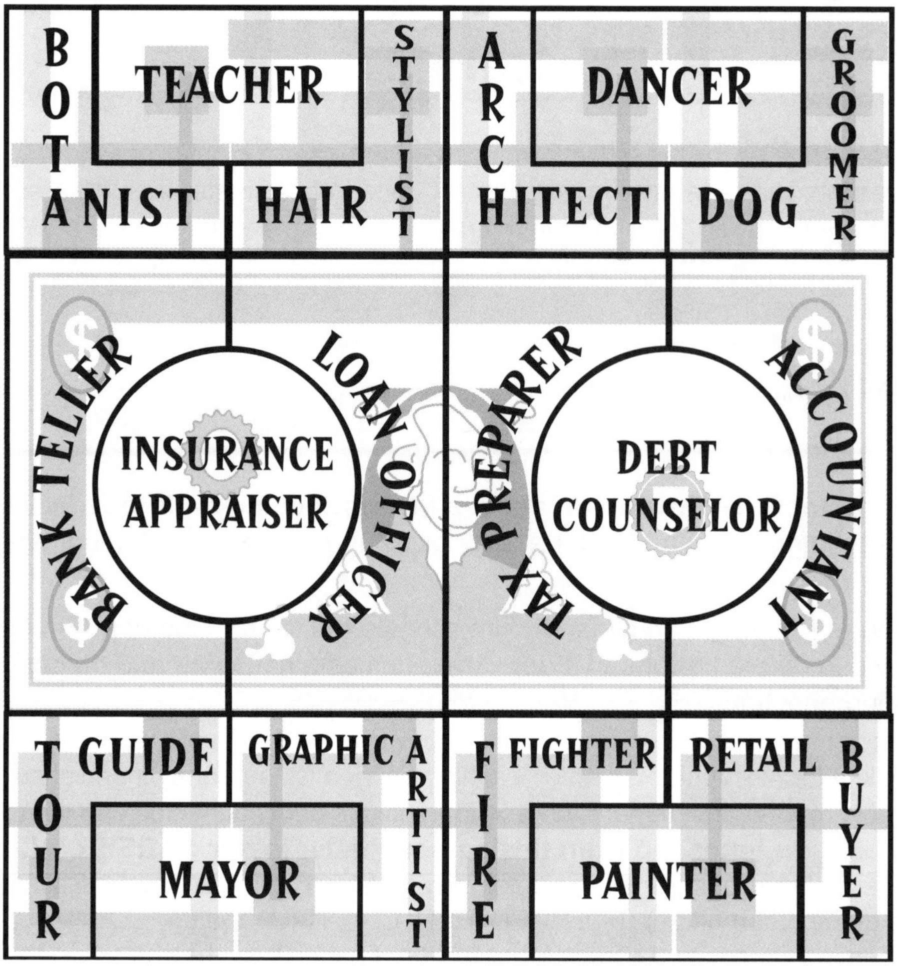

Directions: *Circle the correct answer,* ***TRUE*** *or* ***FALSE****, beside each statement describing the job.*

TRUE	FALSE	1. A cashier needs to know how to give correct change.
TRUE	FALSE	2. A bank teller tells people how to do their jobs.
TRUE	FALSE	3. An insurance appraiser works to know the value of property and helps to settle insurance claims.
TRUE	FALSE	4. A loan officer decides who can borrow money from a bank.
TRUE	FALSE	5. An investment advisor tells you how to best use your time.

Money, Money, Money
Finance

WORK SHEET

List examples of jobs in the area of Finance

Circle one job above and answer the following about that job

	YES	NO
1. Work alone?		
2. Work with people?		
3. Work inside?		
4. Work outside?		
5. Work during the day?		
6. Work during the night?		
7. Work on week days (Monday-Friday)?		
8. Work on weekends (Friday, Saturday, Sunday)?		
9. Does this job require a uniform?		
10. Does this job involve traveling?		
11. Do you need education or training beyond high school?		
If "yes," what:		
12. Will this job be needed in the future?		
13. What is the salary range for this job? Low, average, high?		

Circle the character traits that are especially important with this job

RESPONSIBLE	*RESPECTFUL*	*HONEST*	*SELF-DISCIPLINED*
COOPERATIVE	*GOOD CITIZEN*	*CARING*	*COURAGEOUS*

Circle the subjects in school that would help you with this job

READING	*MATH*	*SOCIAL STUDIES*	*ART*	*HEALTH*
SCIENCE	*MUSIC*	*COMPUTER*	*PHYSICAL EDUCATION*	

OTHER: ______________________________

What's Up Doc?

COLORING SHEET

Activity 87

Activity for WORLD OF WORK

Career Village

What's Up Doc?

Health Services

Overview of the Cluster: This activity focuses on the career cluster of Health Services which includes careers that promote health, wellness and diagnosis, and treats injuries and diseases. Jobs in this cluster include areas of diagnostic services; health information; health support services; therapeutic services; and biotechnology research and development.

Materials

- ✓ Copy of the Career Village poster
- ✓ Copy of the *What's Up Doc?* Activity and Worksheet

Procedures

1. Ask: **What is a detective? How do detectives go about doing their job?** Include that detectives gather information and get the facts by asking questions, listening, observing, and investigating.
2. Invite the students to be a detective and to investigate the career cluster of Health Services. (For added effect you may use different props of a detective such as a hat, coat, and magnifying glass). Ask the following questions:
   - ✯ **What are some jobs in the career cluster of Health Services?** Sample jobs in this cluster include doctor, nurse, dentist, pharmacist, paramedic, medical assistant, veterinarian, physical therapist, athletic trainer, radiologist, audiologist, EEG technologist, medical lab technician, hospital manager, chiropractor, respiratory therapist, pathologist, and microbiologist.
   - ✯ **Where would you find a job from this career cluster in our CAREER VILLAGE?** In our Career Village, jobs from this career cluster may be found at the HOSPITAL (include the paramedics in the AMBULANCE parked out front), SCHOOL (school nurse), FACTORY, a medic in the ARMY, AMUSEMENT PARK (medical staff to help with health problems or injuries), as well as medical personnel on a CRUISE SHIP. Even though the job is not shown in the picture, a veteranarian would be needed to take care of any health problems with the FARM animals.
   - ✯ **Choose a job in the CAREER VILLAGE from this career cluster and answer the following:**
     - **What would be the job responsibilities?**
     - **What skills would you need to do the job?**
     - **What academic subjects would help you prepare for this type of job?**
     - **What other jobs in the community would this person be working with?**
     - **How many people would have this type of job in a community – one, a few, many?**
     - **What jobs from this career cluster, not shown in our Career Village, could be found in a community? You may choose to add it to your career village.**

What's Up Doc?
Health Services

ACTIVITY SHEET

Directions: *Label the objects with the job most likely to use that object. Choose from the list of jobs in the Word Bank.*

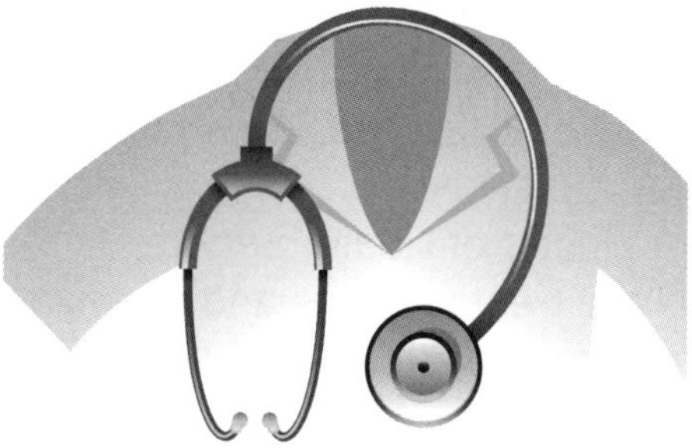

1. ____________

2. ____________

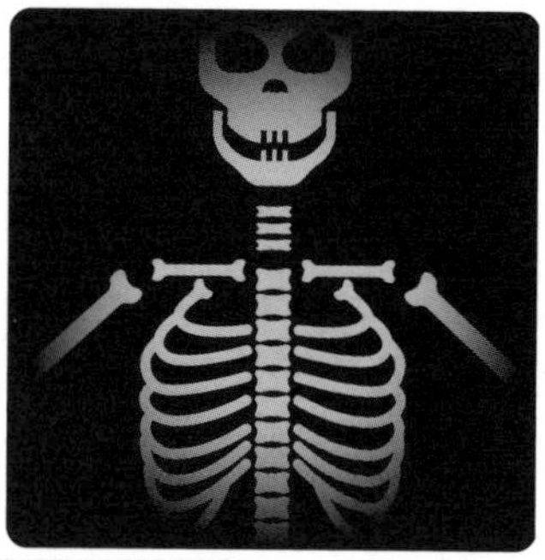

3. ____________

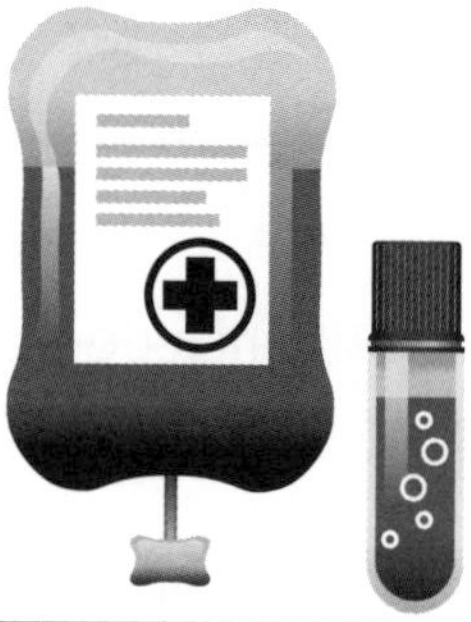

4. ____________

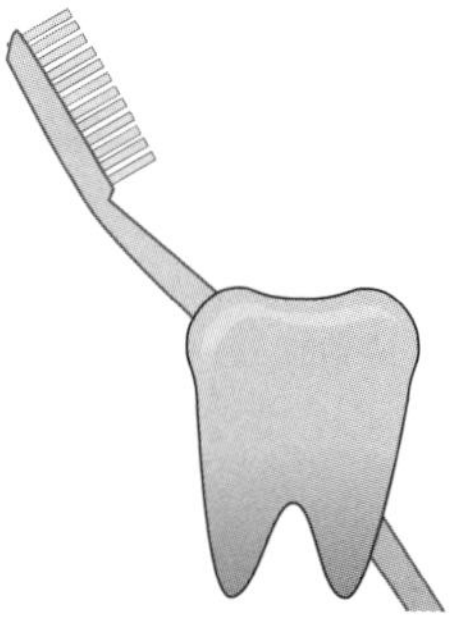

5. ____________

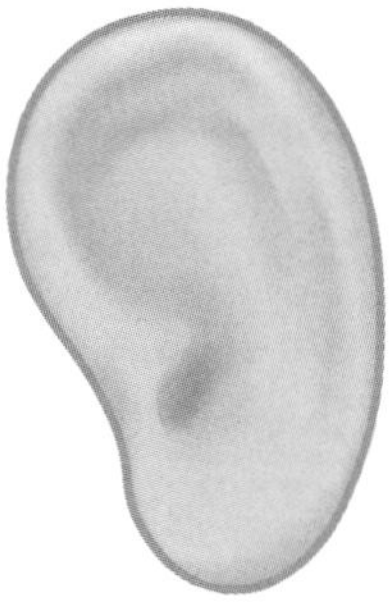

6. ____________

7. ____________

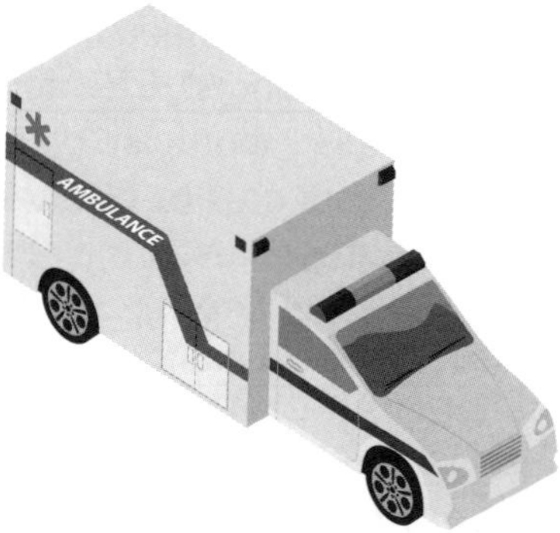

8. ____________

9. ____________

WORD BANK

Dentist	Veterinarian	Pharmacist
Respiratory Therapist	Audiologist	Doctor
Paramedic	Chiropractor	Medical Lab Technician

What's Up Doc?
Health Services

WORK SHEET

List examples of jobs in the area of Health Services

Circle one job above and answer the following about that job

	YES	NO
1. Work alone?		
2. Work with people?		
3. Work inside?		
4. Work outside?		
5. Work during the day?		
6. Work during the night?		
7. Work on week days (Monday-Friday)?		
8. Work on weekends (Friday, Saturday, Sunday)?		
9. Does this job require a uniform?		
10. Does this job involve traveling?		
11. Do you need education or training beyond high school?		
If "yes," what:		
12. Will this job be needed in the future?		
13. What is the salary range for this job? Low, average, high?		

Circle the character traits that are especially important with this job

RESPONSIBLE	*RESPECTFUL*	*HONEST*	*SELF-DISCIPLINED*
COOPERATIVE	*GOOD CITIZEN*	*CARING*	*COURAGEOUS*

Circle the subjects in school that would help you with this job

READING	*MATH*	*SOCIAL STUDIES*	*ART*	*HEALTH*
SCIENCE	*MUSIC*	*COMPUTER*	*PHYSICAL EDUCATION*	

OTHER: ______________________________

Be Our Guest...

COLORING SHEET

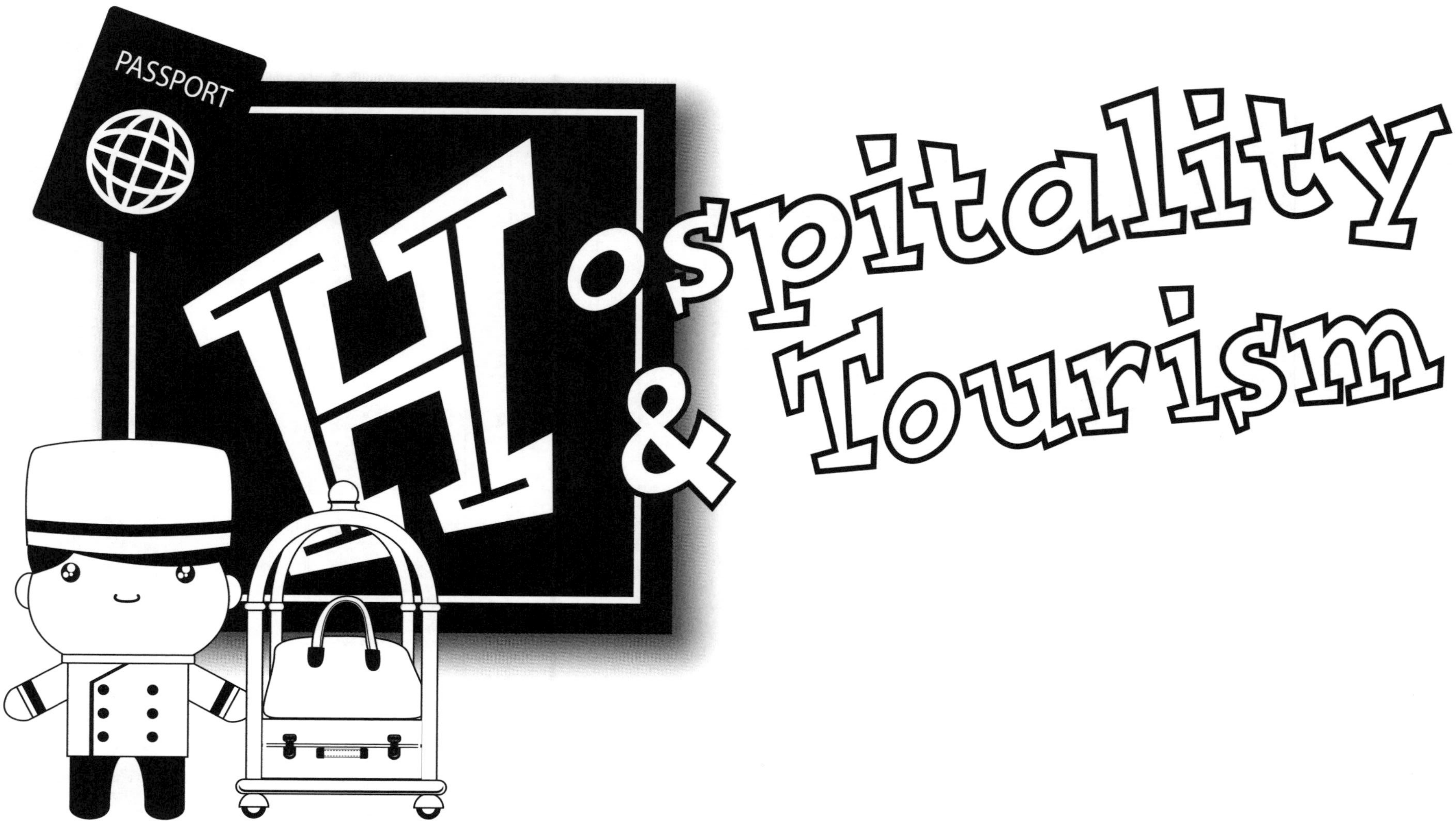

Activity 88

Activity for WORLD OF WORK

Career Village

Be Our Guest...
Hospitality and Tourism

Overview of the Cluster: This activity focuses on the career cluster of Hospitality and Tourism which provides fun and relaxing leisure activities for people. Jobs in this cluster include areas of lodging; recreation, amusements and attractions; restaurants, food and beverage services; and travel and tourism.

Materials

- ✓ Copy of the Career Village poster
- ✓ Copy of the *Be Our Guest...* Activity and Worksheet

Procedures

1. Ask: **What is a detective? How do detectives go about doing their job?** Include that detectives gather information and get the facts by asking questions, listening, observing, and investigating.
2. Invite the students to be a detective and to investigate the career cluster of Hospitality and Tourism. (For added effect you may use different props of a detective such as a hat, coat, and magnifying glass). Ask the following questions:
   - ✯ **What are some jobs in the career cluster of Hospitality and Tourism?** Sample jobs in this cluster include hotel manager/clerk, restaurant owner, waitress/waiter, chef, tour guide, travel agent, welcome center supervisor, resort activities director, cruise director, convention planner, theme park manager/operator/worker, and parks and garden director.
   - ✯ **Where would you find a job from this career cluster in our CAREER VILLAGE?** In our Career Village, jobs from this career cluster may be found at the HOTEL, EATWELL DINER, AMUSEMENT PARK, CRUISE LINE, TRAVEL AGENT, as well as the CITY PARK across from City Hall, and the BOAT MARINA. Cities may also host sports tournaments and special events that invite tourists to visit. Hospitality and Tourism jobs may also be found in the METROPOLITAN AREA (perhaps city tours, carriage rides, restaurants, hotels, etc.)
   - ✯ **Choose a job in the CAREER VILLAGE from this career cluster and answer the following:**
     - **What would be the job responsibilities?**
     - **What skills would you need to do the job?**
     - **What academic subjects would help you prepare for this type of job?**
     - **What other jobs in the community would this person be working with?**
     - **How many people would have this type of job in a community – one, a few, many?**
     - **What jobs from this career cluster, not shown in our Career Village, could be found in a community? You may choose to add it to your career village.**

Be Our Guest...
Hospitality and Tourism

ACTIVITY SHEET

Directions: *The story below includes jobs from the hospitality and tourism career cluster. Choose from the words in the word bank to complete the story.*

OUR FAMILY VACATION

Our family took a trip to Disney World in Florida over Spring Break last year. When planning for our trip, we first visited our __________ __________ in our hometown to help with the travel plans. The details for our vacation were finalized and we would leave on Monday of Spring Break. The day finally arrived. When we crossed into the state of Florida we stopped and talked to the __________ __________ __________ to learn more about what we can see and do there. They even offered us a cup of Florida orange juice to enjoy! Back in the car, we drove all day until we finally arrived where we would be staying on our vacation. We checked into the __________. My parents stopped to talk to the hotel's __________ and found good places in the area to eat. We ate dinner at a nearby restaurant. When we walked into the restaurant, the __________ seated us at a table by the window. Next our __________told us about the specials the __________ would be cooking that evening. Dinner was delicious! After dinner we went straight to bed to get a good night's rest for Disney World.

The next morning we jumped out of bed ready for the big day. We took a shuttle bus to Disney World and arrived at the gate where a __________ __________ took our tickets. Once inside, we rode rides, saw shows, visited with Mickey and Minnie Mouse, and enjoyed the food. There was so much to see, I'm glad we went back two more days to see it all. Wow! What a vacation! I'll never forget our trip to Disney World, one of the world's largest __________ __________.

Word Bank

- welcome center supervisor
- hotel
- chef
- waiter
- travel agent
- concierge
- amusement parks
- hostess
- ticket agent

Be Our Guest...
Hospitality and Tourism

WORK SHEET

List examples of jobs in the area of Hospitality and Tourism

Circle one job above and answer the following about that job

	YES	NO
1. Work alone?		
2. Work with people?		
3. Work inside?		
4. Work outside?		
5. Work during the day?		
6. Work during the night?		
7. Work on week days (Monday-Friday)?		
8. Work on weekends (Friday, Saturday, Sunday)?		
9. Does this job require a uniform?		
10. Does this job involve traveling?		
11. Do you need education or training beyond high school?		
If "yes," what:		
12. Will this job be needed in the future?		
13. What is the salary range for this job? Low, average, high?		

Circle the character traits that are especially important with this job

RESPONSIBLE *RESPECTFUL* *HONEST* *SELF-DISCIPLINED*
COOPERATIVE *GOOD CITIZEN* *CARING* *COURAGEOUS*

Circle the subjects in school that would help you with this job

READING *MATH* *SOCIAL STUDIES* *ART* *HEALTH*
SCIENCE *MUSIC* *COMPUTER* *PHYSICAL EDUCATION*
OTHER: ______________________________

Lend a Helping Hand

COLORING SHEET

Activity 89

Activity for WORLD OF WORK

Career Village

Lend a Helping Hand
Human Services

Overview of the Cluster: This activity focuses on the career cluster of Human Services which includes helping jobs that provide for families and serve human needs. Whether you want to be a social worker, a childcare provider or a hairdresser, you will be addressing human needs. Jobs in this cluster include areas of consumer services; counseling and mental health services; family and community services; and personal care services.

Materials

- ✓ Copy of the Career Village poster
- ✓ Copy of the *Lend a Helping Hand* Activity and Worksheet

Procedures

1. Ask: **What is a detective? How do detectives go about doing their job?** Include that detectives gather information and get the facts by asking questions, listening, observing, and investigating.
2. Invite the students to be a detective and to investigate the career cluster of Human Services. (For added effect you may use different props of a detective such as a hat, coat, and magnifying glass). Ask the following questions:
   - ✯ **What are some jobs in the career cluster of Human Services?** Sample jobs in this cluster include day care provider, nanny, mental health counselor, parent educator, social worker, clergy, personal or home care aide, janitor, recreation worker, athletic programmer or center director, parks and recreation director, tourism director, cosmetologist, hairstylist, florist, housekeeper, and librarian.
   - ✯ **Where would you find a job from this career cluster in our CAREER VILLAGE?** In our Career Village, jobs from this career cluster may be found at the CHURCH, LIBRARY, HAIR SALON, and the human service job of garbage collection represented by the GARBAGE TRUCK. Discuss Human Service jobs you may also find in the METROPOLITAN AREA.
   - ✯ **Choose a job in the CAREER VILLAGE from this career cluster and answer the following:**
     - **What would be the job responsibilities?**
     - **What skills would you need to do the job?**
     - **What academic subjects would help you prepare for this type of job?**
     - **What other jobs in the community would this person be working with?**
     - **How many people would have this type of job in a community – one, a few, many?**
     - **What jobs from this career cluster, not shown in our Career Village, could be found in a community? You may choose to add it to your career village.**

Lend a Helping Hand
Human Services

ACTIVITY SHEET

Directions: *Each job lists three objects. Put a line through the 1 object that does NOT belong with that job.*

HAIRSTYLIST
USES...

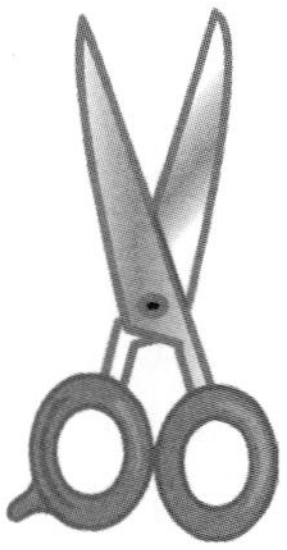
Scissors

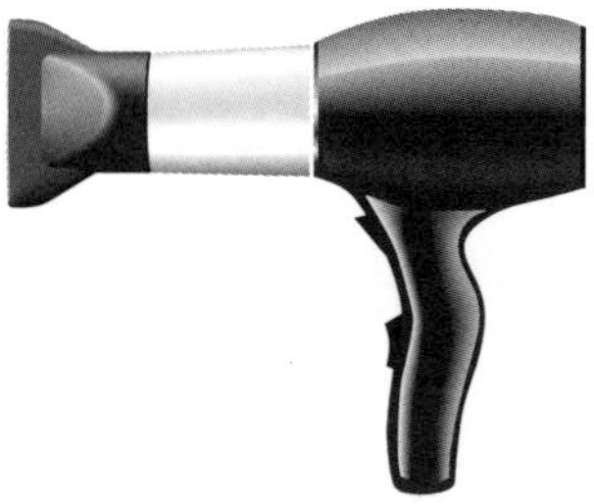
Hair Dryer

Hammer

FLORIST
USES...

Wire Cutters

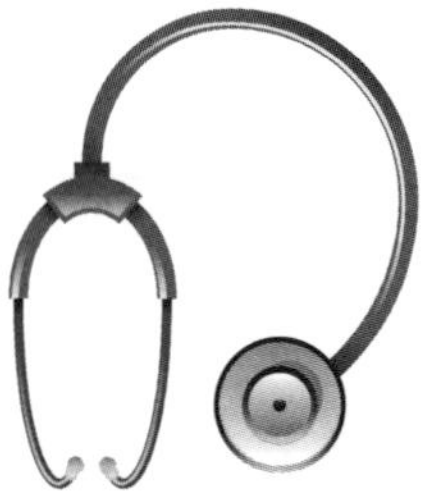
Stethoscope

Vase

HOUSEKEEPER
USES...

Tape Measure

Mop

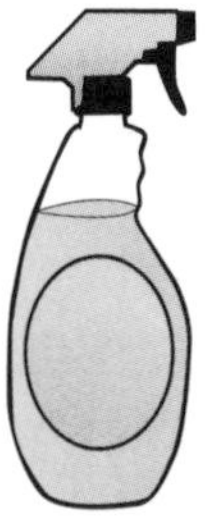
Window Cleaner

LIBRARIAN
USES...

Book

Tractor

Computer

RECREATION CENTER DIRECTOR
USES...

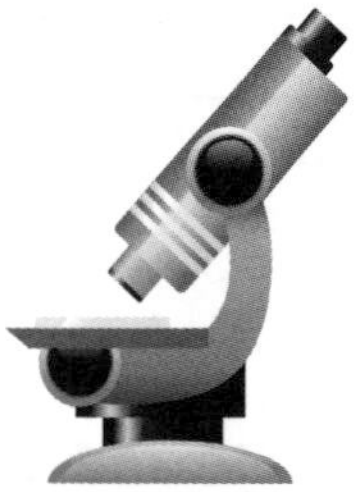
Microscope

Football

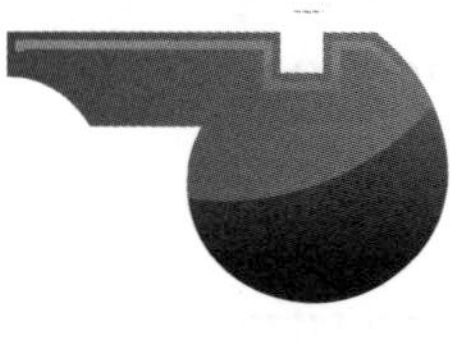
Whistle

Lend a Helping Hand

Human Services

WORK SHEET

List examples of jobs in the area of Human Services

Circle one job above and answer the following about that job

	YES	NO
1. Work alone?		
2. Work with people?		
3. Work inside?		
4. Work outside?		
5. Work during the day?		
6. Work during the night?		
7. Work on week days (Monday-Friday)?		
8. Work on weekends (Friday, Saturday, Sunday)?		
9. Does this job require a uniform?		
10. Does this job involve traveling?		
11. Do you need education or training beyond high school?		
If "yes," what:		
12. Will this job be needed in the future?		
13. What is the salary range for this job? Low, average, high?		

Circle the character traits that are especially important with this job

RESPONSIBLE *RESPECTFUL* *HONEST* *SELF-DISCIPLINED*

COOPERATIVE *GOOD CITIZEN* *CARING* *COURAGEOUS*

Circle the subjects in school that would help you with this job

READING *MATH* *SOCIAL STUDIES* *ART* *HEALTH*

SCIENCE *MUSIC* *COMPUTER* *PHYSICAL EDUCATION*

OTHER: ______________________________

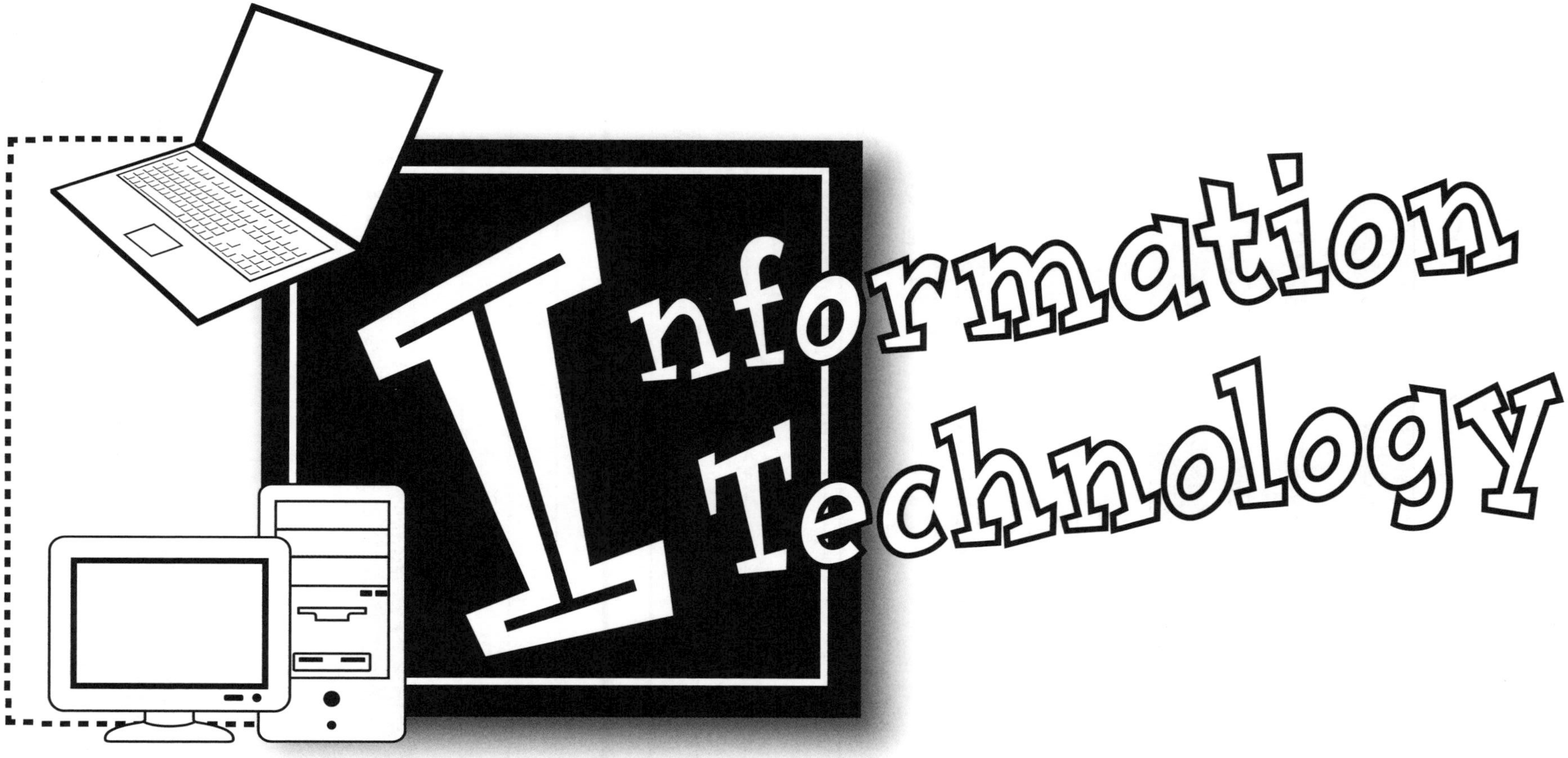
Information
Technology

Activity 90

Activity for WORLD OF WORK

Career Village

Get Connected with the Tech Squad
Information Technology

Overview of the Cluster: This activity focuses on the career cluster of Information Technology which involves careers in design, development, support and management of hardware, software, multimedia, and computer systems and is an ever-changing industry that reaches all areas in our world. Jobs in this cluster include areas of information support and services; interactive media; network systems; and programming and software development.

Materials

✓ Copy of the Career Village poster

✓ Copy of the *Get Connected with the Tech Squad* Activity and Worksheet

Procedures

1. Ask: **What is a detective? How do detectives go about doing their job?** Include that detectives gather information and get the facts by asking questions, listening, observing, and investigating.
2. Invite the students to be a detective and to investigate the career cluster of Information Technology. (For added effect you may use different props of a detective such as a hat, coat, and magnifying glass). Ask the following questions:
   - **What are some jobs in the career cluster of Information Technology?** Sample jobs in this cluster include web designer, computer programmer, game designer/programmer, 3D animator, virtual reality specialist, graphic artist, PC support specialist, broadcast technician, network administrator, telecommunications technician, security or database administrator.
   - **Where would you find a job from this career cluster in our CAREER VILLAGE?** In our Career Village, jobs from this career cluster may be found at the BUSINESS PARK (radio station, newspaper office, YouthLight – graphic artist), the COMPUTER STORE, and perhaps at the AMUSEMENT PARK (3-D animation at a show). Many businesses throughout the Career Village are connected to the Information Technology Career Cluster. Discuss how a web designer or computer/network support specialist may be needed for the business.
   - **Choose a job in the CAREER VILLAGE from this career cluster and answer the following:**
     - **What would be the job responsibilities?**
     - **What skills would you need to do the job?**
     - **What academic subjects would help you prepare for this type of job?**
     - **What other jobs in the community would this person be working with?**
     - **How many people would have this type of job in a community – one, a few, many?**
     - **What jobs from this career cluster, not shown in our Career Village, could be found in a community? You may choose to add it to your career village.**

Get Connected with the Tech Squad
Information Technology

ACTIVITY SHEET

Directions: *Answer the following.*

WHAT IS YOUR FAVORITE THING TO DO ON THE COMPUTER?

____

LIST THE INFORMATION TECHNOLOGY JOBS THAT RELATE TO A COMPUTER:

____

____

____

WHAT IS YOUR FAVORITE VIDEO GAME?

____

LIST THE INFORMATION TECHNOLOGY JOBS THAT RELATE TO A VIDEO GAME:

____

____

____

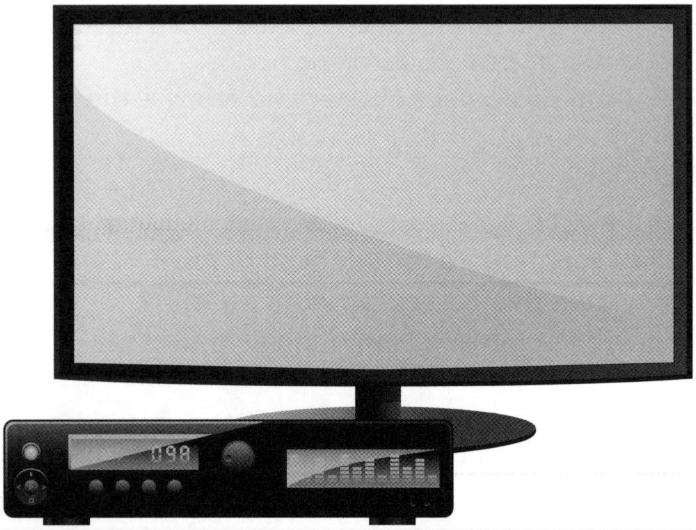

LIST THE INFORMATION TECHNOLOGY JOBS RELATED TO RADIO OR TELEVISION:

____

____

____

____

Get Connected with the Tech Squad
Information Technology

WORK SHEET

List examples of jobs in the area of Information Technology

Circle one job above and answer the following about that job

	YES	NO
1. Work alone?		
2. Work with people?		
3. Work inside?		
4. Work outside?		
5. Work during the day?		
6. Work during the night?		
7. Work on week days (Monday-Friday)?		
8. Work on weekends (Friday, Saturday, Sunday)?		
9. Does this job require a uniform?		
10. Does this job involve traveling?		
11. Do you need education or training beyond high school?		
If "yes," what:		
12. Will this job be needed in the future?		
13. What is the salary range for this job? Low, average, high?		

Circle the character traits that are especially important with this job

RESPONSIBLE	*RESPECTFUL*	*HONEST*	*SELF-DISCIPLINED*
COOPERATIVE	*GOOD CITIZEN*	*CARING*	*COURAGEOUS*

Circle the subjects in school that would help you with this job

READING	*MATH*	*SOCIAL STUDIES*	*ART*	*HEALTH*
SCIENCE	*MUSIC*	*COMPUTER*	*PHYSICAL EDUCATION*	

OTHER: ______________________________

It's the Law

COLORING SHEET

Activity 91

Activity for WORLD OF WORK

Career Village

It's the Law

Law, Public Safety, and Security

Overview of the Cluster: This activity focuses on the career cluster of Law, Public Safety, and Security which focuses on the legal system, public safety, and security. Jobs in this cluster include areas of emergency and fire management; security and protective services; law enforcement; legal services; and correction services.

Materials

- ✓ Copy of the Career Village poster
- ✓ Copy of the *It's the Law* Activity and Worksheet

Procedures

1. Ask: **What is a detective? How do detectives go about doing their job?** Include that detectives gather information and get the facts by asking questions, listening, observing, and investigating.
2. Invite the students to be a detective and to investigate the career cluster of Law, Public Safety, and Security. (For added effect you may use different props of a detective such as a hat, coat, and magnifying glass). Ask the following questions:
   - ✯ **What are some jobs in the career cluster of Law, Public Safety, and Security?** Sample jobs in this cluster include judge, lawyer, bailiff, paralegal, court reporter, police officer, correctional officer, parole officer, customs inspector, emergency dispatcher/911 operator, security guard, armored car guard, private investigator, and firefighter.
   - ✯ **Where would you find a job from this career cluster in our CAREER VILLAGE?** In our Career Village, jobs from this career cluster may be found at the POLICE STATION, FIRE STATION, COUNTY COURTHOUSE, as well as in our METROPOLITAN AREA. Point out that many other areas of the Career Village may also have jobs from this cluster such as a security guard at the BANK and at other places of business.
   - ✯ **Choose a job in the CAREER VILLAGE from this career cluster and answer the following:**
     - **What would be the job responsibilities?**
     - **What skills would you need to do the job?**
     - **What academic subjects would help you prepare for this type of job?**
     - **What other jobs in the community would this person be working with?**
     - **How many people would have this type of job in a community – one, a few, many?**
     - **What jobs from this career cluster, not shown in our Career Village, could be found in a community? You may choose to add it to your career village.**

It's the Law

Law, Public Safety, and Security

ACTIVITY SHEET

Directions: *Where would you find the following people at work? Using the Job Bank, write the name of the job on the line in the correct building/vehicle where they would work.*

JOB BANK	court reporter	parole officer	police officer	firefighter	customs inspector	
	correctional officer	security guard	armored car guard	bailiff	lawyer	judge

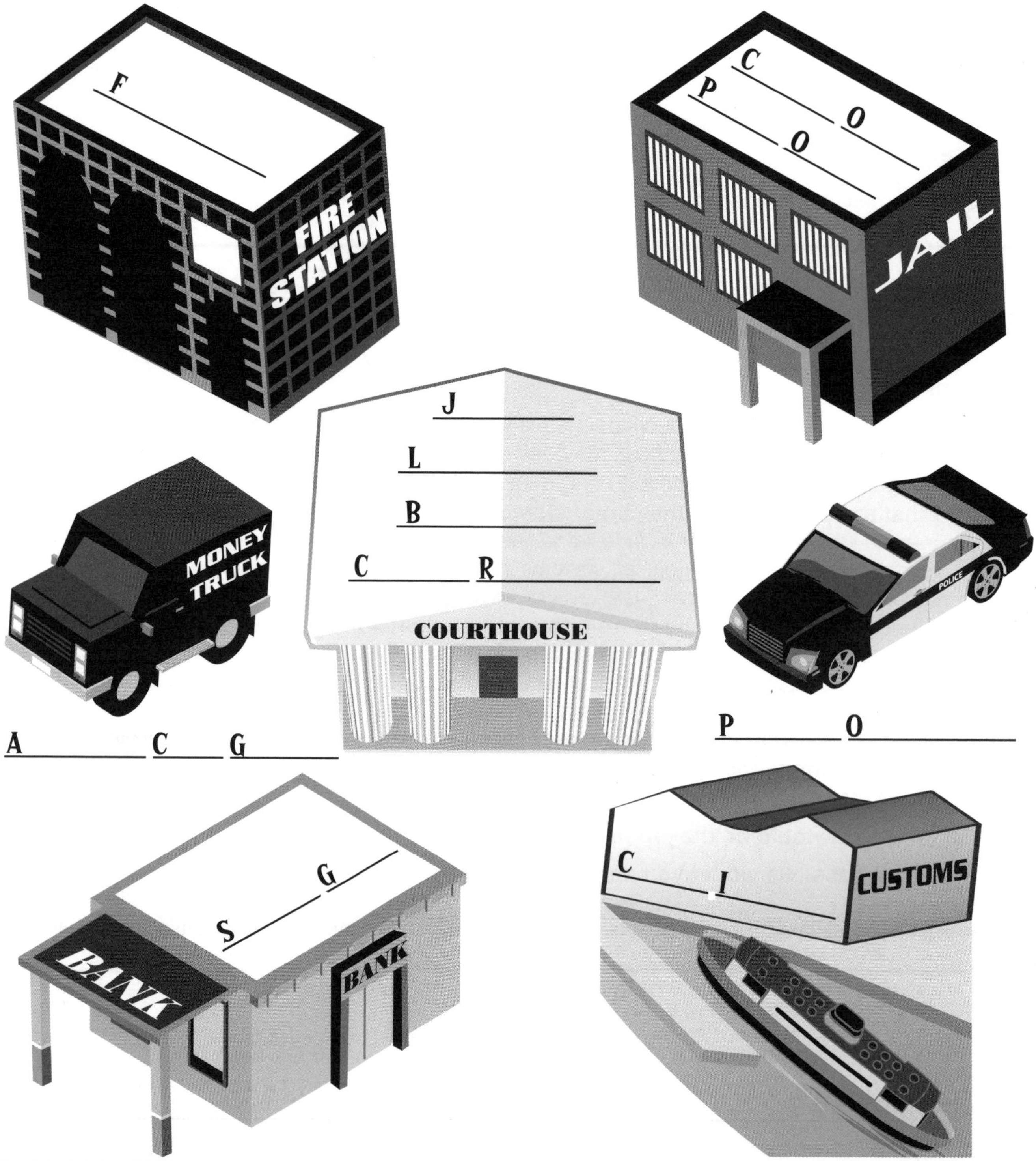

It's the Law

Law, Public Safety, and Security

WORK SHEET

List examples of jobs in the area of Law, Public Safety, and Security

Circle one job above and answer the following about that job

	YES	NO
1. Work alone?		
2. Work with people?		
3. Work inside?		
4. Work outside?		
5. Work during the day?		
6. Work during the night?		
7. Work on week days (Monday-Friday)?		
8. Work on weekends (Friday, Saturday, Sunday)?		
9. Does this job require a uniform?		
10. Does this job involve traveling?		
11. Do you need education or training beyond high school?		
If "yes," what:		
12. Will this job be needed in the future?		
13. What is the salary range for this job? Low, average, high?		

Circle the character traits that are especially important with this job

RESPONSIBLE	*RESPECTFUL*	*HONEST*	*SELF-DISCIPLINED*
COOPERATIVE	*GOOD CITIZEN*	*CARING*	*COURAGEOUS*

Circle the subjects in school that would help you with this job

READING	*MATH*	*SOCIAL STUDIES*	*ART*	*HEALTH*
SCIENCE	*MUSIC*	*COMPUTER*	*PHYSICAL EDUCATION*	

OTHER: ______________________________

COLORING SHEET

Activity 92

Activity for WORLD OF WORK

Career Village

Factories at Work

Manufacturing

Overview of the Cluster: This activity focuses on the career cluster of Manufacturing where products and machines come together to make or package the things that we use everyday like cars, computers, and foods. Jobs in this cluster include areas of production; maintenance, installation and repair; quality, safety and environmental assurances; and logistics and inventory control.

Materials

- ✓ Copy of the Career Village poster
- ✓ Copy of the *Factories at Work* Activity and Worksheet

Procedures

1. Ask: **What is a detective? How do detectives go about doing their job?** Include that detectives gather information and get the facts by asking questions, listening, observing, and investigating.
2. Invite the students to be a detective and to investigate the career cluster of Manufacturing. (For added effect you may use different props of a detective such as a hat, coat, and magnifying glass). Ask the following questions:
   - ✯ **What are some jobs in the career cluster of Manufacturing?** Sample jobs in this cluster include machinist, assembly line workers, labor relations manager, production managers, safety technicians, precision inspector, tool and die operators, and quality control technicians.
   - ✯ **Where would you find a job from this career cluster in our CAREER VILLAGE?** In our Career Village, manufacturing jobs would be found in the FACTORY near the Metropolitan Area. Discuss various types of factories that are needed.
   - ✯ **Choose a job in the CAREER VILLAGE from this career cluster and answer the following:**
     - **What would be the job responsibilities?**
     - **What skills would you need to do the job?**
     - **What academic subjects would help you prepare for this type of job?**
     - **What other jobs in the community would this person be working with?**
     - **How many people would have this type of job in a community – one, a few, many?**
     - **What jobs from this career cluster, not shown in our Career Village, could be found in a community? You may choose to add it to your career village.**

Factories at Work
Manufacturing

ACTIVITY SHEET

Directions: *Crack the code to find the manufacturing job described.*

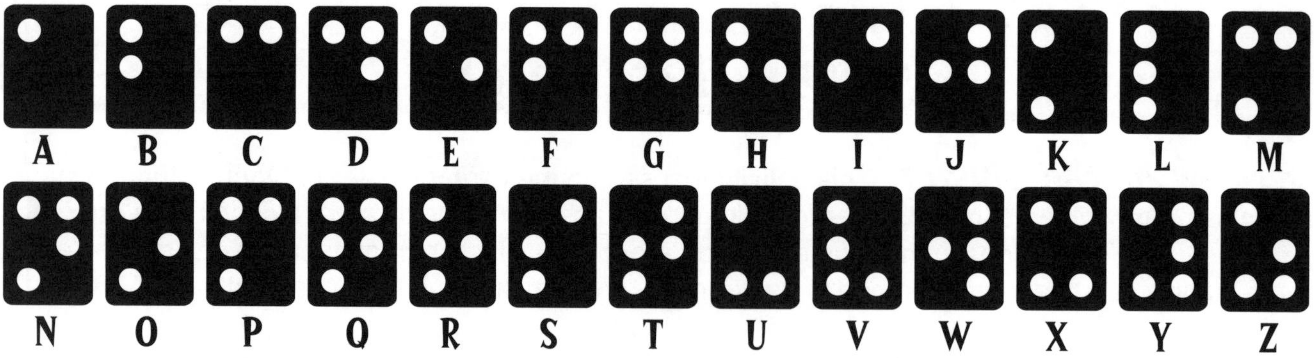

1. A ___ ___ ___ ___ ___ ___ ___ ___ ___ sets up, operates, and maintains machine tools to shape metal to make parts for such things as machines, airplanes, and motors.

2. An ___ ___ ___ ___ ___ ___ ___ ___ ___ ___ ___ ___ worker is responsible for one part of completing a whole unit.

3. A ___ ___ ___ ___ ___ ___ ___ ___ ___ ___ ___ ___ ___ ___ ___ ___ ___ inspects work areas and equipment for safety.

4. A ___ ___ ___ ___ ___ ___ ___ ___ ___ ___ ___ ___ ___ ___ manager serves as a link between worker and manager with the goal of having a positive, productive working environment.

Factories at Work
Manufacturing

WORK SHEET

List examples of jobs in the area of Manufacturing

Circle one job above and answer the following about that job

	YES	NO
1. Work alone?		
2. Work with people?		
3. Work inside?		
4. Work outside?		
5. Work during the day?		
6. Work during the night?		
7. Work on week days (Monday-Friday)?		
8. Work on weekends (Friday, Saturday, Sunday)?		
9. Does this job require a uniform?		
10. Does this job involve traveling?		
11. Do you need education or training beyond high school?		
If "yes," what:		
12. Will this job be needed in the future?		
13. What is the salary range for this job? Low, average, high?		

Circle the character traits that are especially important with this job

RESPONSIBLE	*RESPECTFUL*	*HONEST*	*SELF-DISCIPLINED*
COOPERATIVE	*GOOD CITIZEN*	*CARING*	*COURAGEOUS*

Circle the subjects in school that would help you with this job

READING	*MATH*	*SOCIAL STUDIES*	*ART*	*HEALTH*
SCIENCE	*MUSIC*	*COMPUTER*	*PHYSICAL EDUCATION*	

OTHER: ______________________________

SALES
JANUARY
FEBRUARY
MARCH
APRIL
MAY
JUNE
JULY
AUGUST
SEPTEMBER
OCTOBER
NOVEMBER
DECEMBER
Marketing
Sales
& Service

Activity 93

Activity for WORLD OF WORK

Career Village

Have I Got a Deal for You!

Marketing, Sales, and Services

Overview of the Cluster: This activity focuses on the career cluster of Marketing, Sales, and Service which includes jobs that focus on marketing and selling goods and services for the needs and wants of others. Jobs in this cluster include areas of buying; distributing; and sales and marketing.

Materials

- ✓ Copy of the Career Village poster
- ✓ Copy of the *Have I Got a Deal for You!* Activity and Worksheet

Procedures

1. Ask: **What is a detective? How do detectives go about doing their job?** Include that detectives gather information and get the facts by asking questions, listening, observing, and investigating.
2. Invite the students to be a detective and to investigate the career cluster of Marketing, Sales, and Services. (For added effect you may use different props of a detective such as a hat, coat, and magnifying glass). Ask the following questions:
   - ✯ **What are some jobs in the career cluster of Marketing, Sales, and Services?** Sample jobs in this cluster include salesperson, store manager, sales representative, purchasing agent, distributor, advertiser, car salesperson, e-marketer, advertising manager, wholesale or retail buyer, marketing consultant.
   - ✯ **Where would you find a job from this career cluster in our CAREER VILLAGE?** In the Career Village you will find jobs in the Marketing, Sales, and Services career cluster at the CARS FOR SALE LOT, the DEPARTMENT STORE, the GROCERY STORE as well as other businesses in the area. Discuss jobs in Marketing, Sales, and Services cluster that may be found in the METROPOLITAN AREA.
   - ✯ **Choose a job in the CAREER VILLAGE from this career cluster and answer the following:**
     - **What would be the job responsibilities?**
     - **What skills would you need to do the job?**
     - **What academic subjects would help you prepare for this type of job?**
     - **What other jobs in the community would this person be working with?**
     - **How many people would have this type of job in a community – one, a few, many?**
     - **What jobs from this career cluster, not shown in our Career Village, could be found in a community? You may choose to add it to your career village.**

Have I Got a Deal for You!

Marketing, Sales, and Services

Directions: *Complete the crossword puzzle.*

ACROSS

1. An advertiser ______________ about a service or product in order to increase sales.

2. A salesperson promotes and ________ a product or service.

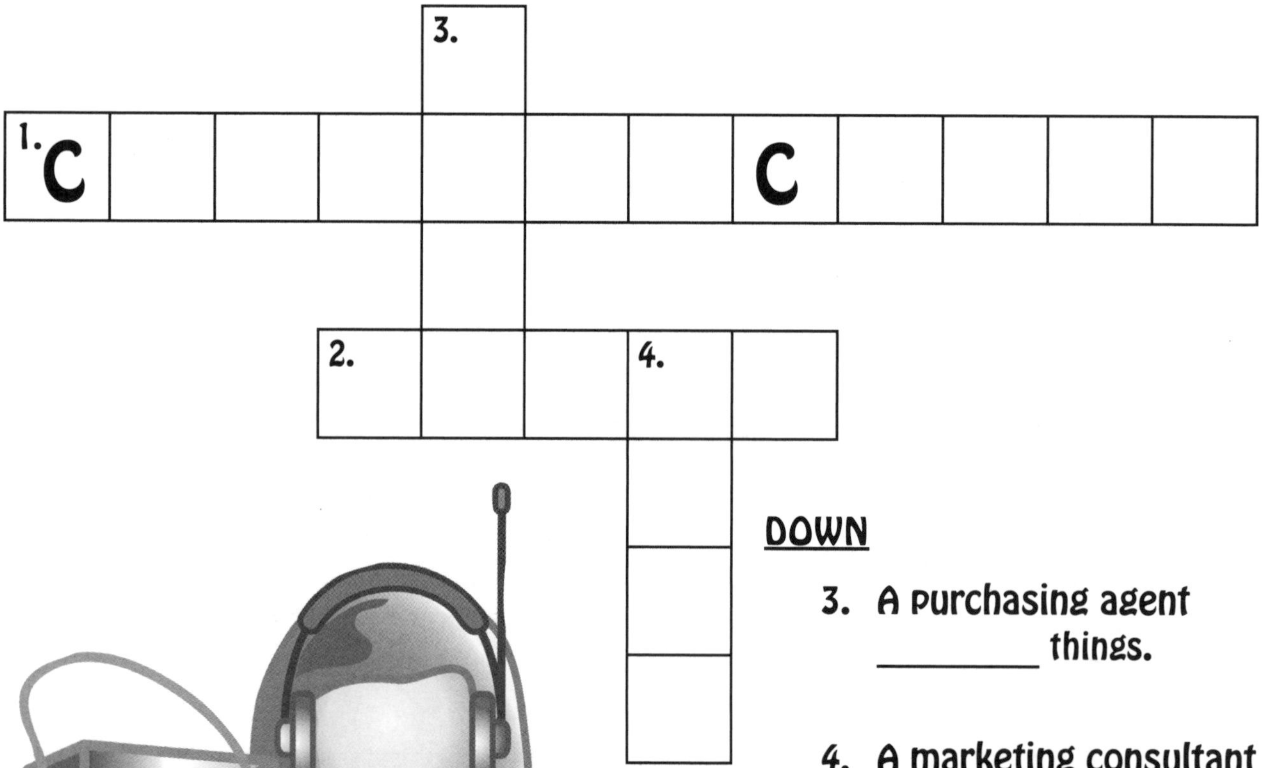

DOWN

3. A purchasing agent ________ things.

4. A marketing consultant studies what people ________ and dislike about the product.

Answers: 1. communicates 2. sells 3. buys 4. like

Have I Got a Deal for You!

Marketing, Sales, and Services

WORK SHEET

List examples of jobs in the area of Marketing, Sales, and Services

Circle one job above and answer the following about that job

	YES	NO
1. Work alone?		
2. Work with people?		
3. Work inside?		
4. Work outside?		
5. Work during the day?		
6. Work during the night?		
7. Work on week days (Monday-Friday)?		
8. Work on weekends (Friday, Saturday, Sunday)?		
9. Does this job require a uniform?		
10. Does this job involve traveling?		
11. Do you need education or training beyond high school?		
If "yes," what:		
12. Will this job be needed in the future?		
13. What is the salary range for this job? Low, average, high?		

Circle the character traits that are especially important with this job

RESPONSIBLE	*RESPECTFUL*	*HONEST*	*SELF-DISCIPLINED*
COOPERATIVE	*GOOD CITIZEN*	*CARING*	*COURAGEOUS*

Circle the subjects in school that would help you with this job

READING	*MATH*	*SOCIAL STUDIES*	*ART*	*HEALTH*
SCIENCE	*MUSIC*	*COMPUTER*	*PHYSICAL EDUCATION*	

OTHER: ______________________________

Scientist at Work!

COLORING SHEET

Activity 94

Activity for WORLD OF WORK

Career Village

Scientist at Work!

Science, Technology, Engineering, and Mathematics

Overview of the Cluster: This activity focuses on the career cluster of Science, Technology, Engineering, and Mathematics which helps design, explore, investigate, and analyze the world around us. Jobs in this cluster include areas of engineering and technology; and science and math.

Materials

- ✓ Copy of the Career Village poster
- ✓ Copy of the *Scientist at Work!* Activity and Worksheet

Procedures

1. Ask: **What is a detective? How do detectives go about doing their job?** Include that detectives gather information and get the facts by asking questions, listening, observing, and investigating.
2. Invite the students to be a detective and to investigate the career cluster of Science, Technology, Engineering, and Mathematics. (For added effect you may use different props of a detective such as a hat, coat, and magnifying glass). Ask the following questions:
   - ✯ **What are some jobs in the career cluster of Science, Technology, Engineering, and Mathematics?** Sample jobs in this cluster include chemist, biochemist, biologist, chemical engineer, robotics engineer, astronomer, astronaut, geoscientist, civil engineer, mathematician, statistician, industrial engineer, and surveying and mapping technicians.
   - ✯ **Where would you find a job from this career cluster in our CAREER VILLAGE?** In the Career Village, you will find engineering jobs which helped with the mechanics of designing and building the ROADS, BUILDINGS, AMUSEMENT PARK, FACTORY, the MARINAS, and the BRIDGE. Science jobs from this cluster will be found at the PLANETARIUM. To broaden the discussion of jobs in this cluster, include the possibility of a Research Lab or Space Center in the METROPOLITAN AREA.
   - ✯ **Choose a job in the CAREER VILLAGE from this career cluster and answer the following:**
     - **What would be the job responsibilities?**
     - **What skills would you need to do the job?**
     - **What academic subjects would help you prepare for this type of job?**
     - **What other jobs in the community would this person be working with?**
     - **How many people would have this type of job in a community – one, a few, many?**
     - **What jobs from this career cluster, not shown in our Career Village, could be found in a community? You may choose to add it to your career village.**

Scientist at Work!

Science, Technology, Engineering, and Mathematics

ACTIVITY SHEET

Directions: *Draw a line matching the jobs to their job description.*

BIOCHEMIST

BIOLOGIST

CHEMICAL ENGINEER

ASTRONOMER

ASTRONAUT

GEOSCIENTIST

CIVIL ENGINEER

STATISTICIAN

- **This person studies living things and their environment.**
- **This person deals with numbers and statistics, and works with businesses to study information to help the company.**
- **This person is trained to pilot and navigate a spacecraft in outer space.**
- **This person studies and learns about the sun, moon, planets, and stars and helps solve problems with space flights and satellites.**
- **This person studies the earth, and may work with oil companies in locating underground resources.**
- **This person applies chemistry, physics, and life sciences with mathematics to produce useful products from chemicals.**
- **This person plans and designs the building of roads, bridges, airports and other buildings as well as oversees their maintenance.**
- **This person studies chemical processes in living things, and may work with companies that make medicines.**

Scientist at Work!

Science, Technology, Engineering, and Mathematics

WORK SHEET

List examples of jobs in the area of Science, Technology, Engineering, & Mathematics

Circle one job above and answer the following about that job

	YES	NO
1. Work alone?		
2. Work with people?		
3. Work inside?		
4. Work outside?		
5. Work during the day?		
6. Work during the night?		
7. Work on week days (Monday-Friday)?		
8. Work on weekends (Friday, Saturday, Sunday)?		
9. Does this job require a uniform?		
10. Does this job involve traveling?		
11. Do you need education or training beyond high school?		
If "yes," what:		
12. Will this job be needed in the future?		
13. What is the salary range for this job? Low, average, high?		

Circle the character traits that are especially important with this job

RESPONSIBLE	*RESPECTFUL*	*HONEST*	*SELF-DISCIPLINED*
COOPERATIVE	*GOOD CITIZEN*	*CARING*	*COURAGEOUS*

Circle the subjects in school that would help you with this job

READING	*MATH*	*SOCIAL STUDIES*	*ART*	*HEALTH*
SCIENCE	*MUSIC*	*COMPUTER*	*PHYSICAL EDUCATION*	

OTHER: ______________________________

Transportation,
Distribution
& Logistics

Activity 95 | Activity for WORLD OF WORK | Career Village

On the Move! All Aboard!
Transportation, Distribution, and Logistics

Overview of the Cluster: This activity focuses on the career cluster of Transportation, Distribution, and Logistics which includes careers and businesses involved in the planning, management and movement of people, materials, and products by road, air, rail, and water as well as the technical support and maintenance of the equipment and facilities. Jobs include areas of transportation operations; warehouse and distribution center operations; facility and equipment maintenance; health, safety, and environment management; logistics planning and management; and sales and services.

Materials

- ✓ Copy of the Career Village poster
- ✓ Copy of the *On the Move! All Aboard!* Activity and Worksheet

Procedures

1. Ask: **What is a detective? How do detectives go about doing their job?** Include that detectives gather information and get the facts by asking questions, listening, observing, and investigating.
2. Invite the students to be a detective and to investigate the career cluster of Transportation, Distribution, and Logistics. (For added effect you may use different props of a detective such as a hat, coat, and magnifying glass). Ask the following questions:
   - ✯ **What are some jobs in the career cluster of Transportation, Distribution, and, Logistics?** Sample jobs in this cluster include air traffic controller, airline pilot, flight attendant, train engineer/conductor, bus driver, ship's captain, tug boat or ferry pilot, truck driver, taxi driver, helicopter pilot, transportation ticket agent, mechanic, chauffeur, railroad safety inspector, cargo and freight agent, and shipping and receiving supervisor.
   - ✯ **Where would you find a job from this career cluster in our CAREER VILLAGE?** In our Career Village, jobs from this career cluster may be found on the TRAIN, PLANE, CRUISE LINE, as a TAXI driver, CHAUFFEUR in the Hummer limo, U.S. MAIL TRUCK, TRANSPORTATION TRUCKS delivering goods to the RETAIL STORES, FACTORY or other distribution areas in the METROPOLITAN AREA. Discuss what each of the above are transporting – people, materials, or products? The GAS STATION also includes the mechanics from this career cluster to help maintain the transportation equipment and keep things moving.
   - ✯ **Choose a job in the CAREER VILLAGE from this career cluster and answer the following:**
     - **What would be the job responsibilities?**
     - **What skills would you need to do the job?**
     - **What academic subjects would help you prepare for this type of job?**
     - **What other jobs in the community would this person be working with?**
     - **How many people would have this type of job in a community – one, a few, many?**
     - **What jobs from this career cluster, not shown in our Career Village, could be found in a community? You may choose to add it to your career village.**

On the Move! All Aboard!
Transportation, Distribution, and Logistics

ACTIVITY SHEET

Directions: *For the following pictures, list different jobs that are connected with the picture.*

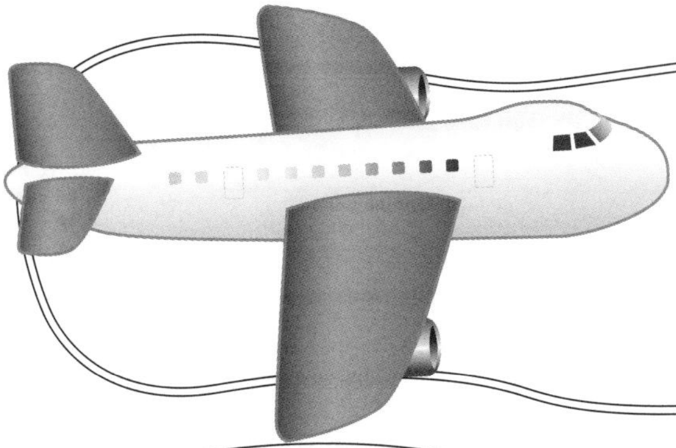

Create your own transportation picture and list the jobs that go with your picture.

On the Move! All Aboard!
Transportation, Distribution, and Logistics

WORK SHEET

List examples of jobs in the area of Transportation, Distribution, and Logistics

Circle one job above and answer the following about that job

	YES	NO
1. Work alone?		
2. Work with people?		
3. Work inside?		
4. Work outside?		
5. Work during the day?		
6. Work during the night?		
7. Work on week days (Monday-Friday)?		
8. Work on weekends (Friday, Saturday, Sunday)?		
9. Does this job require a uniform?		
10. Does this job involve traveling?		
11. Do you need education or training beyond high school?		
If "yes," what:		
12. Will this job be needed in the future?		
13. What is the salary range for this job? Low, average, high?		

Circle the character traits that are especially important with this job

RESPONSIBLE	*RESPECTFUL*	*HONEST*	*SELF-DISCIPLINED*
COOPERATIVE	*GOOD CITIZEN*	*CARING*	*COURAGEOUS*

Circle the subjects in school that would help you with this job

READING	*MATH*	*SOCIAL STUDIES*	*ART*	*HEALTH*
SCIENCE	*MUSIC*	*COMPUTER*	*PHYSICAL EDUCATION*	

OTHER: ______________________________________

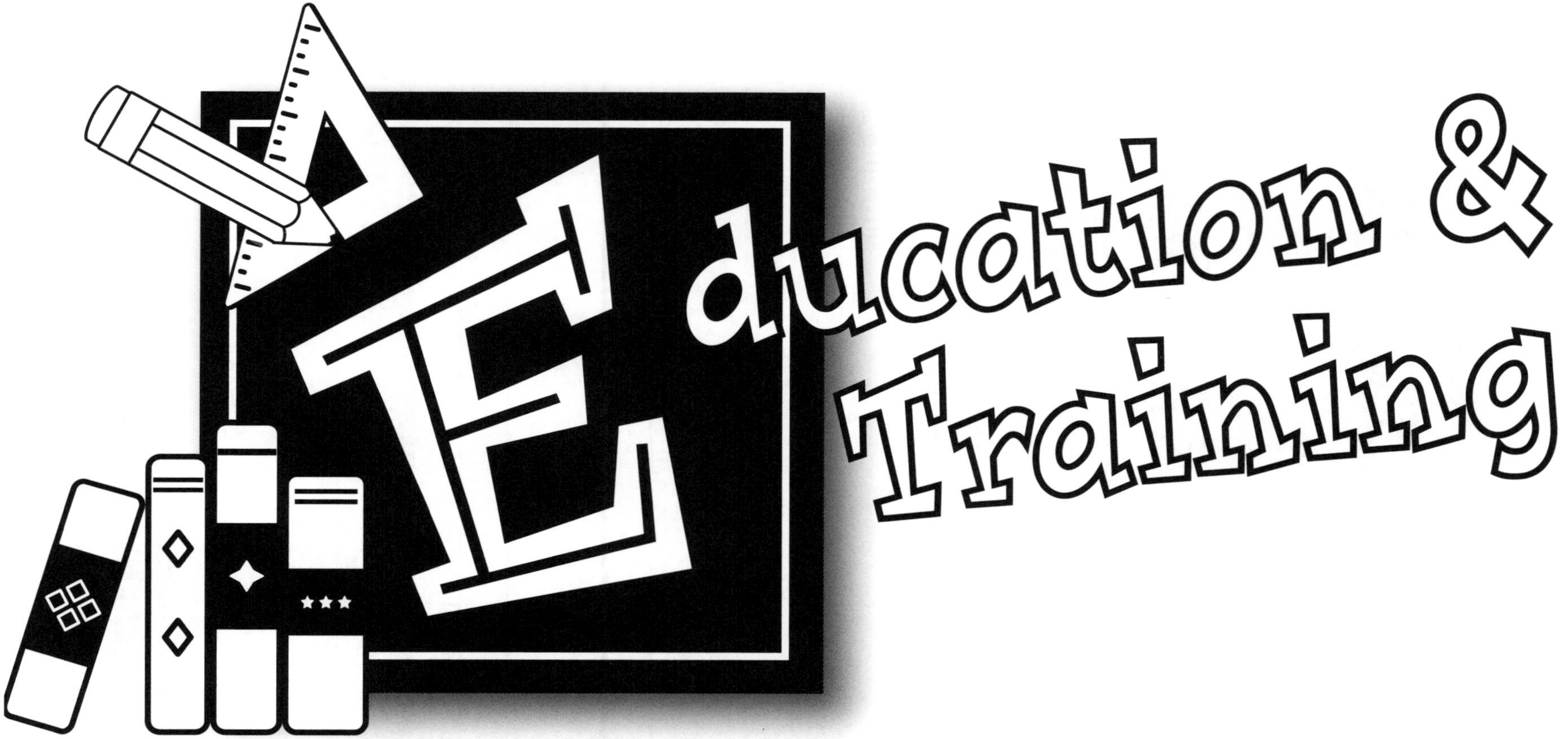
Education &
Training

Activity 96

Activity for WORLD OF WORK

Career Village

Teaching Is What I Love!

Education and Training

Overview of the Cluster: This activity focuses on the career cluster of Education and Training where jobs have a lifelong impact on others and includes teaching, planning and administration in schools, colleges, technical institutes and businesses. Jobs in this cluster include areas of teaching and training; administration and administrative support; and professional support services.

Materials

- ✓ Copy of the Career Village poster
- ✓ Copy of the *Teaching Is What I Love!* Activity and Worksheet

Procedures

1. Ask: **What is a detective? How do detectives go about doing their job?** Include that detectives gather information and get the facts by asking questions, listening, observing, and investigating.
2. Invite the students to be a detective and to investigate the career cluster of Education and Training. (For added effect you may use different props of a detective such as a hat, coat, and magnifying glass). Ask the following questions:
   - ☆ **What are some jobs in the career cluster of Education and Training?** Sample jobs in this cluster include superintendent, principal, teacher, school social worker, school counselor, teacher assistant, school psychologist, headmaster, college president, special education teacher, higher education professor, and speech pathologist.
   - ☆ **Where would you find a job from this career cluster in our CAREER VILLAGE?** In our Career Village, jobs from this career cluster are found in the SCHOOL; however the HOSPITAL and other BUSINESSES may offer ongoing education and training at their facility which would include jobs from the Education and Training Career Cluster. Include in your discussion the possibility of a Technical School, College, or University in the METROPOLITAN AREA.
   - ☆ **Choose a job in the CAREER VILLAGE from this career cluster and answer the following:**
     - **What would be the job responsibilities?**
     - **What skills would you need to do the job?**
     - **What academic subjects would help you prepare for this type of job?**
     - **What other jobs in the community would this person be working with?**
     - **How many people would have this type of job in a community – one, a few, many?**
     - **What jobs from this career cluster, not shown in our Career Village, could be found in a community? You may choose to add it to your career village.**

Teaching Is What I Love!
Education and Training

ACTIVITY SHEET

Directions: *Think of all of the different types of teaching jobs and the different types of schools. Read the questions below and choose a job from the JOB BANK that answers WHO AM I? and write the corresponding letter in the space provided.*

____ 1. I may say "Hola!" instead of, "Hello." Who am I?

____ 2. I may do a lot of experiments with chemicals and test tubes in my class. Who am I?

____ 3. In my classroom, I work with a lot of numbers. Who am I?

____ 4. I help the teacher with students, paperwork, and other duties. Who am I?

____ 5. We read and write stories in my class. Who am I?

____ 6. I talk with students about social, academic, and career learning and/or problems. Who am I?

____ 7. I teach in higher education at a Technology School, College, or University. Who am I?

____ 8. I work at the vocational/technical school teaching to build with bricks and stone work. Who am I?

____ 9. I get to stay active and keep my students active. It's important to get exercise and keep our body in shape. Who am I?

____ 10. I administer and interpret tests about how a student learns and how to best help that student learn. Who am I?

____ 11. I make decisions and oversee activities of teachers and students at the school. Who am I?

____ 12. I work at a vocational/technical school and teach how to fix small engines. Who am I?

____ 13. I work to provide leadership in developing and maintaining the best possible educational programs and services for the schools in my district. Who am I?

____ 14. I teach students how to use the computer to create and design. Who am I?

____ 15. I help students learn how to pronounce words and communicate well. Who am I?

JOB BANK

A. Science Teacher
B. Math Teacher
C. English Teacher
D. Foreign Language Teacher
E. School Psychologist
F. Teacher Assistant
G. Speech Therapist
H. School Counselor
I. College Professor
J. Principal
K. Superintendent
L. Physical Education Teacher
M. Masonry Teacher
N. Small Engine Repair Teacher
O. Graphic Arts Teacher

Teaching Is What I Love!
Education and Training

WORK SHEET

List examples of jobs in the area of Education and Training

Circle one job above and answer the following about that job

	YES	NO
1. Work alone?		
2. Work with people?		
3. Work inside?		
4. Work outside?		
5. Work during the day?		
6. Work during the night?		
7. Work on week days (Monday-Friday)?		
8. Work on weekends (Friday, Saturday, Sunday)?		
9. Does this job require a uniform?		
10. Does this job involve traveling?		
11. Do you need education or training beyond high school?		
If "yes," what:		
12. Will this job be needed in the future?		
13. What is the salary range for this job? Low, average, high?		

Circle the character traits that are especially important with this job

RESPONSIBLE	*RESPECTFUL*	*HONEST*	*SELF-DISCIPLINED*
COOPERATIVE	*GOOD CITIZEN*	*CARING*	*COURAGEOUS*

Circle the subjects in school that would help you with this job

READING	*MATH*	*SOCIAL STUDIES*	*ART*	*HEALTH*
SCIENCE	*MUSIC*	*COMPUTER*	*PHYSICAL EDUCATION*	

OTHER: ______________________________

COLORING SHEET

Activity 97

Activity for WORLD OF WORK

Career Village

The Business World

Business, Management, and Administration

Overview of the Cluster: This activity focuses on the career cluster of Business, Management, and Administration. Jobs in this cluster include areas of business management; financial management and accounting; and administrative support.

Materials

- ✓ Copy of the Career Village poster
- ✓ Copy of the *The Business World* Activity and Worksheet

Procedures

1. Ask: **What is a detective? How do detectives go about doing their job?** Include that detectives gather information and get the facts by asking questions, listening, observing, and investigating.
2. Invite the students to be a detective and to investigate the career cluster of Business, Management, and Administration. (For added effect you may use different props of a detective such as a hat, coat, and magnifying glass). Ask the following questions:
   - ✯ **What are some jobs in the career cluster of Business, Management, and Adminstration?** Sample jobs in this cluster include business owner, receptionist, office manager, entrepreneur, project manager, equal opportunity employment specialist, personnel recruiter, benefits administrator, chief executive officer, human resources manager, and administrative assistant.
   - ✯ **Where would you find a job from this career cluster in our CAREER VILLAGE?** In our Career Village, jobs from this career cluster can be found at the BUSINESS PARK as well as at other businesses in the village. Offices at the BUSINESS PARK include: a radio station, insurance office, realtor, loan office, newspaper, and YouthLight, Inc. Include in your discussion businesses that may be found in the METROPOLITAN AREA.
   - ✯ **Choose a job in the CAREER VILLAGE from this career cluster and answer the following:**
     - **What would be the job responsibilities?**
     - **What skills would you need to do the job?**
     - **What academic subjects would help you prepare for this type of job?**
     - **What other jobs in the community would this person be working with?**
     - **How many people would have this type of job in a community – one, a few, many?**
     - **What jobs from this career cluster, not shown in our Career Village, could be found in a community? You may choose to add it to your career village.**

The Business World
Business, Management, and Administration

ACTIVITY SHEET

Directions: *Answer the following.*

1. Name some businesses in your area. ______________________________

____

____

2. In a business office such as an insurance or realtor's office, who is the person that you usually see first when you enter the office?

____

3. In the larger businesses you may find a personnel recruiter, a benefits administrator, and a human resources manager. Draw a line to match the jobs to their job descriptions.

This person handles the benefits of the job that may include health insurance, vacation days, sick leave, personal leave, incentive bonuses, etc.

This person actively seeks out people who would work well with their company and encourages them to apply.

This person coordinates interviews and hires people to work at the business.

The Business World

Business, Management, and Administration

WORK SHEET

List examples of jobs in the area of Business, Management, and Administration

Circle one job above and answer the following about that job

	YES	NO
1. Work alone?		
2. Work with people?		
3. Work inside?		
4. Work outside?		
5. Work during the day?		
6. Work during the night?		
7. Work on week days (Monday-Friday)?		
8. Work on weekends (Friday, Saturday, Sunday)?		
9. Does this job require a uniform?		
10. Does this job involve traveling?		
11. Do you need education or training beyond high school?		
If "yes," what:		
12. Will this job be needed in the future?		
13. What is the salary range for this job? Low, average, high?		

Circle the character traits that are especially important with this job

RESPONSIBLE	*RESPECTFUL*	*HONEST*	*SELF-DISCIPLINED*
COOPERATIVE	*GOOD CITIZEN*	*CARING*	*COURAGEOUS*

Circle the subjects in school that would help you with this job

READING	*MATH*	*SOCIAL STUDIES*	*ART*	*HEALTH*
SCIENCE	*MUSIC*	*COMPUTER*	*PHYSICAL EDUCATION*	

OTHER: ______________________________

On Stage!

COLORING SHEET

Activity 98

Activity for WORLD OF WORK

Career Village

On Stage!

Arts, A/V Technology and Communication

Overview of the Cluster: This activity focuses on the career cluster of Arts, A/V Technology and Communication which involves careers in designing, producing, exhibiting, performing, and writing or publishing multimedia content. Jobs in this cluster include areas of broadcasting and journalism; performing arts; visual arts; printing technology; audio and video technology; and telecommunications.

Materials

- ✓ Copy of the Career Village poster
- ✓ Copy of the *On Stage!* Activity and Worksheet

Procedures

1. Ask: **What is a detective? How do detectives go about doing their job?** Include that detectives gather information and get the facts by asking questions, listening, observing, and investigating.
2. Invite the students to be a detective and to investigate the career cluster of Arts, A/V Technology and Communication. (For added effect you may use different props of a detective such as a hat, coat, and magnifying glass). Ask the following questions:
   - ✯ **What are some jobs in the career cluster of Arts, A/V Technology and Communication?** Sample jobs in this cluster include TV announcer, newspaper journalist, newscaster, video technician, camera operator, reporter, correspondent, dancer, set designer, musician, actor, playwright, desktop publishing specialist, choreographer, sculptor, cartoonist, photographer, fashion designer, artist, commercial artist, film maker, graphic designer, television studio producer, radio broadcaster, museum curator, costume designer, and art gallery manager.
   - ✯ **Where would you find a job from this career cluster in our CAREER VILLAGE?** In our Career Village the THEATER would offer jobs in this career cluster as well as the radio studio in the BUSINESS PARK. Other job opportunities may be available at a fine arts center, museum, newspaper office, dance studio, art gallery, and music studio that may be found in the METROPOLITAN AREA.
   - ✯ **Choose a job in the CAREER VILLAGE from this career cluster and answer the following:**
     - **What would be the job responsibilities?**
     - **What skills would you need to do the job?**
     - **What academic subjects would help you prepare for this type of job?**
     - **What other jobs in the community would this person be working with?**
     - **How many people would have this type of job in a community – one, a few, many?**
     - **What jobs from this career cluster, not shown in our Career Village, could be found in a community? You may choose to add it to your career village.**

On Stage!
Arts, A/V Technology, and Communication

ACTIVITY SHEET

Directions: *Find and circle the careers in the WORD SEARCH. Can you find all of the jobs listed in the JOB BANK?*

JOB BANK

Choreographer
Camera Operator
Art Gallery Manager
Radio Broadcaster
Video Technician
Costume Designer
Playwright
Cartoonist
Sculptor
Photographer
Newscaster
Artist
Musician
Reporter
Dancer
Actor

r	s	c	u	l	p	t	o	r	e	r	a	l	s	n	r	n
e	e	e	c	e	r	a	b	o	u	e	g	r	e	a	a	a
t	d	p	r	e	p	c	d	t	t	r	a	t	t	i	p	a
s	r	s	o	e	h	i	s	a	t	h	o	t	c	c	o	p
a	a	g	c	r	o	i	h	r	c	s	s	i	a	i	t	l
c	s	c	o	s	t	u	m	e	d	e	s	i	g	n	e	r
d	r	i	t	r	o	e	p	p	d	u	p	s	r	h	e	h
a	r	u	a	o	g	g	r	o	m	t	a	l	o	c	d	r
o	t	h	g	i	r	w	y	a	l	p	n	a	n	e	e	a
r	e	g	a	n	a	m	y	r	e	l	l	a	g	t	r	a
b	e	t	o	a	p	e	s	e	a	e	d	y	s	o	a	o
o	l	h	i	n	h	h	t	m	l	r	t	a	r	e	r	a
i	o	o	i	v	e	o	o	a	a	c	c	a	h	d	h	s
d	o	e	o	s	r	u	p	c	b	s	p	g	r	i	r	c
a	t	i	a	r	v	e	e	c	w	i	r	r	n	v	o	e
r	e	h	p	a	r	g	o	e	r	o	h	c	h	p	e	e
r	c	a	r	t	o	o	n	i	s	t	t	e	c	i	t	v

On Stage!

Arts, A/V Technology, and Communication

WORK SHEET

List examples of jobs in the area of Arts, A/V Technology, and Communication

Circle one job above and answer the following about that job

	YES	NO
1. Work alone?		
2. Work with people?		
3. Work inside?		
4. Work outside?		
5. Work during the day?		
6. Work during the night?		
7. Work on week days (Monday-Friday)?		
8. Work on weekends (Friday, Saturday, Sunday)?		
9. Does this job require a uniform?		
10. Does this job involve traveling?		
11. Do you need education or training beyond high school?		
If "yes," what:		
12. Will this job be needed in the future?		
13. What is the salary range for this job? Low, average, high?		

Circle the character traits that are especially important with this job

RESPONSIBLE	*RESPECTFUL*	*HONEST*	*SELF-DISCIPLINED*
COOPERATIVE	*GOOD CITIZEN*	*CARING*	*COURAGEOUS*

Circle the subjects in school that would help you with this job

READING	*MATH*	*SOCIAL STUDIES*	*ART*	*HEALTH*
SCIENCE	*MUSIC*	*COMPUTER*	*PHYSICAL EDUCATION*	

OTHER: ______________________________

COLORING SHEET

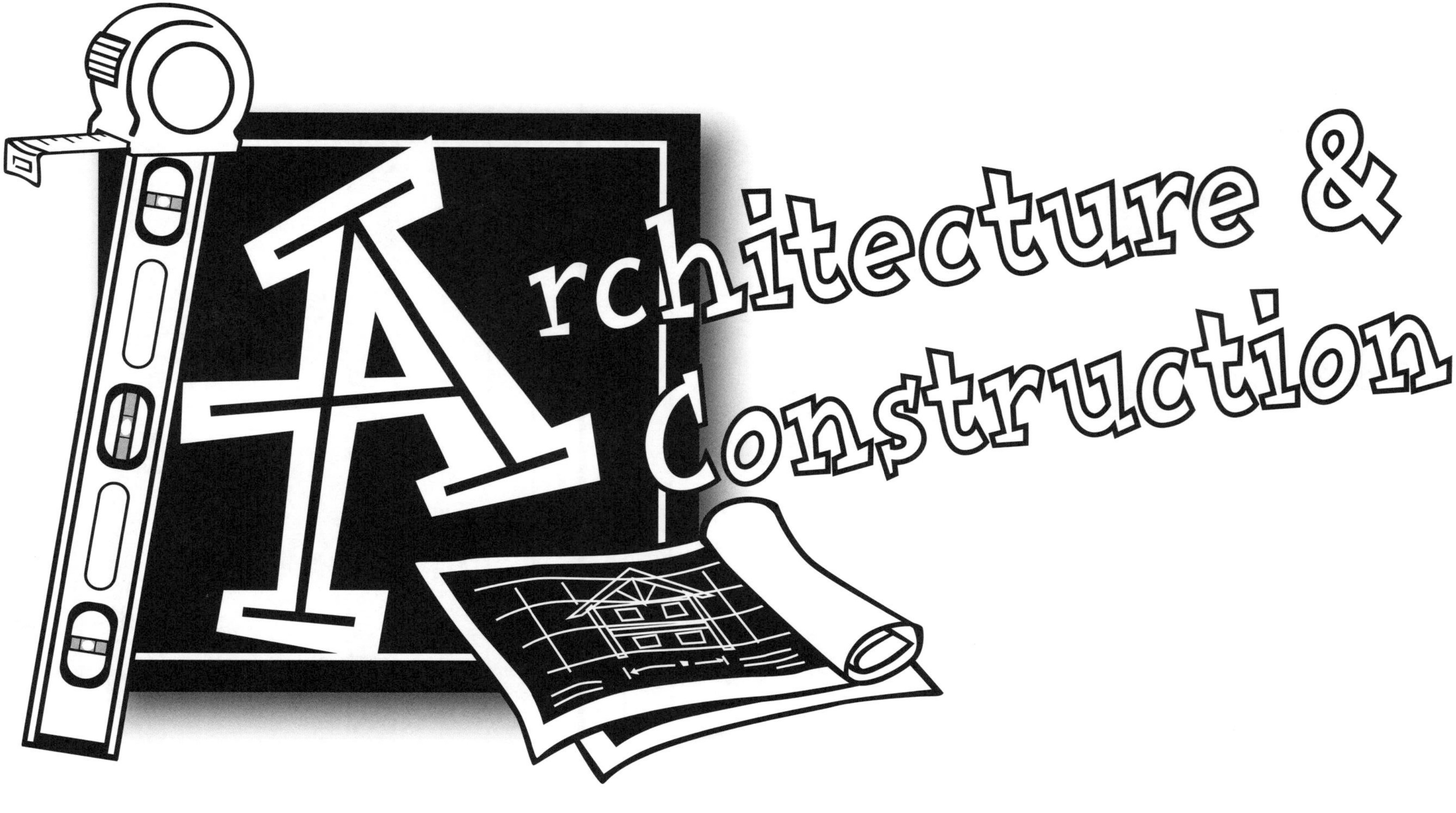

Activity 99

Activity for WORLD OF WORK

Career Village

Designing, Building, and Fixing
Architecture and Construction

Overview of the Cluster: This activity focuses on the career cluster of Architecture and Construction which involves jobs that design, plan, manage, build, and maintain the structures where we live, work, and play. Jobs in this cluster include areas of construction; design and pre-construction; and maintenance and operations.

Materials

- ✓ Copy of the Career Village poster
- ✓ Copy of the *Designing, Building, and Fixing* Activity and Worksheet

Procedures

1. Ask: **What is a detective? How do detectives go about doing their job?** Include that detectives gather information and get the facts by asking questions, listening, observing, and investigating.

2. Invite the students to be a detective and to investigate the career cluster of Architecture and Construction. (For added effect you may use different props of a detective such as a hat, coat, and magnifying glass). Ask the following questions:

   ✯ **What are some jobs in the career cluster of Architecture and Construction?** Sample jobs in this cluster include carpenter, electrician, architect, landscape designer, surveyor, construction worker, painter, highway worker, and brick mason.

   ✯ **Where would you find a job from this career cluster in our CAREER VILLAGE?** In our Career Village, jobs from this career cluster are found in the NEIGHBORHOOD with the house under construction as well as throughout the village for the maintenance of the roads and buildings.

   ✯ **Choose a job in the CAREER VILLAGE from this career cluster and answer the following:**
   - **What would be the job responsibilities?**
   - **What skills would you need to do the job?**
   - **What academic subjects would help you prepare for this type of job?**
   - **What other jobs in the community would this person be working with?**
   - **How many people would have this type of job in a community – one, a few, many?**
   - **What jobs from this career cluster, not shown in our Career Village, could be found in a community? You may choose to add it to your career village.**

Designing, Building, and Fixing

Architecture and Construction

ACTIVITY SHEET

Directions: *Write the name of the job that goes with the tools listed. Choose from the JOB BANK below.*

JOB BANK

ARCHITECT	LANDSCAPER	PAINTER
CARPENTER	ELECTRICIAN	SURVEYOR
ROAD CONSTRUCTION WORKER		BRICK MASON

PAINT BRUSH
LADDER
ROLLER
1. ______________________

PENCIL
SCALED RULER
COMPUTER
2. ______________________

CEMENT
TROWEL
LEVEL
3. ______________________

ASPHALT
PACKER
SAFETY BARRELS
4. ______________________

VOLT METER
PLIERS
SCREWDRIVER
5. ______________________

SHOVEL
AUGER
SPADE
6. ______________________

HAMMER
SAW
SQUARE
7. ______________________

MARKING TAPE
TRANSOM
LASER LEVEL
8. ______________________

Designing, Building, and Fixing
Architecture and Construction

WORK SHEET

List examples of jobs in the area of Architecture and Construction

Circle one job above and answer the following about that job

	YES	NO
1. Work alone?		
2. Work with people?		
3. Work inside?		
4. Work outside?		
5. Work during the day?		
6. Work during the night?		
7. Work on week days (Monday-Friday)?		
8. Work on weekends (Friday, Saturday, Sunday)?		
9. Does this job require a uniform?		
10. Does this job involve traveling?		
11. Do you need education or training beyond high school?		
If "yes," what:		
12. Will this job be needed in the future?		
13. What is the salary range for this job? Low, average, high?		

Circle the character traits that are especially important with this job

RESPONSIBLE *RESPECTFUL* *HONEST* *SELF-DISCIPLINED*
COOPERATIVE *GOOD CITIZEN* *CARING* *COURAGEOUS*

Circle the subjects in school that would help you with this job

READING *MATH* *SOCIAL STUDIES* *ART* *HEALTH*
SCIENCE *MUSIC* *COMPUTER* *PHYSICAL EDUCATION*
OTHER: ______________________________

Down on the Farm

COLORING SHEET

Activity 100

Activity for WORLD OF WORK

Career Village

Down on the Farm

Agriculture, Food, and Natural Resources

Overview of the Cluster: This activity focuses on the career cluster of Agriculture, Food and Natural Resources which includes jobs that ensure that we are responsibly managing our food production and our natural resource consumption. Jobs in this cluster include areas of agribusiness; animal systems; environmental service systems; food products and processing systems; natural resource systems; plant systems; and power, structural, and technical systems.

Materials

- ✓ Copy of the Career Village poster
- ✓ Copy of the *Down on the Farm* Activity and Worksheet

Procedures

1. Ask: **What is a detective? How do detectives go about doing their job?** Include that detectives gather information and get the facts by asking questions, listening, observing, and investigating.
2. Invite the students to be a detective and to investigate the career cluster of Agriculture, Food and Natural Resources. (For added effect you may use different props of a detective such as a hat, coat, and magnifying glass). Ask the following questions:
   - ✯ **What are some jobs in the career cluster of Agriculture, Food and Natural Resources?** Sample jobs in this cluster include farmer, irrigation specialist, horticulturist, beekeeper, gardener, miner, lumberjack, oil rigger, dairy farmer, geologist, USDA inspector, fish and game warden, wildlife manager, zoologist, marine biologist, park ranger, plant nursery, botanist, tree surgeon, ranchers, landscapers, agronomist, hydrologist, archeologist, and forest geneticists.
   - ✯ **Where would you find a job from this career cluster in our CAREER VILLAGE?** In our Career Village, jobs from this career cluster may be found on the FARM, PARK RANGER station, and on the GAME WARDEN boat.
   - ✯ **Choose a job in the CAREER VILLAGE from this career cluster and answer the following:**
     - **What would be the job responsibilities?**
     - **What skills would you need to do the job?**
     - **What academic subjects would help you prepare for this type of job?**
     - **What other jobs in the community would this person be working with?**
     - **How many people would have this type of job in a community – one, a few, many?**
     - **What jobs from this career cluster, not shown in our Career Village, could be found in a community? You may choose to add it to your career village.**

Down on the Farm

Agriculture, Food, and Natural Resources

ACTIVITY SHEET

Directions: *For the following list of jobs, circle the jobs that deal with or protect our NATURAL RESOURCES and underline the jobs that deal with AGRICULTURE. Use a dictionary, if needed.*

fish and game warden

lumberjack

irrigation specialist

wildlife manager

geologist

farmer

USDA inspector

hydrologist

oil rigger

cattle rancher

marine biologist

horticulturalist

miner

NATURAL RESOURCES *are resources that are supplied by nature.*

AGRICULTURE *deals with preparing the land to produce crops and for raising livestock.*

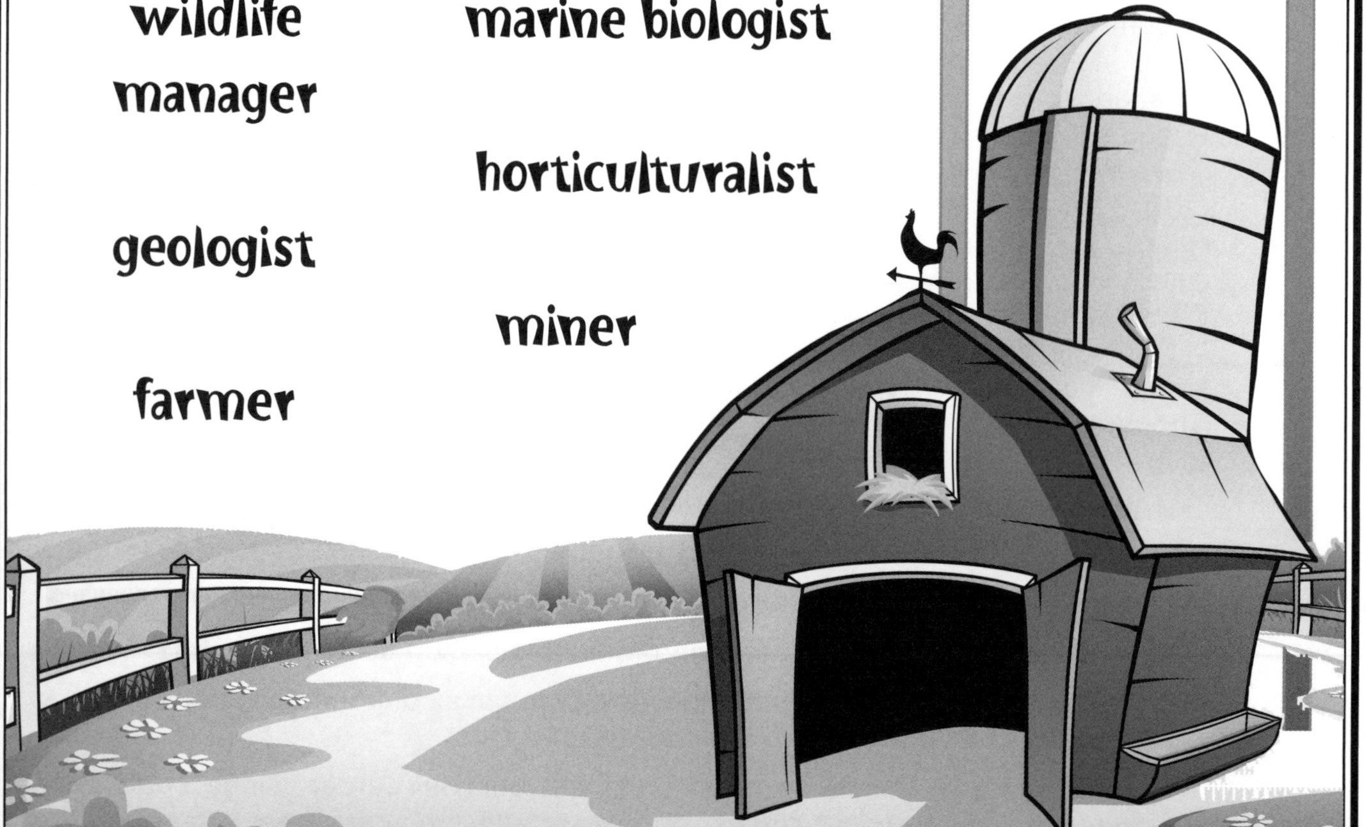

Down on the Farm
Agriculture, Food, and Natural Resources

WORK SHEET

List examples of jobs in the area of Agriculture, Food and Natural Resources

Circle one job above and answer the following about that job

	YES	NO
1. Work alone?		
2. Work with people?		
3. Work inside?		
4. Work outside?		
5. Work during the day?		
6. Work during the night?		
7. Work on week days (Monday-Friday)?		
8. Work on weekends (Friday, Saturday, Sunday)?		
9. Does this job require a uniform?		
10. Does this job involve traveling?		
11. Do you need education or training beyond high school?		
If "yes," what:		
12. Will this job be needed in the future?		
13. What is the salary range for this job? Low, average, high?		

Circle the character traits that are especially important with this job

RESPONSIBLE *RESPECTFUL* *HONEST* *SELF-DISCIPLINED*

COOPERATIVE *GOOD CITIZEN* *CARING* *COURAGEOUS*

Circle the subjects in school that would help you with this job

READING *MATH* *SOCIAL STUDIES* *ART* *HEALTH*

SCIENCE *MUSIC* *COMPUTER* *PHYSICAL EDUCATION*

OTHER: ____________________

AT THE END...

For our students, learning involves not only tuning-in to hear the information but then remembering and applying the new information or skills to their life. There are many ways to help reinforce the skills. The first step is teaching the student good listening skills with eye contact, head nods, staying focused, and processing the information being presented. The next step involves reinforcing and connecting the information to their life. To visually reinforce the information, the use of a summary poster left in the classroom or given to the individual to display can provide a reminder of the new information. Sharing information in a letter or note to the parent and teacher so they can reinforce the new skills for the students each day can also be helpful. Following up with the student individually, at the next group meeting or at a class meeting helps connect and reinforce the new learning. Ask the student to recall the previous learning and ask if he/she had a chance to use the new skill. As they share, compliment, and reinforce their use of the skill. If the student is not able to share how he/she used the new skill, ask: “Think back through your week and decide how you could have used the new skill.” Or ask how he/she might use it in the future.

One of the fun things I like to use at the end of working with a student individually or in a group or to use at the end of a school year to reinforce our learning through class lessons, is the “Bag Pop” trick. Read on to learn about our last activity.

We DO make a difference in the lives of children!

Bag Pop Summary

Overview: This activity provides a fun way to summarize the learning. The activity can be used to summarize learning at the end of working with students individually, in small group, or at the end of the year to summarize the learning through class lessons.

Materials

- ✓ Crayons or markers for students
- ✓ Paper lunch bag for demonstration and for each student

Preparation

You first need to learn and practice the bag pop trick* before performing. The intent of the trick is to give the illusion of tossing imaginary rocks/thoughts into the bag – which is great for summarizing information. The trick involves three steps:

Step one: Hold the paper lunch bag at the open rim with your middle finger inside the bag, hold your thumb outside the bag but pressed against the middle finger with the bag in between. The other fingers can be outside the bag. The trick is to snap your fingers with the bag in between – this makes the noise as if a rock just fell into the bag.

Step two: As you are doing the finger snap with the bag, hold the bag relatively steady but perhaps a quick, small downward motion (dipping the bag) as you snap to add to the illusion that the rock just hit the bottom of the bag.

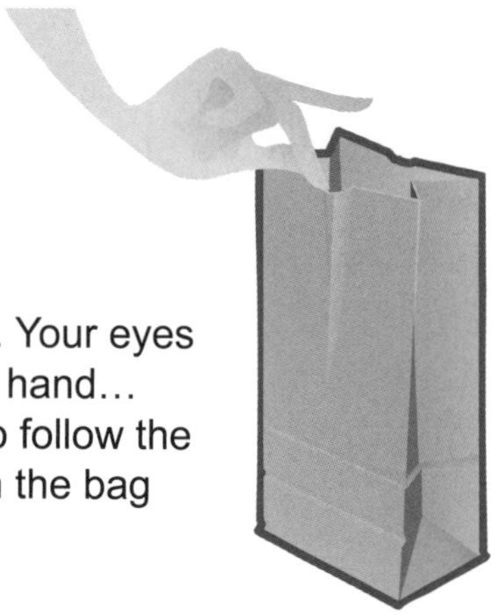

Step three: The final, yet a very important part of the illusion, is the motion of your eyes and head following the rock being thrown. Your eyes need to be focused wherever the rock is – perhaps your other hand… perhaps being thrown by a student. With your eyes, pretend to follow the rock as it leaves the hand, moves through the air, and lands in the bag (make sure to snap the bag as it lands).

Procedures

1. Hold the open paper lunch bag in front of the student(s), and share that it is full of rocks. Share that you need to empty the rocks on the table, so each student can take a rock, write on it something that we have learned and then toss it back into the bag. While you are *pretending* to empty the rocks. Say: **Oh, did I forget to tell you they are *pretend* rocks?** Explain to the students that they need to *pretend* to see the rocks, they need to *pretend* to catch the rocks as

you *pretend* to throw them, and then they need to *pretend* to write on their rock a skill that they have learned. *Pretend* to throw the rocks to the students…

2. Ask for volunteers to *pretend* to read their rock of the skilled learned and to throw the rock back in the bag. As they throw the rock, perform the trick by following the rock with your eyes giving the illusion, snapping the bag for the sound effect and dipping the bag slightly pretending that the rock is back in the bag. Repeat the skill written on the rock for reinforcement. Continue on for other students to share and throw their rock. (If you are using this activity as a review with one student for a follow up to individual counseling, you may ask the student to complete additional rocks to review the skill).

3. Next, explain to the students that you have a bag for each of them that they may first decorate (draw pictures and add words) to help them remember the skills learned. Explain that after they have decorated the bag you will teach them the secret of the trick. Hand out bags and crayons/ markers and allow time. Remind students that this is a time to decorate their bag with skills learned and they are not to pick the bag up to try to figure out the trick…patience…

4. After students have decorated their bag with skills learned, to add a little fun, you may choose for students to take a "Magicians Oath" before you can tell them the secret to performing the trick. Ask students to raise their right hand and repeat after you the following:

   I (and state your name).
   Do hereby pledge.
   To never, ever…
   Tell the secret of the trick.
   Even if
   they beg
   and plead
   I will not tell
   the secret.

5. After the pledge, instruct the student to not pick up their bag until you specifically tell them to do so instead they need to listen to the 3 step instructions. Proceed to first tell them the secret is in a finger snap. You may choose to have students simply practice finger snapping without a bag. Next tell (show them with your bag) how to place the finger with the middle finger inside the bag and the thumb outside the bag against that middle finger ready for the snap (you can typically get a clearer sound if the other fingers are placed outside the bag). Then show the students how to gently dip the bag to indicate the rock has landed in the bag. Finally show the important step of following the throw of the rock with the eyes to complete the illusion of the rock throw.

6. Next instruct the students to stand, open their bag, and practice the trick. Walk around helping, pretending to throw rocks, encouraging and complimenting their ability.

7. Call an end to the practice, ask students to refold their bag, and encourage the student to keep their bag as a reminder of the skills learned.

* adapted from Robert P. Bowman. 2002. 50 Magic Tricks Using Common Objects. Chapin, SC: Youthlight Inc.

References

Bowman, R., 2002, *50 Magic Tricks Using Common Objects*. Chapin, SC: Youthlight, Inc.

Bowman, R, 2004, *The Magic Counselor*, Chapin, SC: Youthlight, Inc.

Hazbry, N. and Roy Condy, 1983, *How to Get Rid of Bad Dreams*, New York, NY: Scholastic, Inc.

Krull, K., 1996, *Wilma Unlimited*, Harcourt.

Ludwig, T., 2006, *Sorry,!* Berkeley, CA: Tricycle Press.

Luthardt, K., 2001, *Mine!*, Simon and Schuster – Antheneum Books for young Readers.

Newport Mill Middle School, 2007 National Schools of Character.

Piper, W., 1976, *The Little Engine that Could*, New York, NY: Platt and Munk Publishers.

Reynolds, P., 2004, *Ish*, Cambridege, MA: Candlewick Press.

Senn, D., 2008, *Bullying in the Girl's World*, Chapin, SC: Youthlight, Inc.

Senn, D. and Gwen Sitsch, 1996, *Coping with Conflict: An Elementary Approach*, Chapin, SC: Youthlight, Inc.

Senn, D., 2004, *Small Group Counseling For Children K-2*, Chapin, SC: Youthlight, Inc.

Sitsch, G. and Diane Senn, 2002, *Puzzle Pieces*, Chapin, SC: Youthlight, Inc.